# Liverpool History

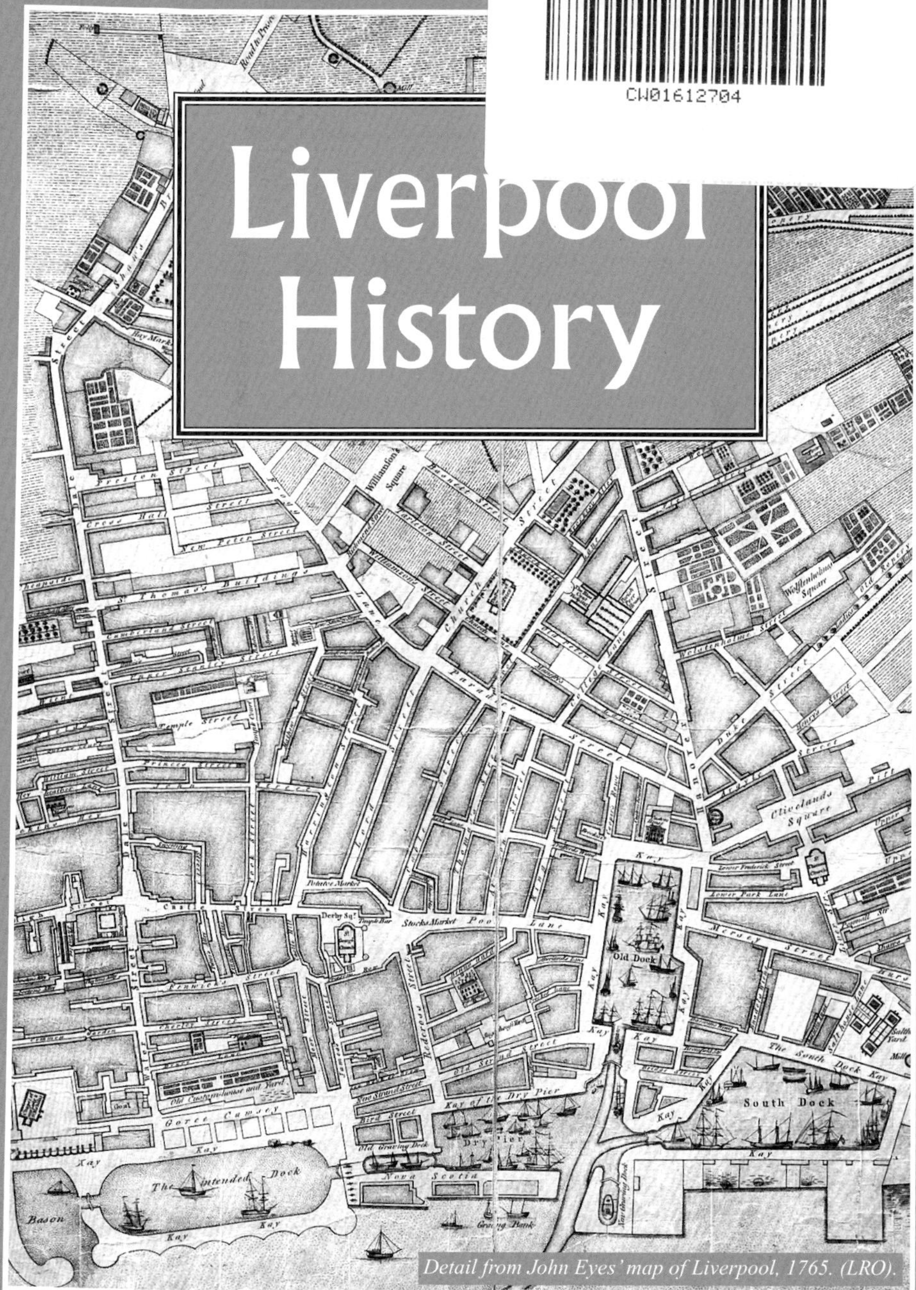


Detail from John Eyes' map of Liverpool, 1765. (LRO).

**Liverpool History Society**
**Journal No. 14**
**2015**

**The Society's Journal *Liverpool History* is published annually by**

## The Liverpool History Society

*(Founded 18th February 2001)*

This issue was edited by Ron Jones and Fred Forrest, Liverpool History Society.

Proofreading – Graham Jones, Liverpool History Society.

Design and production – Ron Jones.



Copies of this edition of *Liverpool History*, and certain earlier editions, are available from:

Fred Forrest, Sales Manager, Liverpool History Society
32 Rugby Drive, Aintree, Liverpool, L10 8JU
(e-mail: fred_forrest@hotmail.com)

**Acknowledgements**

The Society gratefully acknowledges the assistance and permission to use and reproduce material in its custody received from the Liverpool Record Office and Sefton Libraries' Local History & Heritage Service.



**ISBN 978-0-9559428-5-3**

Printed by Mitchell & Wright Printers, Banastre Road, Southport, Merseyside, PR8 5AL

*(The Liverpool History Society is a Registered Charity – No. 1093736)*

# CONTENTS



## Illustrations:

Where details have been supplied by the authors of the various articles in this Journal, the sources of the images used have been acknowledged. In the instances below, acronyms have been used:

(LRO) Liverpool Record Office.

(LOC) US Library of Congress.

(WC) Wikimedia Commons.

(RJ) Ron Jones: either photographed by him or from his personal collection.

*Front cover: RMS Lusitania at the Princes Landing Stage, Liverpool – detail from a Cunard Steamship Company poster produced in 1907, the year of her maiden voyage from Liverpool to New York.*

*RMS Lusitania at the Princes Landing Stage. (RJ).*

# "REMEMBER THE LUSITANIA!" 1915–2015 R.I.P.

## *The life and death of a Liverpool liner*

**Ron Jones**

### 1907: a very special year

1907 was an exceptional year in Liverpool's history for that was the year she celebrated her 700th anniversary. For much of it Liverpool was *en fête*. By comparison, a hundred years later in 2007, with its eye taken off the ball by its nomination as 'European Capital of Culture 2008', the city's 800th anniversary celebrations were somewhat muted, some would even say half-hearted.

Liverpool in 1907 was Britain's premier maritime port city. As the ultimate expression of the port's confidence, wealth and power, the Mersey Docks & Harbour Board had unveiled its stunning new Dock Office at the Pier Head, the first and, in this writer's opinion, the most gracious of the so-called *Three Graces*.

*700th anniversary medals. Top: by C.J. Allen who was later to execute the architectural sculptures for the Dock Office. Bottom: RMS Lusitania and Mauretania by Elkington (RJ).*

The most obvious manifestation of the city's maritime pre-eminence, especially for visitors to the Pier Head or those who travelled along its seven miles of docks on the Liverpool Overhead Railway, was its position as Europe's No. 1 port for transatlantic liners. However, it was not all plain sailing. In 1902, J. Bruce Ismay had sold the White Star Line to J.P. Morgan's International Mercantile Marine Co (IMM). Five years later, as the city celebrated its 700th anniversary, White Star and its crack liners moved to Southampton. Most Liverpudlians were outraged that it had lost one of its biggest and oldest shipping companies to a 'pipsqueak port'. To many it was seen as an act of betrayal.

The pill was sweetened somewhat when, on the 7th September of its anniversary year – a momentous day in its long maritime history – Cunard's new flagship and Blue Riband hopeful, the *Lusitania*, began her maiden voyage to New York.

The patriotic song *Rule Britannia*, originally penned in 1740, was almost like a second National Anthem and demonstrated Britain's perceived worldwide maritime domination – "Britannia rules the waves". It was sung by the vast crowds who had gathered to witness the *Lusitania's* first departure from the Princes Landing Stage

*Lusitania berthed at the Princes landing stage on 8th July 1911. To the right the New Brighton ferry is packed with day trippers enjoying a fine summer's day. (RJ)*

and, seven and a half years later had even been sung by doomed passengers on the wildly sloping decks of the *Lusitania* in the midst of her death throes. Apart from three brief years when it had been in the hands of America, Britain had held the Blue Riband continuously from 1838 for a full 60 years, mostly with Liverpool ships. However, since 1898 the Blue Riband had been held by German 'Kaiser-class' liners and the British Government did not like this dent to its national pride one little bit. For that reason, as well as its determination to stop the country's greatest shipping line, Cunard, from falling into the hands of the American-owned IMM, the Government struck a very special deal with the company in 1903.

The Government would loan Cunard £2.6m to be repaid at the low rate of interest of 2.75% over twenty years. In addition, Cunard would receive a subsidy of £150,000 a year during the loan period. Government largesse did not come without a price. For Cunard's part, it would use the loan to build two new ships to the Admiralty's specifications. Not only would they be enormous passenger liners, they would also double as fast auxiliary naval cruisers to be placed at the Admiralty's disposal during times of war; in fact, the deal meant that the Admiralty could, if it so wished during conflict, requisition the entire Cunard fleet. Furthermore, and importantly, Cunard undertook to remain a solely British company. One of the new ships would be the *Lusitania*; the other would be her sister, *Mauretania*. They were conceived to be the largest, fastest and most luxurious in the world and from the start there was the expectation they would wrest the prized Blue Ribbon from Germany.

**What a send-off!**

Fast forward four years to Saturday 7th September 1907 when the *Lusitania* lay at her moorings in the Sloyne off Tranmere, "Gleaming in all her glorious newness". In fact she had been there for nearly a fortnight having been delivered to her home port from Glasgow builders, John Brown & Co. Ltd. Earlier that week, on the Tuesday, Cunard

had opened her to the public. In five hours, no fewer than 10,000 had paid their half-a-crowns (donated to charity), crowded onto ferry boats, and had "oohed and aahed" as they roamed the *Lusitania's* ten decks and peeped into her sumptuous lounges and dining rooms modelled after apartments in the Palace of Versailles.

That Saturday was a red letter day for Cunard. Also in the Mersey was the *Lucania* which had surrendered the Blue Riband to the *Kaiser Wilhelm der Grosse* in 1898 and was scheduled to depart from the landing stage for New York at 4.30pm, three hours earlier than *Lusitania*. Both liners were fully booked and a frisson of excitement ran through their passengers and the waiting crowds as they asked themselves: would they 'race' each other to New York and would *Lusitania* go flat out at her service speed of 25 knots per hour and bring the Blue Riband back to Britain? It was a supposition that Cunard was quick to deny: "The *Lusitania* would not be pushed on her first voyage." Moreover, another former Cunard Blue Riband holder, the ageing *Umbria*, which would be pensioned off the following year, was due to arrive from New York as the *Lusitania* departed. One can only marvel at Cunard's mastery of logistics that day. Arriving at or departing from the Pier Head were thousands of passengers and their baggage, as well as the crew and staff of the companies that serviced the three great liners, supplying them with everything from coal to caviare. On top of that there were tens of thousands of sightseers to contend with.

On that Saturday morning *Lusitania* slipped her moorings and moved up river where she dropped anchor between Birkenhead and Seacombe in readiness for the short crossing to her berth at the Pier Head later that day. The Mersey Docks & Harbour Board was taking no chances. Earlier that week it had dredged the area around the landing stage to ensure there was sufficient depth for *Lusitania's* 33ft 6in draft. That afternoon tenders ferried the third-class passengers to board *Lusitania* in mid river. First and second-class passengers, many of them arriving on 'long trains de luxe' from Euston to Riverside railway station, would not be so inconvenienced. They would be boarded from the landing stage.

At 5pm the *Lucania* edged away from the Pier Head and headed up river, her place soon to be taken by *Lusitania*. Just shy of 800ft., she took up virtually the entire length of the landing stage. As reported in the *Liverpool Daily Post & Mercury* two days later, "Amid a scene of enthusiasm and jubilation unprecedented in the maritime history of Liverpool, the largest and fastest vessel afloat – the Lusitania – on Saturday night left the Princes Landing-stage on her maiden voyage to New York." As was the custom at that time, newspapers rarely made do with just one headline for their lead story. In this instance, alongside photographs of the *Lusitania* and her skipper, Captain Webb, no less than five headlines were employed: "The Lusitania Sails" / "Historical Event" / "Enthusiasm in Liverpool" / "Magnificent send-off" / "Huge Crowds on the Landing-stage". Eventually, at 9.10pm, four hours after the *Lucania* had sailed for New York, Cunard's new flagship cast off to the strains of *Rule Britannia*, cheered by a crowd estimated at some 200,000 that had occupied every vantage point on both sides of the river.

The transatlantic voyage itself was uneventful with the *Lusitania* behaving impeccably, if chastely. True to Cunard's word, but disappointedly for most passengers, its captain did not attempt a new speed record, although the *Lucania* was overtaken between the Sunday night and the Monday morning off the coast of southern Ireland. The crossing took a very respectable 5 days and 54 minutes at an average speed slightly over 23 knots: the *Deutchland's* record for a west-bound crossing was safe...but only by half an hour.

Most were fulsome in their praise of the new liner with West Virginia Senator, Howard Sutherland, declaring in a speech that the *Lusitania* was, "more beautiful than Solomon's Temple" and, "large enough to hold all his wives and mothers-in-law." On board, the British MP Rober Balfour flagged her up as yet another link in the friendship between America and England whilst first-class passenger George Copewell, Vice-President of the Copewell Horse Nail Company of Hartford, Connecticut, described the *Lusitania* as being, "more like a great hotel than a ship."

*Above left: Lusitania arriving in New York. Above right: berthed on arrival at New York at the end of her maiden voyage on 13th September 1915 (both images LOC).*

If anything *Lusitania's* arrival in New York was greeted with even wilder scenes of enthusiasm than her departure from Liverpool five days earlier. The *New York Times* reported, "Fully 1,000,000 spectators lined the landing stage and river banks in the immediate vicinity and yelled themselves hoarse." There were scenes of utter pandermonium as 15,000 people in the streets outside the pier fought for the chance to see her. Yet more people crowded from every tall building in Lower Manhattan. Fittingly, one observer described her as, "like a skyscraper adrift." Interestingly, stood on end, *Lusitania* was nearly 200ft taller than the tallest skyscraper in the world at that date (even today she would be as tall as Liverpool's tallest 'skyscraper', West Tower, *and* the Anglican Cathedral standing one on top of the other). One onlooker gushed, "The beautiful profile of the thoroughbred liner put to shame all previous liners."And what a sight she must have been, dressed overall with the US flag fluttering from her mainmast and the Blue Ensign from her stern as she edged her way alongside Cunard's liner terminal, her New York home for the next seven and a half years.

The following month, *Lusitania* did what was expected of her all along: she took the east-bound Blue Riband away from the *Kaiser Wilhelm 11* ending Germany's boast of having the fastest ships on the Atlantic. For the next two years, *Lusitania* shared the east and west-bound records with her sister *Mauretania*, with the latter holding on to the Blue Riband for twenty years, in itself a record that stands to this day. The *Mauretania*, which entered service just two months after her sister, was slightly longer, heavier and faster. More important, she had a much longer and more illustrious career, retiring in 1934 after 27 years' service.

For the next seven years both ships were familiar and thrilling sights on the River Mersey and the Hudson River. In that curious habit Liverpudlians have for foreshortening names, the sisters were soon affectionately dubbed the 'Lusi' and the 'Maury'. In New York, the *Lusitania* was known as 'The Big Lusi'.

**Into the war zone**

At a meeting with First Lord of the Admiralty, Winston Churchill, on 19th February 1913, Cunard's Chairman, Alfred Booth, was left in no doubt that war between Britain and Germany was on the horizon; the estimated date was given as September 1914. Churchill asked Booth to modify the *Lusitania*, *Mauretania*, *Ivernia* and *Aquitania* (then under construction) in preparation for their role as armed cruisers. Churchill further instructed that as soon as that work had been completed another six ships were to be converted.

*Lusitania* entered dry dock in Liverpool on 12th May with Cunard's public explanation that she was being withdrawn from service to be fitted with the latest turbines. That was true but it was only part of the story. She was also being made ready for war. Apart from certain strengthening modifications and the conversion of some areas for shell storage, twelve gun rings were fitted on her decks so that, when the time came, six-inch quick-firing guns could be lowered onto them and bolted into place. Ten weeks later *Lusitania* resumed her normal Liverpool – New York service. By the following March Churchill was able to report to the Commons that

*Lusitania arriving in New York at the end of her second, and record-breaking, voyage from Liverpool on 11th October 1907. By 1910 she was docking at the newly-built Pier 54 at Chelsea Piers. (LOC).*

some forty British merchant ships had been, in political speak, 'defensively armed'. In fact, *Lusitania* and her other Cunard sisters could offer more firepower than some Royal Navy cruisers guarding the English Channel.

On 4th August 1914, as *Lusitania* readied herself in New York for her 92nd round-trip to Liverpool, war was declared and she was handed over to the Admiralty. Her trademark orange-red funnels were painted black and her gleaming white superstructure and black hull gave way to sombre grey. Among the other designated Cunarders singled out for war service was the company's newest and biggest of the 'grand trio' of luxurious express liners, *Aquitania*, the so-called 'Ship Beautiful'. The start of her maiden voyage from Liverpool to New York on 30th May that year was a muted affair: the previous day, the Liverpool-based liner *Empress of Ireland* had sunk in the Saint Lawrence River and Liverpool was mourning the loss of over 1,000 souls. First *Titanic*, then *Empress of Ireland*; it couldn't get any worse. But it did. Within the space of just three years, a trio of Liverpool-registered 'Cursed Queens' would be consigned to watery graves at a cost of over 3,700 lives.

Within four days of the outbreak of war *Aquitania* had been fitted with her guns and soon after *Lusitania* entered Canada dry dock to have hers installed. She was now war-ready. In September 1914, barely a month later, *Lusitania's* game plan changed. The Admiralty told Cunard that her services as an armed cruiser would no longer be required; she was to operate a high speed passenger and cargo service between Liverpool and New York. The Admiralty would, however, still be pulling the strings: the cargo space on *Lusitania* and all other Cunarders on that run was to be put at the disposal of the Government. Any space not used by the Govenment could be used by Cunard but the authorities' cargo needs were to take priority and all eastbound cargo needed clearance by the Admiralty's US-based staff. Cunard was not best pleased. By now the war was in full swing, the Atlantic passenger trade was in the doldrums and Cunard had wanted to lay *Lusitania* up for the rest of the war.

On 30th January 1915 U-21 lay in wait in the approaches to Liverpool and sank three unarmed merchant ships. *Lusitania* herself had two, albeit at-a-distance, encounters with German U-boats before her fateful final journey. On 1st May, the day of her sailing from New York, a strongly worded warning by the German Embassy aimed at transatlantic travellers in British liners and those of her allies started to appear in US newspapers. That this notice appeared next to an advertisement for the *Lusitania* made many believe that Germany was intent on targeting the great ship.

Some prominent passengers, including the wealthy Alfred Vanderbilt, had also received telegrams that morning warning them not to travel on *Lusitania.* Whilst some people cancelled their sailings or transferred to other ships, the warnings largely went unheeded. After all hadn't Cunard's response been that *Lusitania* could outrun anything afloat with Captain Turner deriding the very notion – "It's the best joke I've heard in many days this talk of torpedoing."

***The final voyage***

The story of the sinking of the *Lusitania* is almost as well known as that of the *Titanic* and cannot adequately be covered in this short article. However, briefly, at 2.10 on the afternoon of Friday 7th May 1915, on her home run into Liverpool and eight miles off the Old Head of Kinsale, the German submarine U-20 under the command of Walther Schwieger, without warning, fired one torpedo which struck the vessel just below the wheelhouse on the starboard bow. Seconds later there was a second (and still unexplained) explosion. The great ship was doomed. Within eighteen minutes she was on the sea bed. As a result 1,191 passengers and crew lost their lives, mainly through drowning and hypothermia. Many of the crew, including Captain William Turner (a *Lusitania* veteran and survivor), were from Merseyside. There was also a large contingent of Americans – 159 of whom 128 died. Poignantly, of the 129 children on board, 94 perished; this included 35 infants of whom only four were saved.

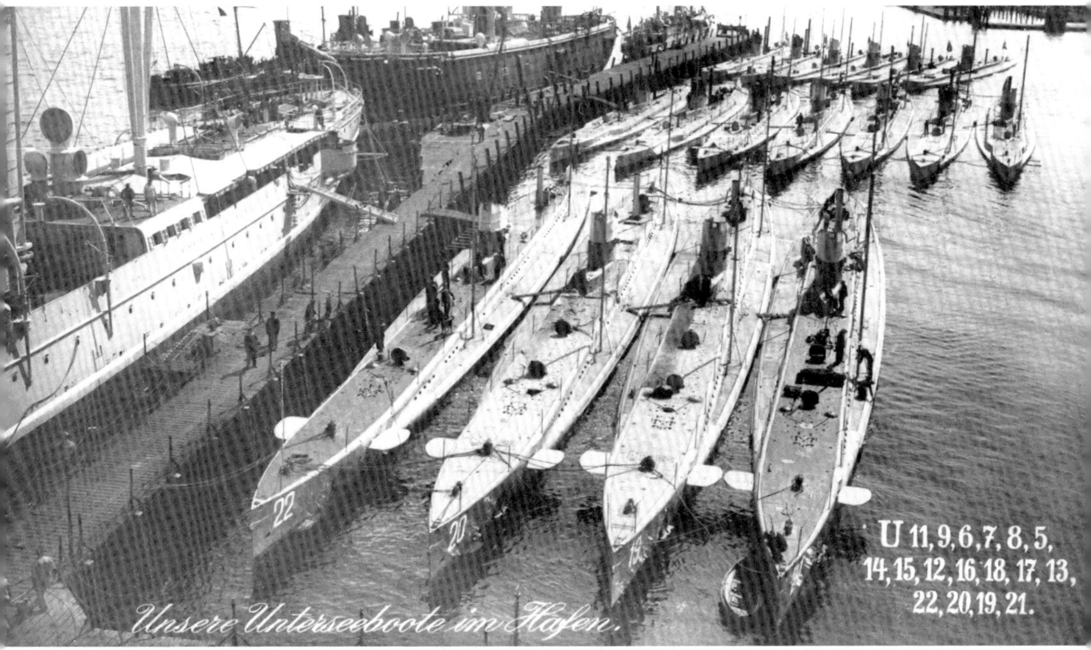


*A flotilla of seventeen U-boats: on the front row, second from left, is Lusitania's nemesis, U-20. She was responsible for sinking 37 ships and damaging two others. The four U-boats in the front row collectively sank a total of 152 ships, damaged another ten and also sank five warships. Not pictured is U-35 which alone sank 226 ships. Conversely, a total of 202 U-boats were lost during the war. (RJ).*

***What the papers said: how Liverpool heard the news***

Slowly word was beginning to reach Liverpool: "By and by a little crowd began to gather round the Cunard offices, grave men with pale anxious faces, and be-shawled women, many in tears – the wives, mothers, sisters, and sweethearts of those who had staffed the great vessel." Beyond midnight the crowd had grown considerably and staff were bombarded by questions.There was no inkling of how many had been lost or saved. Many people simply refused to believe that the great ship had gone. It was even rumoured that it wasn't the *Lusitania* that had been torpedoed but another vessel of the same name. In fact, another Liverpool ship, also named *Lusitania,* had indeed been lost but that had been in 1901.

*'Avenge the Lusitania'. Detail from recruitment poster for the Irish Regiment. (LOC).*

The full scale of the disaster was beginning to be revealed in the *Liverpool Daily Post & Mercury* the following day. As was the custom at that time, you would have had to search the front page hard for *any* news story, even one this big. But there it was, a tiny single-column piece, "The incoming Cunard liner was torpedoed and sunk by a German submarine eight miles south by west of Kinsale at half-past two yesterday. She had on board altogether 1918 souls." The full terrible story was to be found on pages 5, 6 and 7. Beneath headlines that included, "Liverpool Moved"; "How the News was Received"; and "Surprise, Sorrow and Anger", the lead paragraph highlighted the close bond between Liverpudlians and the great liner:

> *'No shipping disaster of the war affecting Liverpool has struck so wide and deep a blow as the loss of the Lusitania. She was the pride of the Mersey, and people loved her like a personal friend. The sense of loss will be felt by everyone, whether they had direct association with the vessel or not, because she was essentially Liverpool's own ship.'* adding, *'The faith which Liverpool people had in the Lusitania was tremendous...',* and, *'No more sumptuous vessel than the Lucy ever ploughed the seas. She surpassed both Titanic and Aquitania in every quarter – the gracefulness of her lines, lavishness of her internal equipment, great speed etc.'*

The *Daily Post's* Naval Correspondent waded in with the purplest of prose: "Culminating Point of Barbarism" and "Cresecendo of Atrocity". Later that week, the *Liverpool Weekly Mercury* ran photographs of the *Lusitania* and Captain Turner and thundered: "nowhere in the annals of human wickedness and human depravity is there a record of a deed so hellish as the deliberate sinking of the Lusitania and the wilful, premeditated murder of the children, women and men who were on board."

Winston Churchill's measured statement in the wake of the disaster, as well as the use of poison gas against British troops the previous month, reflected the mood of 'civilised people' everywhere, "The outrage is unparalled and the grounds for it are shameless in their insincerity. We shall not whine, but we shall take steps to give punishment and exact reparation for this brutality, and the whole world will be with us in our efforts to put an end to the flagrant outrages which Germany has heaped upon civilisation and humanity."

*Nearly three days after the sinking of the Lusitania 150 of her victims were buried in three mass graves in the Old Church cemetery near Queenstown (renamed Cobh in 1922). Eighty of them were never identified. Cunard paid $25 for the recovery of a body. The 'bounty' offered for Alfred Vanderbilt's body was $5,000. It was never found. (courtesy The Times).*

As there were so many Americans on board the USA took unprecedented interest in the *Lusitania* story as it unfolded: "Great Indignation in USA" reported the *Liverpool Daily Post* whilst the *New York Herald* trumpeted "American women and children give up their lives to German pirates." The *New York Tribune* went further calling the sinking of the *Lusitania*, "an act of war" and, "If she continues on the course, a declaration of war is the inevitable consequence." adding, "Many millions will regret that no American soldiers are in those lines doing America's part in the battle to defend civilisation. For let no one mistake the fact. A wild beast is loose in the world, a creature combining the ferocity of the animal with the lust of the degenerate human being. The struggle is not a struggle of nations, it is a battle between civilisation and barbarism.' German-American citizens who sympathised with the Kaiser were branded as, '...traitors to the United States of America."

The US had previously warned the German Government that it would hold Germany to strict account for any damage or destruction that might be done to American lives or property and many, on both sides, thought that the *Lusitania* incident would propel America into the war. Small wonder that Count von Bernstorff, the odious German Ambassador in Washington, scurried to the Department of State and, with much hand-wringing and weasel words, expressed Germany's deep regret at the loss of American lives by the torpedoing of the *Lusitania*. At the same time, the German press was euphoric in its praise of the sinking of Britain's greatest liner as this editorial from the Catholic newspaper *Kölnische Volkszeitung* demonstrates: "The sinking of the Lusitania is a success for our submarines which must be placed beside the greatest achievements in this naval war. The sinking of the great British steamer is a success the great moral significance of which is still greater than the material success. With joyful pride we contemplate this latest deed of our navy, and it will not be the last."

Whilst President Wilson did send a lengthy strongly-worded, if belated, note to the Kaiser, as we know, a further two years elapsed before America eventually entered the war. The sinking of the *Lusitania* may not have been the prime reason, but it was certainly a deciding factor.

Rescued passengers arriving at Lime Street station.

### *The survivors return*

In the early hours of the 9th May the first of the surviving passengers started to arrive by train at Lime Street station. Cunard had done all it could to help the returning crew and passengers, reportedly placing all available taxi-cabs at their disposal. The *Daily Post's* reporter on the platform described the distressing scenes: "Among them were hundreds of women with heavy hearts scanning the faces of the home-comers with hope hand-in-hand with despair. Other women searched frantically for relatives who were not to be found." There were cases of hysteria. Whilst the crew were reported as being 'stolid', their womenfolk, "gave free vent to their feelings. Some wives clutched their husbands convulsively and wept. Some were embraced and swooned away."

Many arrived as 'walking wounded'. One man wore just his trousers and a singlet. A gentleman, well-known in the town, was seen to leave the crowd and walk towards him. He removed his fine overcoat, placed it round the shoulders of the shivering man then simply walked away without a word. Another man, clad from head to toe in a light-coloured dressing garment, looked, "singularly strange, perhaps also because he was still clutching his lifebelt, from which he refused to be parted." A group of young women heartbroken at the presumed loss of a dear brother were buoyed by the remark of a stranger – "Another train shortly." A glimmer of hope had been raised. There were similar pathetic scenes at London's Euston station where American survivors were met by Dr Page the US Ambassador.

When news of the sinking had first reached Liverpool it had been a city in shock. That quickly turned to a fierce rage and a desire to avenge which found expression in ways both good and bad. Recruiting figures rocketed over the weeks that followed spurred on by a stirring appeal by Lord Derby for recruits – "to hunt down and crush once and for all a race of cold-blooded murderers." A recruitment tent was set up on the George's Landing Stage and recruiting officer Captain Townroe addressed audiences estimated at 14,000 at the city's theatres exhorting men to sign up to "cage the wild beast". Shaming was another tactic used – "Every able-bodied Liverpool man who is free to enlist and who feels the loss of the *Lusitania* and yet remains without a uniform should consider himself eternally disgraced."

'Remember the Lusitania!' became a watchword as well-known as Nelson's at the Battle of Trafalgar. A first-person report in the *Daily Post* described what it was like going into battle – "I heard men going into battle with the cry 'Remember the Lusitania!' on their lips and, when that cry was heard it had a terrible meaning for the Germans." It was emblazoned on recruitment posters in Britain and Ireland and in America after April 1917 when the US eventually declared war on Germany.

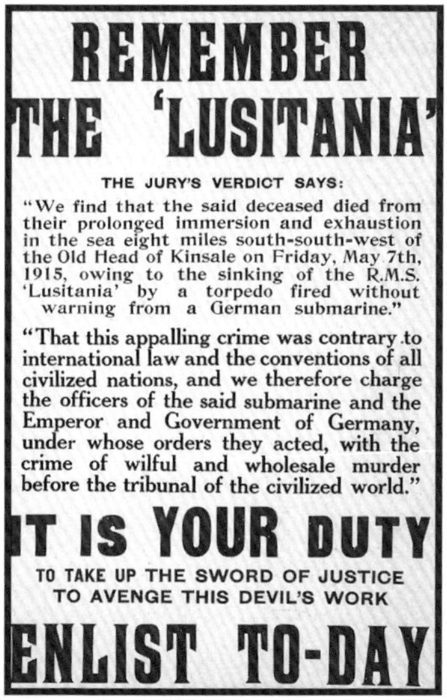

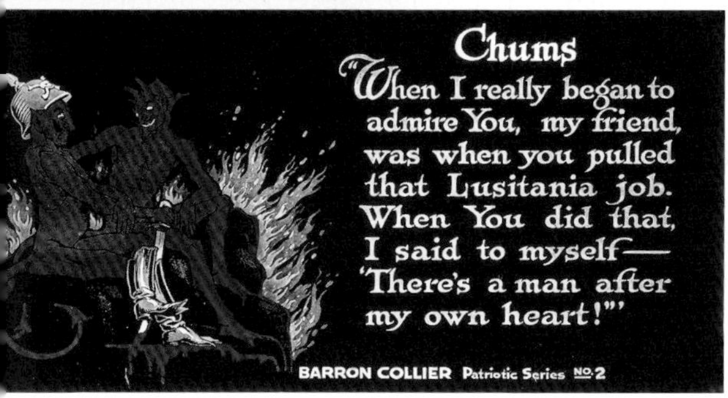

*Top row: emotive recruitment posters. Bottom row: One of many cartoons published in the wake of the Lusitania disaster (all LOC) and, one of the two port-side propellers salvaged from the wreck of the Lusitania on permanent display on the quayside at the river entrance to Canning Dock. Every year, on the anniversary of her sinking, a service to commemorate her loss is held there. (RJ).*

*Left: Yaag's German Pork Butcher's shop, Great George Street and, above, another German shop were pictured in The Illustrated London News on 15th May 1915. The caption for Yaag's shop read – "In Liverpool, the home of most of the Lusitania's men, a German shop wrecked by the crowd by way of revenge."*

***Sausage fights in the streets of Liverpool***

By Tuesday 11th May, the *Daily Post* was filing its first reports of the disturbances which began in the city on the previous Saturday and were continuing on a daily basis during the daytime and into the evenings: "Anti-German Riots" / "Liverpool Outburst" / "Fire and Pillage" / "Homes Invaded and Shops Wrecked" / "Aliens to be Interned." The principal targets were shopkeepers of (supposed) Teutonic nationality and in particular owners of pork shops, not all of whom were German either by birth or descent. That did not concern the rioters, many of whom were women who had lost relatives on the *Lusitania*. First they broke the windows, then looted the shops before entering the living quarters and smashing the furniture or throwing it into the streets where it was either spirited away or set on fire.

Pork butchers were not the only ones targeted. Furniture dealers, outfitters, jewellers, even hairdressers came under attack. It seemed that the inflamed mob needed only the flimsiest of excuses – a "foreign name, be of German extraction, have married a German or have done something at some time in his life to have aroused suspicion". Kaufmann's furniture store in Ellenborough Street off Scotland Road was the scene of one spectacular riot where all the furniture ended up in the street and the premises set on fire whilst the crowd danced in the street and sang 'Tipperary', the chorus led by a large woman wearing a military cap. It was Liverpool's 'Kristallnacht'.

Anti-German rioting was particularly strong in the Brownlow Hill area, but it was taking place all over the city. In the city centre an outfitters in Paradise Street was completely ransacked whilst in Fenwick Street the American barber's shop, supposedly owned by Germans, was attacked and looted by a hostile crowd. Bootle, Wallasey and Birkenhead did not escape the attentions of the mob either. In Birkenhead's Cleveland Street a woman married to an alien (who had been sent away), and her children, were rendered homeless when a rampaging mob, reportedly 2,000-strong, attacked her home. Everything was smashed to smithereens and the house made uninhabitable. The poor woman (who had been taking in washing to make ends meet), and her five children, had to find refuge in the workhouse.

But it was the pork shops that bore the brunt of the actions of the restless mobs roaming the streets of Liverpool. In the Smithdown Road / Lodge Lane areas women were seen going home with their aprons full of pork and bacon. Other women were streaming up Smithdown Road carrying looted furniture, including heavy sofas, to be "borne away to slum houses". In nearby Arundel Avenue where a large pork butchers had been raided, women hurled sausages at each other. One woman even went on her hands and knees and scrubbed the pavement with a joint of pork.

A rare participant's account is contained in Pat O'Mara's *The Autobiography of a Liverpool Slummy*. A number of his pals went down with the 'Lusi' and his account of rioting in the Scotland Road and Park Lane areas is illuminating, amusing at times, but ultimately shameful. After a hard day's rioting he went to bed that night feeling ill, a result of all the raw sausages he had gorged on earlier.

His account confirms that much of the rioting was indiscriminate and the result of drunkenness and sheer hooliganism. Sometimes it was enough just to be 'foreign'. Non-Teutons resorted to placing hastily scrawled notices in their windows – "Italians live here who are on the side of the British." and "We are Russian." The authorities did what they could. Mounted police and special constables were drafted in, licensed premises closed at 6pm, pleas for calm were made by the Bishop of Liverpool and Lord Derby, and many of the miscreants were hauled before the Stipendiary Magistrate under the Riot Act for sentencing. One woman 'of this sort'; (i.e. "of the class of habitual offenders, a class prone to fly to drink at each opportunity and eager to join in any display of hooliganism") up before the 'Stipe' for putting in the plate glass windows of a Russian tradesman, despite the fact that Russia was one of Britain's allies, "didn't see why Chinamen, Scandinavians, Russians and Italians had any title to be spared." For their own safety all Germans and Austrians were interned – the Main Bridewell in Cheapside was almost full to bursting. They were subsequently ferried in Black Marias to Lime Street station to board a special train for Scotland. The hostile crowd that gathered were kept in order by soldiers of the Kings (Liverpool) Regiment. As the trainload of Germans drew away they were booed mightily.

After a week or so Liverpool calmed down and the city gradually returned to normal; well, as normal as any city in the middle of a world war could be.

***Epilogue***

One hundred years on controversies about the sinking of the *Lusitania* still intrigue us, perhaps as much as those surrounding the *Titanic*: for certain the international repercussions of '*The Lusitania Incident*' were far graver. What caused the second massive explosion that almost certainly sealed the liner's fate in so rapid a manner? Was Captain Turner (who had made 42 crossings in *Lusitania*) negligent in the manner that he handled his vessel? Why did she not receive timely warnings that German submarines were active in the area and why did no Royal Navy escort vessel accompany her in the dangerous waters off the Irish coast? Was her sinking part of political manoevering by Churchill to drag the US into the war? Apart from millions

*Contemporary postcard showing the enormous size of the Lusitania. Until the completion of the 'Shard' in London in 2012, the length of the Lusitania surpassed the height of every tall building in Britain. (RJ).*

of rounds of small arms munitions and gun cotton, was she carrying other high explosives? Was there a cover-up by Lord Mersey's Inquiry? And, ultimately, was *Lusitania* a legitimate target of war?

Depressingly, a mere twenty years after the end of "The war to end all wars", history was about to repeat itself. This time German atrocities, including the genocide of six million Jews and the mass murders of five million other victims, were far worse, giving credence to the adage – "Times change. People don't".

## *Main sources*

**Newspapers**:

1. *Liverpool Daily Post & Mercury* September 1907 and May 1915. Liverpool Central Library.
2. *Liverpool Weekly Mercury* May 1915. Liverpool Central Library.
3. *Liverpool Echo* May 1915. Liverpool Central Library.

**Books**:

1. *Wilful Murder: The Sinking of the Lusitania* Diana Preston, Walker & Co., New York, 2002.
2. *Lusitania* Updated Merseyside edition, Colin Simpson, Avid Publications, Merseyside, 1983.
3. *Lusitania An Illustrated History of the Ship of Splendour* J. Kent Layton, Lulu Press, 2007.
4. *The Autobiography of a Liverpool Slummy* Pat O'Mara, Bluecoat Press, Liverpool, 2007.

**Websites**: ● www.liverpoolmuseums.org.uk/lusitania ● www.rmslusitania.info ● www.lusitania.net ● en.wikipedia.org/wiki/Lusitania ● en.wikipedia.org/wiki/Blue_Riband ● www.uboat.net

## *Notes*

1. Recent research by independent historian Peter Kelly, has led to an update of passenger and crew data for the *Lusitania's* final voyage: Total number on board – 1962 (previously 1959); Survived – 771 (previously 761); Lost – 1191 (previously 1198); Passenger survival rates – 480 (786 lost); Total passengers – 1266 (previously 1257); Crew survival rates – 291 (405 lost); Total crew – 696 (previously 702). More than 600 of those on board had connections with Liverpool and the wider region.

2. As might be expected the 100th anniversary of the sinking of the *Lusitania* has spawned a number of new books, none of which have been consulted due to the timescale for completion of this article.

3. *Lusitania: life, loss, legacy* is the title of a special long-term exhibition that opened at the Merseyside Maritime Museum on 27th March 2015 to mark the centenary of the disaster.

# THE OLD DOCK RE-VISITED:
## Some 300th Anniversary Musings

*Adrian Jarvis*

The Liverpool Dock, or Old Dock as it became known with the passing years (and how it is referred to throughout this article), has a lengthy historiography which might be taken to begin with Henry Peet's paper on Thomas Steers, its engineer. The works which have followed have tracked down much of the story both of The Dock and of Steers, gradually extending our knowledge, and very little has got cut out along the way. The result, and it is one in which I am as guilty as anyone, is that authors of new works on the subject seem to recognise no limit to the number of times a good tale can be well told. That may well cause the reader to ask whatever am I doing now, starting another hare, using little new information. The answer is that there may come a time when it is necessary to take stock of where we have got to, for, shame to admit it, much of what has been written recently has not weighed the new information against the old. In some cases we find authors posing some new question arising from new work (it does happen!) exhibiting complete failure to take the new work on board. To take a personal example, in *The Liverpool Dock Engineers* I published puzzlement at where Steers was able to secure large numbers of skilled workers, especially stonemasons and bricklayers. I thought it was a reasonable question to ask, one which is usually answered in narrative accounts of engineering construction, but in this case it was greeted with a profound silence. Finding the appointment of contractors in the Corporation minutes is fairly easy, but when we ask where those contractors recruited men on Steers' behalf, no answer is forthcoming.

Could it be that people expect that something which is a 'world first' must be free of blemish and that it is somehow improper to criticise it? Peet certainly thought that way. The answer in the case of the labour problem was quite simply that Steers *did not* hire large numbers of skilled men. When the walls of Old Dock were exposed in the Oxford Archaeology North excavation of 2006-2008, some of their workmanship, especially bricklaying, could be seen to be of poor quality. None of the later Liverpool dock engineers would have tolerated it nor any proud craftsman perpetrated it. There were two obvious reasons for this. In common with many other works of civil engineering, Old Dock involved heavy expenditure for years before any of the anticipated income materialised. In this respect, if not in others, the ramshackle Old Dock performed better than its successors. From receiving Parliamentary sanction (itself a cost incurred in anticipation of income) to a rather low-key opening took a highly efficient five years. On the other hand, the time and cost overrun to 'carry the works through to completion' left much to be desired. The completed works suffered from a need for frequent 'scuttling' (manual dredging) which continued down to closure in 1826, and retaining wall failures were not unknown. Occasional requests for permission to take down part of a wall for ship-repairing purposes during the summer (when the demand for berth space was minimal because ships tended to be

*Botched brickwork exposed in a section of the Old Dock preserved beneath the Liverpool One shopping development. It is suggested that the use of unskilled labour resulted in dock walls that would not have passed muster by later dock engineers such as Jesse Hartley. (RJ).*

at sea) were not necessarily rejected out of hand, suggesting that the walls lacked the precision and permanence of Jesse Hartley's work. We know enough of that gentleman to imagine his reaction to any suggestion of interfering with his walls.

Anyone who has worked for a present-day public body knows that part of its expenditure is simply paying for the taxpayer/ratepayer to know that everything is 'above board'. By bending the rules it is possible, quite honestly but not properly, to reduce costs. In the case of Steers and the Councillors this principle was taken to extremes, with Steers involved as a consultant, as a salaried employee, as an elected representative, and eventually as Mayor. Council members both received and disbursed public money through their personal accounts and took major policy decisions in those proverbial 'smoke-filled rooms'. It must be stressed, however, that while there was the *potential* for serious fraud, there is no proof that any ever occurred on the Old Dock project. Just as engineering errors might occur through the novelty of the problem, so procedural problems might arise in the same way. And here lies an important point: Old Dock was not the first in the world on any engineering grounds: it was the first *commercial* dock. The crucial problem did not lie with the standard of brickwork or in the novelty of its silt control. It was a commercial answer to a commercial problem, and it was that quality of that answer which would determine the issue of whether Liverpool could or could not turn itself into an international port.

It could and did, but there was no inevitable link between building the dock and a gratifying growth of trade. In the event, it was the port's collective business acumen, not Steers' dodgy bricklayers, which achieved it.

It has taken a long time, but the revisionists, or at least some of them, have finally caught up with the reputation of Bad King John. This places a serious strain on the traditional explanation of his part in the evolution of Liverpool from a small town in which some of the inhabitants did a bit of trading or fishing, into a seaport. It is arguable that had John been a better king, and specifically had he succeeded in maintaining better relations with those who are often known collectively as 'The Barons' he might never have had cause to notice Liverpool, much less to change its fundamental character by the grant of his famous 'Charter'. But he had been left holding a poisoned chalice in the shape of extensive land in Ireland, Scotland and Wales, a chalice handed to him early in his public life by his father, Henry II. Seen from John's viewpoint, what was wrong with that situation was that these lands were inhabited by people who (often with good reason) liked John not at all. Communications around and between these various lands were difficult, and could be brought to a standstill by the geographical position of Chester, where Earl Ranulph controlled road and river. There does not seem to have been any specially bitter or long-standing acrimony between them, but Ranulph could fairly be termed a chancer and John had more sense than to put himself in the position of depending on him. He needed an alternative.

Just a little to the north he found what he wanted. The Mersey, it is true, was far from ideal, but it was reasonably sheltered from the prevailing wind, had deep water and parts at least of the middle Mersey offered good holding ground for anchors. Its tiny merchant community was willing to deal at prices which even 'Lackland' could afford. As King, he, could of course, do a better deal by selling or leasing other people's land and a better one still (as Lloyd George could later testify) by granting or leasing a right or title which he had just created for the purpose – which cost him nothing and had the probable side-effect of making the recipient grateful for a while. John was not slow to repeat this wheeze: nationwide he granted a total of 57 Borough charters, often, as in the case of King's Lynn, with considerable and lasting benefit to the recipients.

It was not just a matter of avoiding dependency on Ranulph. There is also the question of total handling capacity – John's Ireland expedition of 1210 is said to have involved no less than 700 ships, which would have caused severe strain on the shallow Dee estuary, meaning that Liverpool was probably not just an alternative but also an adjunct. And there was more: the 'Royal Navy' was normally made up of merchant ships requisitioned to fight for the king when necessary and returned to their owners when no longer required. John wanted complete control of access to Ireland, to say nothing of Scotland and Wales, which made him embark on probably the greatest English royal warship building programme between King Alfred and Henry V.

*Known as 'The Peters Painting', it dates from about 1680 and shows, in the centre, Water Street at the foot of which ships could be beached and unloaded at low tide. On the extreme right is the original 'Pool of Liverpool', the site of the town's first dock. Courtesy National Museums Liverpool – the painting is normally on display in the Merseyside Maritime Museum.*

Warships needed berths, whether at quays, anchorages or mud docks. John's ships were probably seriously neglected in peacetime (purpose-built warships usually were: recall the fate of Henry V's mighty *Grace Dieu*), but John was not a strikingly pacific character, so there would most likely have been an ongoing need for at least some maintenance and supplies. Road transport to and from Liverpool was dire, so those supplies would almost inevitably have arrived by sea. The terms on which burgage tenure had been granted would probably mean that procuring the 'logistics vessels' should not have been too difficult, but what arrangements were made for supplying fresh water to the warships?

There have been many 'woulds' and 'must haves' in this section, which even if sustainable in general terms are, and will presumably remain, unquantifiable. Unfortunately, when we begin in the fourteenth century to find occasional sources for real documentary history, it is difficult to establish even a basic narrative to explain the growth of trade which would eventually drive the desire of the townsmen to build a dock. In 1709, Sir Thomas Johnson and Richard Norris, Liverpool's two MPs, were charged with seeking parliamentary powers to borrow what proved to be the wildly insufficient sum of £6,000 to build the dock, and within the year these were granted. The following year, work began. The exact price when all was complete (which was not until 1721) is not clear, but was of the order of three times the estimate.

As we have already seen, the dock they were setting out to build was not just any old dock: it was the first commercial wet dock in the world, and its construction required the bringing together at the same place and time of several factors, of which the first was, as usual, money. Historically, commercial docks in Britain came to be funded in one of several ways, including local magnates, ad hoc bodies and local authorities. All were likely to face money problems, for such is the way of the world when confronted with novelty with its attendant overspends. The problems might be practical matters

*'Prospect of Liverpool' c1725, believed to be the earliest known depiction of the Old Dock. Also shown is the wooden pier or jetty and the new Custom House, completed in 1722. Courtesy National Museums Liverpool – the painting is normally on display in the Merseyside Maritime Museum.*

of engineering, or legal squabbles, but either way there had to be a source of funding which already had, or could borrow, five-digit sums. Quite as important was the ability to make the decision to build, and then to stand by that decision until the project was completed: cold feet led to failure. These factors first came together in Liverpool towards the end of the seventeenth century – and the first port to follow Liverpool's lead was Hull in 1774. Not only was the Hull dock far from snapping at Liverpool's heels – it was designed by Henry Berry, Steers' successor as Engineer to the Liverpool Dock Trustees and 'doing a foreigner' with their consent. The Hull Dock was, however, considerably larger than any of Liverpool's eighteenth century docks, because its natural harbour was better and larger than Liverpool's, allowing the postponement of major engineering.

What is important and not always recognised is that this mixture of motives and problems could not be resolved using just one of the tools in the would-be dock-builder's box: the problem was not solely an engineering one, and hence the solution could not be either. But the solution of the strictly engineering part of the project was not as difficult as has sometimes been thought. The traditional view is that, in the absence of any acknowledged specialist in dock-building, the necessary skills to build the Liverpool dock must have been assembled by involving people each of whom had some of the knowledge required and who together had all or nearly all of it. So it was that Thomas Steers was able to embark on, and eventually successfully complete, the construction of the dock. That, of course, is not quite how it happened: in 1708, Johnson and Norris approached George Sorocold, perhaps the most accomplished hydraulic engineer of his generation, who, assisted by Henry Huss, produced a report in September 1709. What happened next is unclear: in the following May the Council adopted Steers' plan, of which this is the first we hear, for reasons unknown. It seems possible that Steers' political involvement may have had some bearing on the matter.

But we have run far ahead of the other strands of the story. The trade of the port is very ill-documented, but authors have generally agreed that after the kick-start by King John, a small coastwise trade gradually grew, centring on the Irish Sea. The Town Books show a gradually increasing Corporation expenditure on what we may loosely describe as port services, including a public quay, a public warehouse and some modest efforts at marking the channel into the Port. These did not involve major expenditure, but they did mark an acceptance of responsibility. They also comply with Jackson's well-known obiter dictum that 'in the final analysis, a port is not a place, but a community of merchants'. The merchants may not have yet become specially large, wealthy or numerous, but they were acting as a community, and that enabled them to hedge trading risks, which in turn allowed them to become involved in larger-scale ventures. These larger ventures had two effects: they widened the range of goods in which the port could trade and they encouraged the use of larger ships, especially desirable for facing the horrors of the North Atlantic. So began the conflict, which continues to this day, between shipowners wanting the increased efficiency of larger ships and port authorities wishing to avoid capital expenditure to provide deeper berths for them. In Liverpool, however, the shipowners and the 'Port Authority' were largely the same people, a situation which would later be resolved by the concept of 'hat-wearing', which did not exist at the time. The result was that, while there might be the odd squabble, there was a rough consensus which evolved in Tudor times and lasted until the Municipal Reform Act. This is not to say that all was sweetness and light, merely that the people who mattered were generally prepared to sink their differences in the interest of the benefit of the port.

Another favourable circumstance is that Liverpool was generally on the right side of the country: at the time when Liverpool men were beginning to give serious thought to the idea of port improvement, Britain was involved in a series of wars, which one might expect would have had serious effects on Liverpool's trade. In the event, most of the naval campaigning took place in the Channel and some of the wars had little or no actual naval involvement at all. It might be expected, for example, that the War of the Spanish Succession (1701-14) would make money-raising difficult. Liverpool did lose some ships to French privateers, but in fact, the war had relatively little effect for two reasons: it was primarily a land war in which the land battles were characterised by thumping victories won by the future Duke of Marlborough, and Louis XIV had a novel foe to face – the fund-raising power of the Bank of England. Britain did succeed in acquiring Gibraltar, but it was not then seen as being as important as it later became. The war of the Spanish Succession may have produced some impressive victories for British arms, but wars can usually be relied upon to inhibit major civilian investment: why were Liverpool men willing and able to form an exception? The fact that Sir John Houblon, Governor of the Bank of England, was a Portuguese Merchant who lobbied powerfully for the Royal Navy to protect his trade may have helped create a friendly climate. A weak argument perhaps, but it is a strange and counter-intuitive fact that not one of Liverpool's eighteenth century docks was built entirely in peace-time.

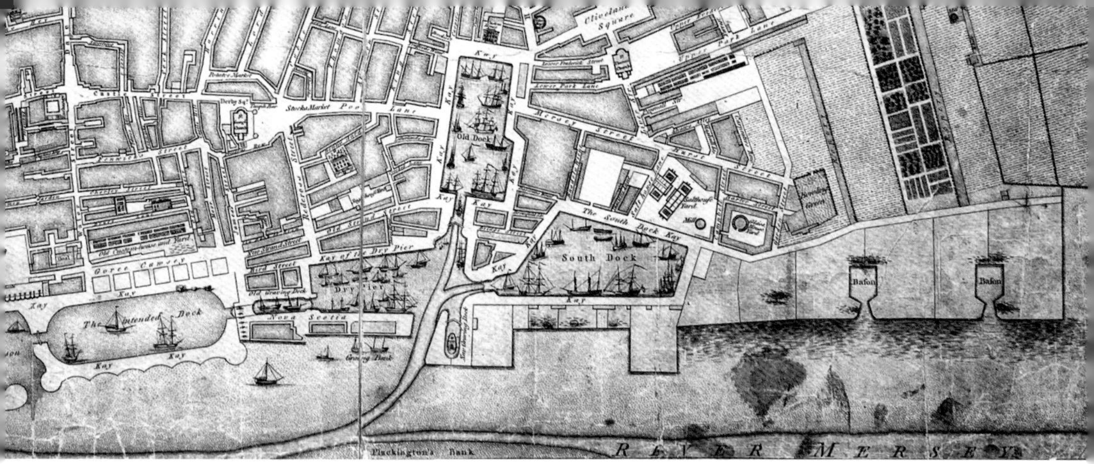


*Produced just fifty years after the Old Dock opened, John Eye's map of 1765 illustrates the growth of Liverpool's embyro dock system. Courtesy Liverpool Record Office.*

Liverpool's Corporation Estate gave the town a unique advantage over every other port in the country. It was, and remains, exceptionally rare for major works of engineering to be built without large-scale borrowing. Liverpool's estate was not made up of land only, but also of rights variously granted by King John and leased from the Molyneux family. The land could not be mortgaged (though it appears that it was!), but the rights, and especially the Town Dues, levied on goods entering and leaving the port, could. The Dock Dues, which would be chargeable on the goods in and out of the new works, could be anticipated. Liverpool could raise funds for dockbuilding, and in 1711 all seemed set fair.

At this point it is necessary to think back to the beginning of this paper and beware of triumphalism setting in, starting with Old Dock's reputation and moving on to its finance and construction. Not everything went right, and we may begin with Johnson and Norris' part: they had been charged to agree for the dock's design and construction with a 'proper person'. They appeared to be on the brink of success when they agreed a plan and estimate for the dock with George Sorocold and Henry Huss. But they were dealing with a man who specialised in water supply and navigation and liked living in Derby to the point he would not leave it. Second choice, Thomas Steers, was duly appointed. It would be possible to attack him for not being a specialist dock engineer – but who was? We might as well criticise Robert Stephenson, whose 'Rocket' did not contain a single completely novel idea but which in Robert's hands became a brilliant synthesis. Steers could do that, because he had experience in a range of relevant employments, beginning as a soldier in the Fourth Foot. In 1702 he was Quartermaster, a highly suitable post for one with transferable talents in logistics and in civil engineering. It appears that he was involved in at least two of the lengthy sieges (Huy, Namur) which characterised war at the turn of the century and might provide spells of enforced leisure. The Duke of Bridgewater resorted to technological tourism (or espionage) when he got bored: may we assume that Steers might have done the same? There was no shortage of high-tech water control engineering in the Low Countries to stimulate his interests, but perhaps more striking and more relevant was the work of Louis XIV's great military engineer Sebastien de Vauban whose fortified dock system at Dunkirk[1] was completed in 1678, complete with fully-locked entrances. It was intended to provide over-winter berths for 30 major warships, but Louis' navy did not do very well at the Treaty of Utrecht (which ended the War of the Spanish Succession) with the result that Vauban's handiwork was demolished in 1713. By then, however, Steers, whose knowledge had probably been enhanced by his connection with the Howland Estate in Rotherhithe and its Howland Great Dock of 1697, may well have learned all he could from others.

The outline of construction which has been attempted above shows some of the difficulties in construction, but there were more to come. Owing to a lack of funds during construction and of operational experience – at times one might even say of ambition – it was soon found that the little octagonal entrance basin, itself apparently a retro-fit, was nowhere near large enough, and it was supplemented with a timber pier which may have been Steers' response to an instruction of 1718 to extend the tidal part of the system. When a sailing ship is approaching a dock entrance it needs to get its speed down to a point where a heaving line and a mooring line will get it fully under control. This is a critical operation especially if the tide is running and/or the water in the approach less than calm. This, and not overcrowding betokening immediate success, was what mandated the early 'extension' of Old Dock. It might be argued that this penny-pinching caused difficulties right through until 1842 when a thorough-going remodelling by Jesse Hartley solved the problem for good. The irony, of course, is that by then Old Dock had been infilled for six years.

When Old Dock opened it was not immediately inundated with new trade from parts of the world with which there had been little or no previous trade. The Town Dues are a reasonable guide, albeit a rough one, to the growth in trade, and their income multiplied by about 2.4 between 1720 and 1744. This indicates that there was no huge latent demand as there was for the Liverpool & Manchester railway's passenger (but not freight) services. With growing experience in port management, Liverpool learned to judge (admittedly not perfectly) the relationship between projects which caught up with existing demand and those which also anticipated growing traffic. But in the eighteenth century finding that balance was a pretty hit and miss affair.

In some 30 years studying various aspects of the history of ports I would not care to guess how many times I have been asked what sort of goods were carried in a particular type of ship or stored in a particular block of warehouses. They are questions to which it is very difficult to provide an answer, and the reason for that difficulty takes us back to the need to view a port or even a single dock as a manifestation of mercantile activity. Of course we may find that Old Dock handled Cheshire salt travelling coastwise, but even that, as a single cargo, is unusual. The greater part of Liverpool's trade in the eighteenth century was carried as a multiplicity of comparatively small consignments and the ships that carried them were frequently in multiple ownership. A 'venture' which staked to the normal perils of the sea, and not infrequently those of French privateers as well, was bold, verging on the reckless. Spreading risks was a much commoner, and wiser, way of doing things.

*'A view of the Cuftom Houfe, taken from Traffords Wyent' showing the head of the Old Dock c1770. In the middle distance is St Thomas' Church, Park Lane (opened 1750, closed 1905, bombed 1941). From an engraving by P.P. Burdett and Edward Rooker. (LRO).*

That is the reason why the question 'what did Old Dock handle?' can only yield limp answers about 'mostly the Irish trade' or 'mostly high-value goods whose total transport cost would bear the cost'. It did not necessarily handle the largest ships: the small but valuable trans-Atlantic trade was established before Old Dock was even thought of, much less built or put into service.

Old docks usually suffered the fate I have previously dubbed 'gravitating', where they gradually sank from the highest-value goods carried in the largest ships to those carried in small and decrepit vessels. After about 20 years, the obsolete dock would be either modernised or (much less commonly) in-filled. This was not what happened to Old Dock: too small and too shallow for general trade, still having problems with its walls, and with the lift bridge which crossed its entrance, still needing frequent scuttling, it was totally obsolete. In 1811 Parliamentary authority for its closure and the reclamation of its valuable site was granted. But for those who expected rapid action, disappointment loomed, for the Old Dock was not closed until the summer of 1826. The reason for this, at a time when trade was growing rapidly, was that the Old Dock had become a 'pet dock', that is to say it possessed attributes other than the ability to maximise ship and cargo handling. These included proximity to such services as the Custom House, suppliers of charts or navigational instruments, chandlers, anchor smiths. It was, in short, possessed of the assets which turned a dock system into a port. That is why Old Dock survived beyond its apparent usefulness.

Convenient access to those assets, in their turn, turned a piece of engineering infrastructure from being 'any old dock' into a critically important mercantile dock and its port authority – the Dock Trustees – into a world-beater.

## *References and Notes*

[1]It should not be assumed that Dunkirk was the only wet dock to predate Liverpool's: Portsmouth Great Stone Dock of 1648 was another. Before that, in the 1560s, the Exeter Canal had the first pound locks in Britain to control its waters - a technology which was not even considered for Liverpool docks until John Rennie's Report, commissioned in 1809 (proposing the construction of Princes Dock), came out strongly in favour of fully-impounded rather than half-tide entrances. The importance of the word '*commercial*' is critical when claiming Liverpool's precedence!

## *A Bibliographical Note*

Early mentions of Thomas Steers and his dock in classic accounts of Liverpool by such as Picton and Touzeau are justly castigated by Peet, on grounds both of excessive brevity and of inaccuracy. Peet himself may be credited with the first serious attempt at the subject, but his biographical approach is marred by 'the invisible hand' of Smiles, whose influence in the 1930s was ubiquitous. The Smiles formula includes both unqualified admiration of Steers and exaggeration of his achievement by over-estimation of the difficulties he faced.

There is no inherent reason why a biographical approach need be problematical. On the contrary, Mike Clarke's updated and revision of Nancy Evett's entry in the Oxford Dictionary of National biography avoids the difficulties above, and his 2002 entry on Steers in the Biographical Dictionary of Civil Engineers is a more substantial essay. Clarke's most substantial offering is in a collection of papers given at a research day school at Merseyside Maritime Museum in February 1993, one of a series organised with the University of Liverpool.

Clarke did not only improve the overall knowledge of the subject, he broadened it as well, particularly with regard to Steers' other works.

There are two works which cover the Old Dock from an archaeological viewpoint, which of their nature would be unlikely to adopt a biographical tone. Nancy Ritchie-Noakes' work is centred on the standing structures for which the Merseyside Development Corporation took responsibility in 1981. It was known that substantial remains of Old Dock remained under ground but that they were buried in very expensive places, which mostly confined her work to ancillary structures, but it remains a valuable contribution. The opportunity, indeed the obligation, to excavate arose in 2006 and one of its outputs was a volume by Richard Gregory et al which first summarised then enhanced our knowledge of the archaeology of Old Dock. Additions to the history had been fewer, and the amount of new source material slowed, perhaps with the work of Power and others new effort was going into the interpretive side. By then, if not sooner, it would be a rash scholar who ventured into the field without reading at least some of the following works.

## *Bibliography*


Clarke, Mike. Thomas Steers in *Dock Engineers*: Papers Delivered at a Research Day School at Merseyside Maritime Museum on 13 February 1993, National Museums and Galleries on Merseyside.

Clarke, Mike. *Thomas Steers* in Biographical Dictionary of Civil Engineers (Vol 1) Institution of Civil Engineers (2002).

Gregory, Richard et al. *Archaeology at the Waterfront: Investigating Liverpool's Historic Docks*, Lancaster Imprints (2014).

Peet, H. Thomas Steers, the Engineer of Liverpool's First Dock. A Memoir. *THSLC* LXXXII (1932) 163-181.

Power, Michael. Creating a Port: Liverpool 1695-1715, *THSLC* 149 (2000) 10-71.

Ritchie-Noakes, Nancy. *Liverpool's Historic Waterfront* (1984) HMSO.

Weir, Ian. *Port of Liverpool Quay Walls, An Investigation into the Development of their Design and Construction, 1710-1900*. MSc in History of Science and Technology, University of Liverpool, 1993.

# WALKING ON WATER STREET, Part 8
# VANISHED STREETS: CHORLEY STREET, 1725-1925

*Graham Jones*

Vanished streets are perhaps somewhat like long-departed relatives; gone but fondly remembered through family records and a few fading black-and-white photos taken in their advancing years. Chorley Street is like that. Shown on the first contemporary map of Liverpool – Chadwick's '*Mapp of all the Streets Lanes & Alleys*' of 1725 (detail in fig. 1)[1] – it survived for two centuries, watching first the town and then the city grow all around it.

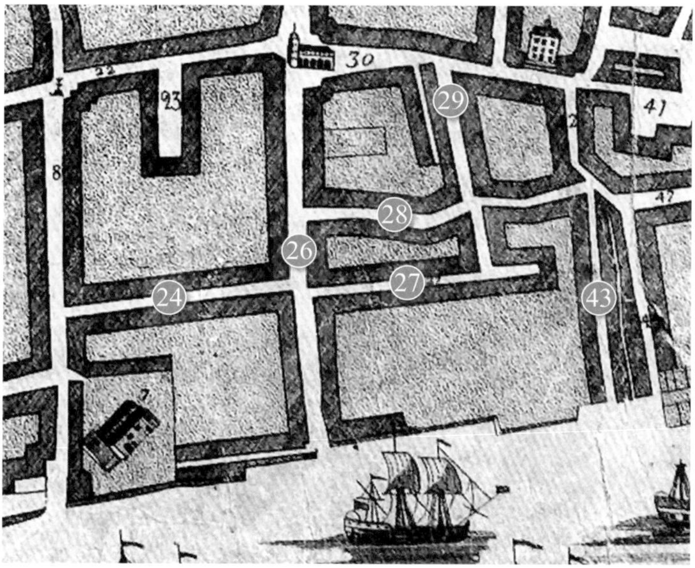


*Fig. 1. Not mentioned in Queen Anne's rate assessment of 1708, Chorley Street appears in the legend to John Chadwick's map as 'Entwisle [sic] Street' (no. 27), an almost straight continuation of Covent Garden (24), and running from Water Street (26) towards Moor Street (43). Immediately above it, Fenwick Street (28) is listed as "Phenwick Street". Later in the century, Phenwick Alley (29) would be replaced by Brunswick Street.*

Increasingly the poor relative of the likes of Water Street and Castle Street, its fate was sealed by the decision to construct the 20th century India Buildings beneath which it now lies buried. But Chorley Street does have a history, albeit fragmentary, and deserves to be celebrated for what it was: a street which at different times bore the names of mayors, recorders and bailiffs (Table).

Mayors, recorders and bailiffs from the Appendix to *Gore's Directory*.

| | | |
|---|---|---|
| 1602-1619 | Leonard Chorley | recorder |
| 1662-1708 | John Entwistle | recorder |
| 1678 | John Chorley | mayor |
| 1706 | William Squire | bailiff |
| 1707 | Henry Chorley | bailiff |
| 1709-1722 | Bertie Entwistle | recorder |
| 1715 | William Squire | mayor |

John Stonehouse mentions '*an old and highly respectable as well as influential family of Liverpool, of which two members held the high office of recorder for many years*'.[2] John Entwistle (who resigned after a remarkable 46 years service) was succeeded by his son Bertie (who died in office) and hence, although Chadwick misses off the second 't' of '*Entwistle*' in his map's legend, it is by their name that Chorley Street was first recorded on a map.

Thomas Steers is remembered as the engineer responsible for Liverpool's first dock but is perhaps not as well known for his association with Chorley Street. However, in 1727, John Entwistle is recorded as leasing to Thomas Steers (for 2,000 years!) property described as '*All those new-erected buildings, being in the upper end of the further orchard or garden... commonly called Chorley Street... which buildings were frequently made use of as a play-house and dancing-school*'.[3] As late as 1852 a delightfully evocative *Dancing School Lane* was still listed as running off Chorley Street.[4]

John Eyes' sketch of 1753 and his map of 1765 (fig. 2)[5] both show the street with its eventual name of Chorley, whilst George Perry's plan of 1769 is unique in marking it as '*Chorley Street or Squire's Garden*'.[6] Indeed, the first three editions of *Gore's Directory* all refer to the street as Squire's Garden prior to its becoming Chorley Street from 1772.[7] When John Gore, '*Bookseller near the Exchange*', published his first directory in 1766 just three names appeared: those of Thomas Eden (merchant), Henry Grimbalston (cooper) and William Hill (tide waiter).[8]

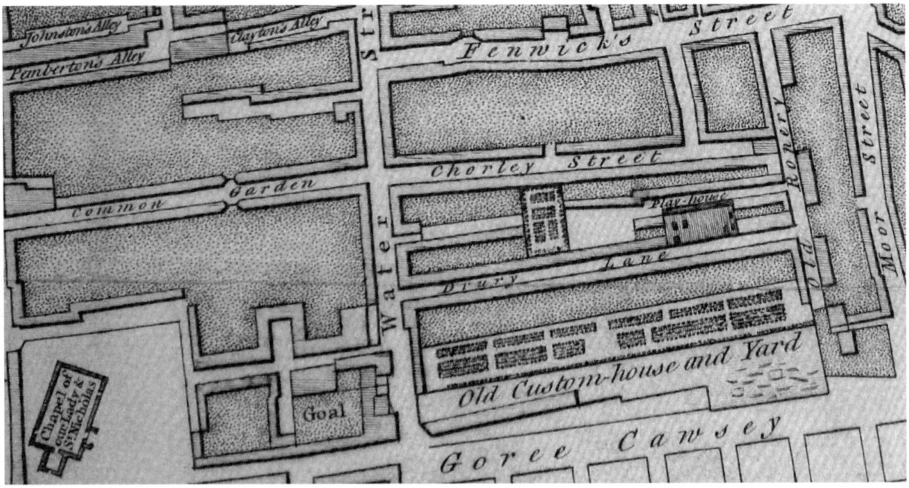


*Fig. 2. Chorley Street on one of John Eyes' maps of 1765. Note the arrival of Drury Lane and Old Ropery, the reversion to the ancient name of Common Garden (from the days when the land was in use as such) and the unusual but common spelling of 'Goal' (the prison and former Tower of Liverpool). Image courtesy of the Athenaeum.*

In 1786, as part of a street improvement scheme, a new street was laid out from Castle Street to George's Dock. Replacing Phenwick Alley (no. 29 in fig. 1), and cutting through Chorley Street, Drury Lane and the Playhouse, it was named Brunswick Street, and Richard Horwood's highly detailed map of Liverpool '*showing every house*' in 1803 indicates the result (fig. 3). In the section of Chorley Street between Water Street and Brunswick Street, and excluding the buildings on each of the four corners which probably were listed in the directories under the main streets, Horwood's survey shows 28 buildings, and between Brunswick Street and Old Ropery a further 10.

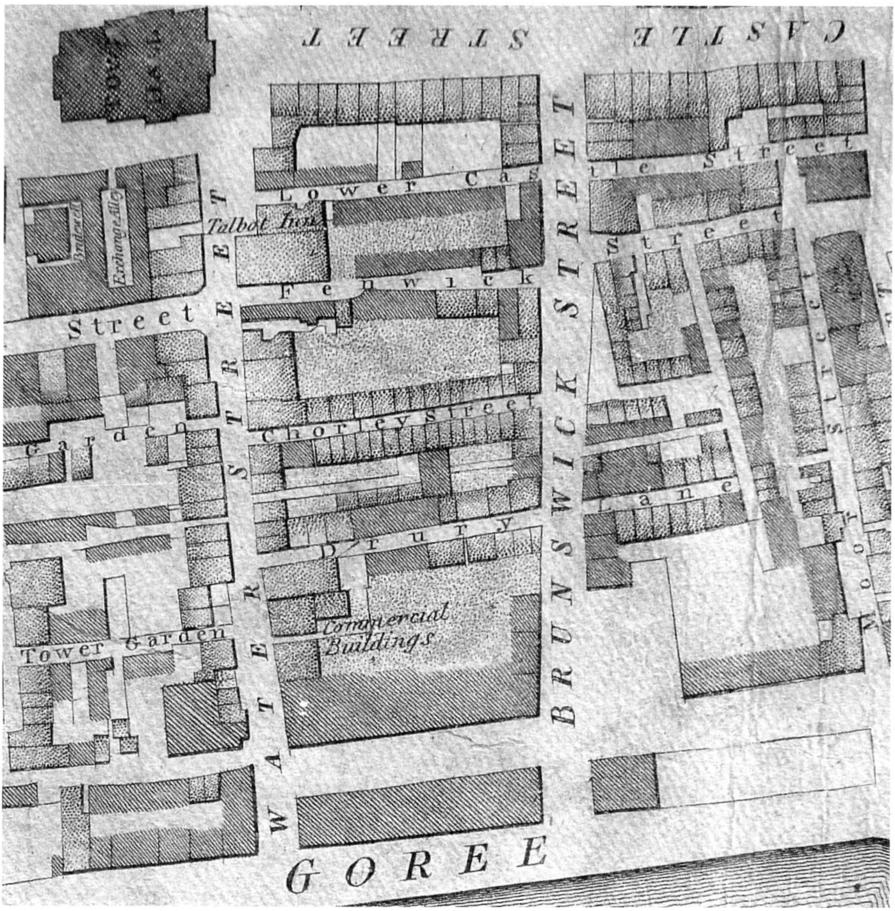


*Fig. 3. Chorley Street in 1803 on Richard Horwood's highly detailed map. Image courtesy of the LRO, ref. Hf 912 1803.*

*Gore's Directory* for 1790 lists the names of 21 people who lived in Chorley Street in a total of 18 properties (some of which would also have been their places of work). They comprised an auctioneer, brewer, cooper, joiner, two shoemakers, two shopkeepers, three tailors, a tinplate worker, an upholsterer, two victuallers, and – given that the street was a matter of yards from George's Dock – a mariner and no less than five pilots. A 22nd person, a merchant, was the only one listed as living elsewhere but with his premises – a counting house – in the street, and one other building was listed as the Court of Request Office. This therefore accounts for only 20 of the 38 buildings on Horwood's map and also gives no clue as to the total number of occupants or of the true extent of activity in the street.

However, a population survey, '*Taken by M Simmons, from October 13th, 1789, to January 13th, 1790*' (reproduced in the 1790 directory) provides a more complete picture. Chorley Street is listed as having 36 front houses (accommodating 254 people) and two back houses or cottages (11 people) (38 buildings in total, in good agreement with Horwood's map) plus an additional eight cellars within those buildings (29 people). The total of 294 people that were living there may be compared with the totals in the surrounding streets: 242 in Water Street, 178 in Drury Lane, 173 in Moor Street, 140 in Covent Garden and 125 in Fenwick Street. In 1790 therefore, even with the disruption caused by the arrival of Brunswick Street four years earlier, Chorley Street had maintained its historical importance.

In the 19th century, however, things would begin to change dramatically. By 1805 the number of people listed as living or working in Chorley Street had dropped to 12. In 1810 Troughton's *History of Liverpool* depicted the arrival of the first Corn Exchange in Brunswick Street (fig. 4) which had required the obliteration of the 10 Chorley Street buildings between Brunswick Street and Old Ropery. And by 1824 the list for Chorley Street in *Baines' Directory* had shrunk to nine names.

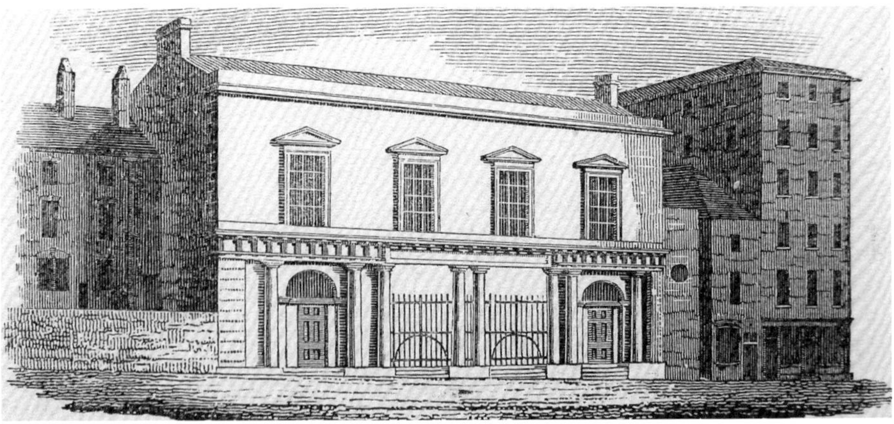

*Fig. 4. From Troughton's History of Liverpool, 1810, showing the town's first Corn Exchange in Brunswick Street. Image courtesy of the LRO, ref. Photographs & Small Prints (P&SP): Commerce & Industry: Trades: Corn Exchange (old).*

*Gore's Directory* for 1829 contains just seven names: the street was the residence of Elijah Airey (victualler), Ann Balmer (rabbit dealer), Ellen Davies (victualler), Robert Hunter (warehouseman) and Samuel Warburton (joiner), whilst it also contained the cooperage of William Harrison and the office of the merchant Robert Syers (both living elsewhere).

And it was Robert who, a year later and just before his retirement, published his famous '*The History of Everton*', about which James Picton would later be full of praise for its '*Boswellian minuteness of portraiture, and a naivete which is racy and amusing in the highest degree*'.[9]

Michael Alexander Gage's detailed survey of 1835 reveals the considerable redevelopment of the commercial area that had begun to take place by then (fig. 5). The street widening scheme, begun in Castle Street in 1786, had been completed in Water Street as far as the newly constructed Liverpool Union Bank, most if not all of Chorley Street's ancient dwellings had been replaced by offices and warehouses, and (thc first) India Buildings had also arrived.

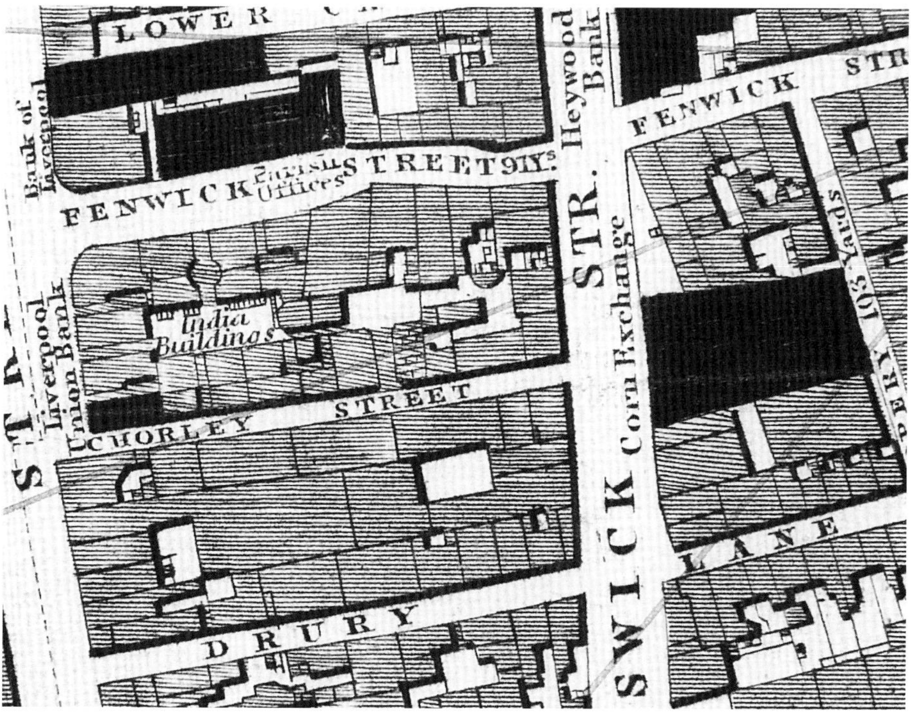


*Fig. 5. From Michael Alexander Gage's plan, surveyed in 1835 and published in 1836, showing where a section of Chorley Street had been replaced by the Corn Exchange and where the dwellings in the remaining section had also been superseded by larger buildings. Private collection. The LRO copies are under ref. Hf 912 1836.*

It was not until 1839 that *Gore's Directory* began to provide a numerical (street by street) index in addition to the alphabetical list of names. By then, however, Chorley Street had been so transformed that it did not justify its own listing, and the 1848 O.S. provides an indication of what had taken place (fig. 6).

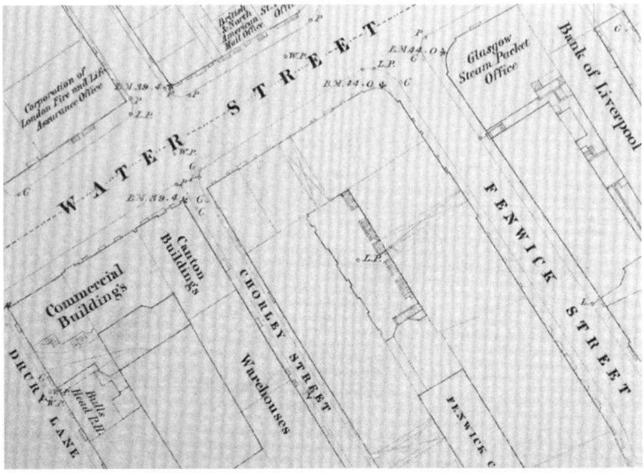


*Fig. 6. A detail from the bottom edge of sheet 24 of the 1848 O.S. (correctly oriented to the north in contrast to the other maps) showing Chorley Street as having become a passageway between offices and warehouses. Image courtesy of the Athenaeum.*

When *Kelly's Directories* took over publication of the directory at the end of the 19th century, it introduced a listing for Chorley Street and this shows just what little remained (fig. 7).[10]

**CHORLEY ST.—W**
*Water st*
Hetherington's vaults
**Mawdsley James and Son,**
***TELEPHONE* No. 727**
printing and lithographing works
Mawdsley J. P. warehouse keeper
*Brunswick st*

*Fig. 7. The entry for Chorley Street in the directory for 1900, the third issue published by Kelly's Directories. Image courtesy of the Athenaeum.*

Relegated to life as an alleyway for the collection and discharge of goods at warehouses, its ultimate fate had been sealed. In the next century, in a further street improvement programme, it would finally vanish. And it was not until 1923, two hundred years after its creation, that a view of the street first came to be recorded – or a view of it, whether sketch or photograph, first came to be preserved (fig. 8). It forms part of the City Engineer's immensely valuable collection at the LRO. Seen from Water Street and with the Corn Exchange visible in the distance, warehouses on either side of Chorley Street are linked by a makeshift covered bridge.

*Fig. 8. 5th July 1923, the earliest known view of Chorley Street in a detail from a City Engineer's Department photograph. Image courtesy of the LRO, ref. P&SP: Streets & Districts: Chorley Street.*

The photographer was standing with his back to Covent Garden, Lloyds Bank's Colonial & Foreign Department was still open for business in Canton Buildings, three women had paused for a chat outside Frank Lamb's shop, and a bread van was passing by. How many of them, other than the Engineer's Department photographer, knew what was to come so soon?

A year later and seen from Brunswick Street (fig. 9), a photograph shows Chorley Street's redundant warehouse hoists on the right whilst, on the left, wooden chutes can be seen discharging rubble into heaps. Beyond the pedestrians on Water Street, the view extends along Covent Garden to offices on Chapel Street.

*Fig. 9. June 1924, a view along Chorley Street seen from Brunswick Street. Image courtesy of the LRO, ref. P&SP: Streets & Districts: Brunswick Street.*

*Fig. 10. June 1924, and another view of Chorley Street from the Water Street end. Image courtesy of the LRO, ref. P&SP: Streets & Districts: Chorley Street.*

During that same month in 1924 a city engineer walked down from the Town Hall, stepped into Covent Garden, turned around and focused his camera again upon Chorley Street (fig. 10). Hoarding had now arrived to block the entrance and, ominously for the middle of the day, Frank Lamb's doorway had a gate across it. Lloyds had moved to India Buildings in Fenwick Street, two boys posed for the engineer, and a bowler-hatted man chatted to a street trader and glanced at the man's basket of wares. And the buildings stood empty, awaiting their fate.

Then, in 1925, the photographer J F Smith captured the final obliteration of Chorley Street in a view which would have reduced two centuries of its ghosts to tears (fig. 11). On the left the foundations were being laid for the western section of '*Holt's Buildings*' (the second India Buildings) and, standing silently in the background, Oriel Chambers had watched Canton Buildings vanishing and was wondering which other of its neighbours would go next.

*Fig. 11. Left: 24th March 1925, and a dramatic image by the photographer J F Smith captures the final disappearance of Chorley Street. Image courtesy of the LRO, ref. P&SP: Commerce & Industry: Firms: India Buildings.*

*Fig. 12. Below: In 1927 and viewed from the Water Street / Rumford Street junction, the new and half-completed second India Buildings towers over the old one. Image courtesy of Liverpool University Press.*

Two years later in a remarkable photograph (fig. 12), subsequently reproduced in *Blue Funnel* by Francis Hyde,[11] two India Buildings – both the old and the partially completed new – stand alongside each other. A reminder of Chorley Street is marked by the break in the pavement prior to the demolition of the old India Buildings and, with it, the completion of another section of street widening.

Chorley Street thus disappeared from maps (fig. 13) and before the end of the 20th century, with the '*Commercial Quarter*' having moved a few hundred yards northwards into St Paul's Square taking with it several important businesses, the Water Street area had become a ghost town, and India Buildings – together with many of its once busy neighbours – was struggling to remain viable.

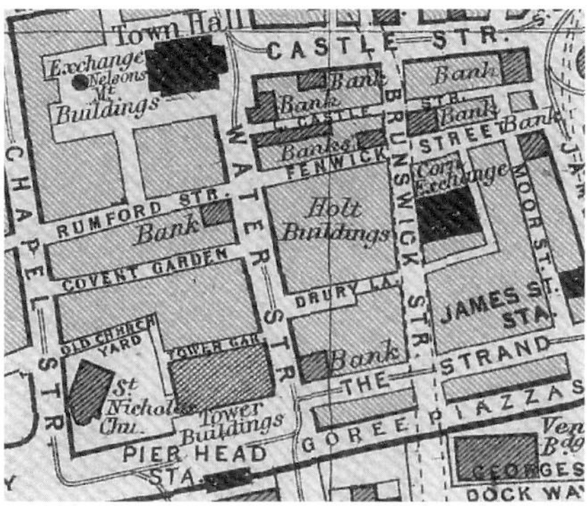


*Fig. 13. From a 1930s Bartholomew's map of the city centre marking Holt's Buildings and the Corn Exchange – memories of where Chorley Street once ran. Image courtesy of Harper Collins.*

Then, in 2012, the *Liverpool Post* reported that '*The future of one of Liverpool's most famous buildings appears in crisis, with tenants fearing eviction and its owner cautioned by the council for illegally removing its eight bronze entrance plaques*'.[12] Liverpool's planning conservation officer issued a caution to the owner, and with the developer's threat to close Holt's Arcade and convert it into offices – an arcade which, as the successor to Chorley Street, was considered a right of way between Water Street and Brunswick Street – two of the arcade's shopkeepers launched an SOS campaign.[13] At the time of writing things remain uncertain for this once vibrant arcade (fig. 14), but the owners of the antique shop, barbers and newsagents that have survived are "*just hanging on*".

*Fig. 14. December 2014. Christmas in 21st century Chorley Street, looking towards the Water Street entrance and with many of the Holt's Arcade shops standing sadly empty. Author's photograph.*

The eventual sweeping away of Chorley Street was an inevitable consequence of commercial growth. The Entwistles, the Chorleys, and the Squires had given it their names and dignity at a time in Liverpool's history when most eyes were perhaps focused on the hoped-for success of the first dock. However, thanks to John Gore and his initiative in producing a Liverpool directory, it is not only their names that can be remembered, but also those of a variety of the townsfolk who arrived and departed through two centuries of growth and decline. If there are ghosts that inhabit the travertine marble arcade – perhaps including Ann Balmer's rabbits – maybe they will ensure that a memory of Chorley Street lives on.

## *References and notes*

[1] Chadwick's map, of which there is an original at the Liverpool Record Office (as used here, ref. Hf912 1725), has many copies, a good quality version being in *Pictures from the Post*, Daily Post & Echo, 1946 (LRO ref. 942.7214 LIV, 1946). Most early maps of Liverpool, even after the 1848 O.S., are oriented towards the east.

[2] James Stonehouse, *Transactions of the Historic Society of Lancashire and Cheshire* (THSLC), 1852-53, vol. 5, p. 193 (LRO ref. 942.7206 HIS). Stonehouse mistakenly suggested that Entwistle Street was the original name for Drury Lane, a misunderstanding which has been repeated in some subsequent histories despite James Picton's correction (*Memorials of Liverpool,* 2nd edn., 1875, vol. II, pp. 90-91) that '*Chorley Street was originally called Entwistle Street; afterwards Squire's Garden,*' and that Drury Lane was a new street laid out in the late 1840s.

[3] Henry Peet, *THSLC*, 1930, vol. 82, p. 230.

[4] *A List of the Streets, Lanes, Squares, Alleys, &c. in the Town of Liverpool, in 1752*, tabulated in *Gore's Directory*, 1805, pp. 109-111. This was the first directory published by Johnson Gore, his father having died in 1803.

[5] Eyes' 1753 sketch: LRO ref. *Binns collection*, vol. 9, Hf942.7204. 1765 map: Hf912 1765.

[6] LRO ref. Hf912 1769. The LRO also has six documents (part of a collection under ref. 354 EVE/5) dated 1716 and signed by William Squire whilst mayor.

[7] A possible explanation for the eventual decision to settle on the name Chorley Street was perhaps in memory of the fact that '*A Seamen's Hospital for aged sailors and their families was established in 1752, drawing upon a legacy for this purpose left by John Chorley*.' Noted by Jane Longmore in *Liverpool 800* (ed. John Belchem), Liverpool University Press, 2006, p. 151.

[8] G T Shaw, *THSLC*, 1906, vol. 58, pp. 113-162. Shaw remarked that the number of houses in Liverpool in 1766 was estimated at 6000 and yet the directory contained only 1134 names, and wondered on what basis John Gore had made his selection. '*On the title-page the directory is described as 'an alphabetical list of the merchants, tradesmen, and principal inhabitants.' What was the 'hall-mark' of respectability on those included?*' The three residents in Chorley Street in 1766 may be compared with the 42 (mainly merchants and traders) in Water Street.

[9] James Picton, *op. cit*., p. 339.

[10] James Mawdsley & Son had taken over publication of *Gore's Directory* earlier in the century and had retained the Gore's name. 1897 was their final year as publishers, using their printing and lithographing works in Chorley Street. It then passed into the hands of *Kelly's Directories* who likewise retained the Gore's name for several years. The penultimate entry for Chorley Street in 1922 was for *Oriental Import Co. fine art dealers*, and the final entry in 1923 was for *Alfred Holt & Co. (stewards' dept)*. Both were on the west side of the street and were therefore in the first buildings to be demolished (the left hand side of fig. 11). *The Liverpool Review*, 26 January 1889, p. 4, carried a fascinating account of Mawdsley's production process in an article entitled, *How a Directory is Made. 200 Liverpudlians at the Game*. It is available on microfilm at Liverpool Central Library.

[11] Francis E Hyde, *Blue Funnel*, Liverpool University Press, 1st edn., 1956.

[12] Peter Elson's article in *The Liverpool Post*, 22 November 2012, p. 7.

[13] See, for example, the article in *Private Eye*, 14 December 2012, p. 11.

# EISTEDDFODS IN LIVERPOOL

## *Brian Woodbridge*

As a schoolboy at the Liverpool Collegiate in the late forties, I had a choice of travelling by the number 19 tramcar from my house in Anfield or taking a three mile hike to Harvey Lonsdale Elmes' great sandstone building on Shaw Street, and if it was dry I often chose the latter. In those days the streets of Liverpool were paved with gold. I could walk all the way to town along pavements of York stone. My route would take me through the Victorian suburbs of Everton and it was littered with history all the way. It began with a long trek up Beacon Lane to the top of Everton Hill where a beacon was said to have been lit in 1588 to warn of an imminent Spanish invasion.[1] This had been replaced by St George's, the world's first iron framed church and within its churchyard lay a Russian consul and his family.[2]

*Heyworth Street, Everton, at its junction (on the extreme right) with Wentworth Street, 1949. Note the York stone pavements. (RJ).*

Walking along the ridge of the hill and Heyworth Street (pictured above), I was crossing the campfield of the royalist army of Prince Rupert, who had laid siege to the castellated town of Liverpool below, during the Civil War. Rupert Street, named after him, took me through the old Everton Village, past the ancient lock-up tower[3] and down Everton Brow, probably the steepest street in the whole of Liverpool. This brought me to level ground on Shaw Street, with Whitley Gardens on my left. Through the railings I could see a large cross with inscriptions commemorating the Indian Mutiny of 1857,[4] and then further on was a huge outcrop of sandstone with the tower of St Augustine's Church overlooking what appeared to be a druid circle with a much bigger stone in the middle. Had they been erected by the druids in days gone by? Surely Liverpool didn't have a monument of ancient times, I asked myself. But the bell was already ringing for morning assembly as I passed through the Collegiate's majestic entrance to sign the punishment book for being late again.

*Remains of druid circle with Shaw Street in the background. Author's image.*

For the next few years I pestered a long line of history teachers with the questions about the stones and their significance. None of them knew and I could not find the answer in the library so eventually I stored the question away in my memory bank. It was not until many years later that it was all brought back to me. Exploring Wales with my young family, I began to notice that many of the towns had a similar ring of stones. On enquiring with the locals, I was informed, "*Oh, they were put up for the Eisteddfod.*" and of course I knew about those festivals of music and verse that were held in a different place in Wales every year.

Shortly after, we were crossing the Stanley Embankment on Anglesey and the elderly Welshman, who collected the toll money, asked where I was from. When I told him, he responded with a smile, "*Liverpool, Capital of North Wales.*" As I drove off, I knew I had the answer to my question regarding the Shaw Street stones. As a boy in Anfield, the clues had all been around me. At school many of the boys in my class had Welsh surnames: Davies, Hughes, Griffiths, Jones, Parry, Roberts and Williams, and many more. The phone book was full of them. Most of the houses had been built by Welsh builders with bricks from Ruabon and they often named the roads after their birthplaces: Kemlyn, Bala, Dinorwic, Wylva, Valley and Skerries immediately sprang to mind.

The same could be said of other parts of Liverpool. The Welsh streets of the Dingle in South Liverpool were another example and of course there were the big department stores T.J. Hughes and Owen Owen to name but two. My mother's maiden name was Foulkes, and to cap it all, my wife was an Evans. So it was obvious, the Welsh had flooded into Liverpool during its evolution as 'The second City of the Empire'. The establishment of this strong Welsh community in the area would certainly justify holding an Eisteddfod here, and the ring of stones in Shaw Street, I now realised, was where it was held.

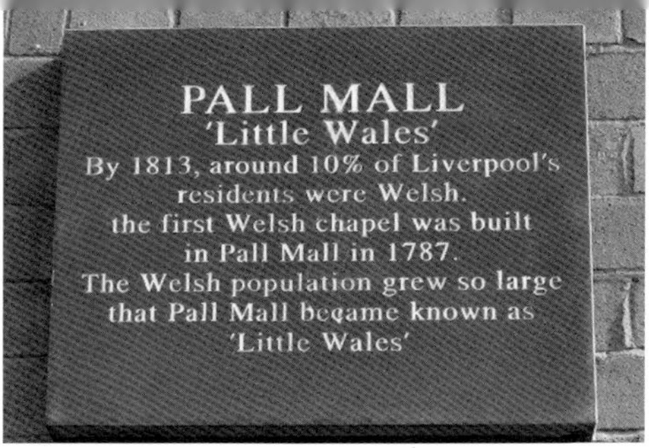


*Above: plaque erected on the wall of J. Thompson Office Furniture, 78 Pall Mall, on 21st August 2007.*
*Right: Bardic chair in Liverpool Town Hall from the 1900 Liverpool Eisteddfod.*
*Below: panel detail from chair. All author's images.*

A visit to the Town Hall proved I was right, for in the Entrance Hall on either side of the fireplace were two Bardic Chairs, obviously used in the ceremonies and suggesting that there had been more than one Liverpool Eisteddfod. Further research in the Central Library revealed that Liverpool had in fact hosted three of these events, in 1884, 1900 and 1929.

The first began on Monday 15th September 1884, during W.E. Gladstone's second time in office and with the backdrop of the war in the Sudan. From early in the morning, thousands of people arrived on special trains from Wales. An arena had been constructed and suitably decorated in the North Cornmarket on Cazneau Street to accommodate at least ten thousand spectators. Also, a circle of unhewn stones had been created in the gardens in Shaw Street for the bardic ceremonies which were an essential part of the Eisteddfod. The first of these, known as the Gorsedd, took place on the Tuesday morning when the procession of bards, all draped in their colourful masonic-like garments and headdresses, paraded along Shaw Street and made their way through the vast crowds into Whitley Gardens.

*Above: the author tries out the bardic chair.*

*Gorsedd Bards at the Liverpool Eisteddford. Photograph by John Thomas, 1884, courtesy of the People's Collection Wales website.*

The ceremony was conducted in Welsh and each bard bore a special name. The Archdruid, Hyfa Mon, took up his position, facing east towards the sun, standing on the centre stone, known as the Maen Wog or Logan stone. Twelve druids assembled at each of the outer stones which represented the signs of the zodiac, and the rest stood inside the circle with the sacred sword and harp, representing war and peace. They were surrounded by thousands of spectators. The sword was unsheathed and the question, "*Is it peace?*" was asked in Welsh. The response was in the affirmative, so the sword was returned to its scabbard. After a roll call of the bards, the Gorsedd prayer was read, the following being a translation: "*Grant oh God thy protection; and in protection, strength; and in strength, understanding; and in understanding, knowledge; and in knowledge, knowledge of the just; and in knowledge of the just, the love of it; and in that love, the love of all existences; and in the love of existences, the love of God. God and all goodness*." The Archdruid gave the Eisteddfod address, after which the meeting was closed. The crowds parted to allow the druids to leave in procession through the crowded streets to the North Haymarket. Here, the Eisteddfod festival was held throughout the week.

On the first day, the Lord Mayor, Thomas Holder, presided over the opening ceremony to great applause and after further speeches and the singing of the Eisteddfod song, adjudications eventually began. Prizes were awarded for poetry, prose, art, musical performances and singing, as well as wood carving, sculpture and handicrafts. Later in the afternoon choirs competed and in the evening there was a grand miscellaneous concert, presided over by William Rathbone MP.[5]

The next day continued with the Lord Lieutenant of Denbighshire, Cornwallis West, presiding. In his opening remarks he reminded the audience that Liverpool was always regarded as the metropolis of North Wales. The main events of the day were the choral competitions and the Liverpool Philharmonic choral society performed at the evening concert.[6]

On Thursday, there was another meeting of the Gorsedd at St Augustine's mount in Shaw Street and again there was a large crowd to greet the bards in their ceremonial dress. The archdruid addressed the crowd, thanking the organisers for giving them sunny weather and for successfully transplanting the Eisteddfod to English soil, adding that Liverpool had probably more Welshmen than any town in Wales. He also stressed the importance of keeping up the Welsh language, and announced that the next Eisteddfod would be in Aberdare. The procession then made its way to the Pavilion where the adjudications continued. The highpoint of the afternoon was when the winner of the bardic chair for poetry was announced. With sounding trumpets and deafening applause Evan Rees was enthroned.[7] Further contests and musical

LAST DAY.

ROYAL NATIONAL EISTEDDFOD

AND

MUSICAL FESTIVAL,

TO BE HELD IN THE GRAND PAVILION IN THE HAYMARKET, LIVERPOOL.

SEPT. 15TH, 16TH, 17TH, 18TH, 19TH, AND 20TH.

THIS DAY (SATURDAY),

AT ELEVEN O'CLOCK,

PRESIDENT, ALDERMAN CHAMBRES, J.P.

GRAND BRASS BAND CONTEST.

(Twenty-five Bands Entered.)

THIS (SATURDAY) EVENING, AT SEVEN O'CLOCK.

PRESIDENT, JOHN HUGHES, ESQ., J.P., C.C.

GRAND CONCERT.

ARTISTES.

MADAME EDITH WYNNE,

MADAME ANTOINETTE STERLING,

Mr. LUCAS WILLIAMS, Mr. DYFED LEWYS,
Mr. HIRWEN JONES, IORWERTH AP GWAIN.

Mr. W. H. JUDE,

LIVERPOOL CYMRIC VOCAL UNION,
THE LIVERPOOL CAMBRIAN QUARTETTE,
PENILLION SINGING BY IDRIS VYCHAN,
HARPIST, TELYNOR SIRIOL.

ACCOMPANISTS:
Miss MAGGIE EVANS and Mr. J. SKEAF.
CONDUCTOR—Mr. DAVID WILLIAMS.

*Above: Liverpool Daily Post, Saturday 20th September 1884. Left: poster for the Liverpool Eisteddfod 1900, courtesy of the People's Collection Wales website.*

performances took place on Friday, and on the final day, brass band competitions were held throughout the day, with a final concert in the evening.

The first Eisteddfod of the 20th century was held in Liverpool in 1900 against the backdrop of the Boer War and it was patronised by Queen Victoria and the Prince of Wales. Again the Welsh poured into the city in their thousands from trains and boats to attend their annual event. It was bright, genial weather that favoured the bards as they assembled in their colourful robes of blue, white and green, in front of the Alexandra Hall in Islington Square. The band of the training ship *Indefatigable* led the parade through the dense crowds along Shaw Street playing *March of the Men of Harlech*. The crowds parted to allow them to enter Whitley Gardens where the Gorsedd ceremony would be enacted with the tower of St Augustine overlooking the scene. Archdruid Hyfa Mon and his deputy Cadfan took up their places on the central 'Maen Log' stone and the rest of the bards assembled on the outer ring of sacred stones. The gorsedd prayer was recited by Gwynedd in Welsh in a loud majestic voice, followed by the Heddwch ritual. As the sword was partly unsheathed, Hyfa Mon put the question three times "*A ces Heddweh?*" (Is it peace?). The response was an emphatic "*Heddeh!*" (peace). The sword was returned to its scabbard and the Gorsedd song was sung with harp accompaniment. The Archdruid addressed the meeting followed by other bards. Lord Mayor Louis Cohen and his wife were given the honorary titles of Cohenydd and Mai Cohenydd and were introduced to Hyfa Mon, who invested them with the degree of ovates (beginners). The Lord Mayor and Lord Mostyn briefly addressed the gathering, and then the meeting was brought to an end.[8]

The band led the procession from the gardens through the crowded streets all the way to the pavilion in the North Haymarket, which had been the venue in 1884. The Lord Mayor addressed the packed audience, welcomed all the Welsh visitors and formally opened the Eisteddfod. The competitions began in art, poetry and music. Adjudications were given in both Welsh and English, and medals and cash prizes were awarded. Concerts were held each evening throughout the course of the event.

*Photograph courtesy the People's Collection Wales website.*

The crowning of the bard ceremony took place on Wednesday, the recipient being the Rev. John T. Job, with the winning ode. The following day, there was a final meeting of the Gorsedd, with the fine weather continuing. The afternoon opened in the Pavilion with a selection by the band of the *Indefatigable*. During all the events the Chairing of the Bard ceremony took place. The Rev. John Owain Williams of Liverpool or Pedrog, to give him his bardic name, was enthroned amidst great enthusiasm. It was the third time he had won the chair.[9]

On the Friday morning, the Archdruid paid an eloquent complement to the city of Liverpool and its organisers for a very successful Eisteddfod. In the evening the proceedings were rounded off with a popular concert held in the Pavilion with the band of the Coldstream Guards, the Royal Eisteddfod Choir and many popular Welsh singers of the period.[10]

*Below left: workmen in April 1928 at Princes Park seen placing the centre stone for the Gorsedd circle in readiness for the Archdruid of Wales, J.O. Williams, to make the Proclamation for the 1929 Liverpool Eisteddfod. From the Daily Post, April 1928, courtesy Trinity Mirror plc. Below right: Photograph courtesy the People's Collection Wales website.*

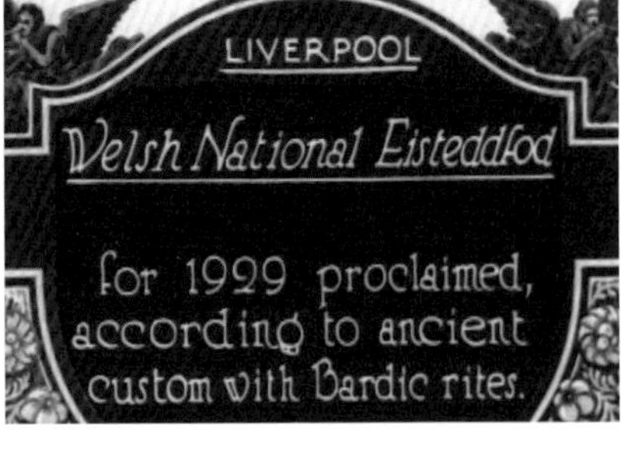

During the reign of King George V, the Eisteddfod returned to Liverpool for a third time. Opening on 6th August 1929, this time a venue had been chosen in the south end of the city. A druid stone circle had been prepared in Princes Park and close by in Sefton Park a huge pavilion had been erected capable of accommodating eleven thousand people. This parkland area was known in ancient times as Esmedune,[11] and had been acquired by King John as his private hunting forest. Once again the city was taken over by the Welsh, pouring out of vehicles of every description. The Cunard liner *Laconia* arrived at the landing stage, flying the Eisteddfod flag, and carrying 533 Welsh Americans. The event began with the procession of the Gorsedd (the Guild of the Bards), from the Welsh Wesleyan Chapel in Princes Avenue. A band led the way playing familiar Welsh airs. Then came the herald bard on horseback, followed by the bearers of the Gorsedd standard and the red dragon of Wales. Next was the Archdruid Pedrog, dressed in white robes with a gold celtic breastplate, a laurel wreath adorning his head, and all the leading bards who were dressed in robes of blue, green, white and red. It was appropriate that Pedrog had been made Archdruid for this return to Liverpool as he was the popular Reverend John Owain Williams of Kensington Chapel, who had won the bardic chair on three previous occasions, the last being at the 1900 event in Liverpool.

*Gorsedd Bards at the third Liverpool Eisteddfod.*
*Photograph courtesy the People's Collection Wales website.*

The procession finally made its way through the packed crowds in Princes Park. Pedrog entered the circle and mounted the central logan stone and the bards took up their positions all around him. The druids in white to signify purity, piety, learning and truth; poets in sky blue were associated with peace and tranquillity and the ovates, or beginners, were bareheaded and wearing green to symbolise growth. Among the ovates were Lord Mayor Henry Morley Miller and his wife who were later given honorary titles of Melinid and Mym e Melinid (miller and miller's wife). Together, they awaited the ceremony of graduation when the Archdruid would confer on them their bardic titles and they could then assume their hoods. The Gorsedd opened with the Corn Gwlad trumpet sounding a call to the four cardinal points and summoning the bardic brotherhood. The Gorsedd prayer was chanted, followed by the familiar ceremony of the sword. A female bard presented the Hirlas horn to the Archdruid who then gave his address, proclaiming the opening of the Eisteddfod. In his speech, he compared the Gorsedd to an oak tree rooted in the heart of the country. After a benedictory hymn was sung, the new members were admitted and the meeting was closed. The procession reformed and made its way from the park through the crowded streets to the pavilion in Sefton Park where there were competitions and adjudications throughout the day and the first of the evening concerts.[12]

On the Wednesday, Dr David, the Bishop of Liverpool, presided remarking that he was half Welsh but felt wholly Welsh this week. He was presented with an altar cloth for the cathedral.

The highlight of the afternoon was the crowning of Caradog Prichard. The Lord Mayor was presented with a presidential chair by the Australian Welsh, who were in attendance, made from many of their native woods.[13]

On Thursday, the Gorsedd was attended by thousands. It began with the cornet summons and was followed with the Gorsedd prayer. Miss Katie Williams and two little girls brought offerings of corn, flowers and honey to the Archdruid who gave thanks for the symbolic gifts. Candidates were admitted to their degrees and there was robing of the bards, followed by honorary aspirants including Captain Prothers of the *Laconia*. The ceremony drew to a close with the spirited singing of *The Land of my Fathers*.[14]

In the afternoon, trumpets announced the arrival of the procession as they entered the arena, which was filled to capacity to witness the Chairing of the Bard ceremony with special guest, Lloyd George, in attendance. Dr. D. Emrys James of Aberystwyth mounted the platform to the strains of *See the Conquering Hero Comes* and was duly installed in the chair. At three o'clock, Lloyd George received a tremendous reception as he rose to address the audience: "*It is 45 years since I first came to the Liverpool Eisteddfod*," he began, "*I was a little lad from Criccieth and came by excursion*." Speaking in Welsh and English, he quoted Abraham Lincoln, "*God loved the common people, that's why he made so many of them*" and he added that the common people had kept the Eisteddfod alive. The old Prime Minister had not lost any of his eloquent oratory powers and after his speech it was almost an anti-climax as the business returned to the customary competitions and awards. Overall, the Eisteddfod was declared a huge success and it left Liverpool the following day, never to return again.[15]

In 2008, when Liverpool was awarded European Capital of Culture status, it was hoped that the Eisteddfod would be brought to the city again as part of the festivities, but sadly the suggestion was not pursued.

Today if you visit Princes Park, you will search in vain for any trace of the druid circle, but in Shaw Street, Whitley Gardens has become part of the huge Everton Park which sprawls across the hillside. There, below the sandstone outcrop, the stones that aroused a young boy's curiosity all those years ago are still standing. Despite the ravages of time and that area, they somehow survived. Some stones are missing and others out of place and the site is badly in need of some restoration and a suitable information plaque to tell their story.[16] But, the city's links with Cymru are still strong and if you climb the hill on a clear day and look out across Liverpool Bay, you will be rewarded with a wonderful panoramic view of the mountains of North Wales: the Land of my Fathers.

*View from Everton Park looking west over the Mersey and Dee to the hills of North Wales. Author's photograph.*

Before I close, I must mention that we did have two other Eisteddfods in Merseyside on the other side of the river. These were held in 1879 and 1917 in Paxton's wonderful Birkenhead Park. The second one was held during the first World War and came to be known as 'The Eisteddfod of the black chair'. When the winner of the bardic chair was announced, nobody came forward. It was later discovered that the winner. Ellis Evans, had been killed in the Battle of Paschendale a few days earlier. Ironically his poem was entitled, 'The Hero', in Welsh of course. Sadly the chair was draped in black and transported all the way back to his village at Tresfynydd, in Mid Wales.

***References*:**


[1] There was a number of these beacons erected around the coast of Britain to act as an alarm and to summon resistance to an attack by King Philip II's fleet (see: Pye, Ken, www.discover-liverpool.com)

[2] Nicholas Mahs of St Petersburg, Consul for Russia at Liverpool died 18th June 1891

[3] Inaugurated in 1787, a depiction of the tower has appeared on Everton Football Club's crest since 1938

[4] Memorial to the Eighth (King's) Regiment. See Cavanagh, Terry, *Public Sculpture of Liverpool*, Liverpool University Press, 1997, p 211-2

[5] *Liverpool Echo*: Proclamation of the Gorsedd and Inaugural Eisteddfod Meeting at the Pavilion, Tuesday 16th September 1884

[6] *Liverpool Echo*: Report on the Day's Proceedings, Wednesday 17th September 1884

[7] *Liverpool Echo*: Report on 2nd Meeting of Gorsedd and Proceedings, Thursday 18th September 1884

[8] *Liverpool Echo*: Opening of the Gorsedd, Tuesday 18th September 1900

[9] *Liverpool Echo*: National Eisteddfod, Wednesday 19th September 1900

[10] *Liverpool Echo*: The Eisteddfod. Close of the Festival, Friday 21st September 1900

[11] The area now known as Smithdown was listed in the Domesday Book as Esmedune, commissioned by William I. See: Syers, Robert, *The History of Everton*, G & J Robinson, 1830 p 42 (available online as free e-book)

[12] *Liverpool Echo*: Welsh Americans Here, and The Gorsedd Ceremony, Tuesday 6 August 1929

[13] *Liverpool Echo*: Eisteddfod Welcomes the Bishop, Wednesday 7th August 1929

[14] *Liverpool Echo*: Thousands at Gorsedd, Thursday 8th August 1929

[15] *Liverpool Echo*: Lloyd George's Speech at the Eisteddfod, Thursday 8th August 1929

[16] The 1917 Eisteddfod at Birkenhead Park, for example, is commemorated by a monument inscribed with a Celtic design (see: http://www.pmsa.org.uk/pmsa-database/5115/)

# A HEALTHY FINAL JOURNEY

## The development of Liverpool's cemeteries – c.1760 to 1910

*F.T. Forrest*

*Fig.1. Low Hill General Cemetery (The Necropolis). Engraving by Robt. Wallis from drawing by T. Allom.*

The population movement within Britain from the countryside to the town and city as a consequence of the Industrial Revolution created a number of public health problems that were for a while a very serious threat to the life expectancy of all urban dwellers, rich and poor alike. Many towns expanded very rapidly and in a largely unplanned manner, leading to outbreaks of cholera, typhus and other infectious diseases caused mainly by poor or non-existent water supply and sewerage as well as inadequate and overcrowded housing. Liverpool saw serious cholera outbreaks in 1832 (when 1500 people died) and 1849 that began in poor areas but, with so many people crammed into then such a small area, all were under threat.

Valiant work by engineers, doctors and politicians locally and nationally to help to alleviate these problems is well documented but not so well known are the health dangers posed by small cemeteries, usually in urban churchyards, which rapidly became overcrowded with the dead of the rising population. In time these corpses, inevitably buried closer and closer to the surface as unused space declined, became a health hazard to the living. In the sloping graveyard of St John's Church, which was situated on today's St John's Gardens, opened by the Parish of Liverpool in 1767 and largely used for burial of the poor, over time some coffins buried close to the surface are said to have gradually descended the slope towards Old Haymarket! Stonehouse tells us that there were 27,000 burials there from 1800 to 1820 and that in 1806 a huge pit was dug in it, covered by folding doors or flags, the dead being deposited into this and earth thrown upon each layer of coffins as it was completed! A writer to the

*Liverpool Mercury* in 1816 advocated a similar solution to a smell problem at Our Lady & St Nicholas. In another article in the *Liverpool Mercury* dated as late as 28th March 1856, William Wordley, an architect involved in the building of the adjacent St George's Hall, is quoted as saying of the cemetery that "The bulk of the ground was a mass of putrefying matter" and that "very offensive exhalations proceeded from the graveyard". According to one source, the last interment here was amazingly as late as 1865! It sounds as if the smell of the cemetery was as offensive to the noses of passers-by as the architecture of the church was to the eyes of the likes of James Picton.

Non-conformist and minority churches with limited land were usually even more pushed for space. O'Connor tells the story of a very small Jewish cemetery founded in the backyard of a house on Frederick St., off Park Lane, in 1773 and closed by 1800, the house being used as a synagogue. He quotes the following from Margoliouth, "The Cemetery in Frederick St. was filled and covered again and again until at last the door was blocked and the key thrown over the wall". The 1922 photograph of it in O'Connor's book shows a small space with half a dozen gravestones closely surrounded by decaying properties.

Referring to the early 1820s, Picton says that, "Public attention had recently been directed to the disgraceful state of the graveyards in large towns, and to the necessity for some better provision for interment". He goes on to tell us that this led to the opening of The Necropolis (literally "city of the dead") on West Derby Rd., Everton, then in open fields outside the town, by Protestant Dissenters in 1825. It was, however, a private venture joint stock company (one of the first in the country) and the cemetery was open to all comers, the first burial being of a member of the dissenting Hope family. Its architect was the younger John Foster and, according to Hollinghurst, the influence of Foster's experience of the Grand Tour could certainly be seen in the design, its Propylaea style entrance resembling that of the Acropolis in Athens (see fig.1). Not one renowned for praising other architects, Picton describes the style as "massive and grave, well suited to the purposes of the structure". It was surrounded by a high wall, much of the inside of which was lined with an arcade containing family enclosures (Hollinghurst).

Another local private initiative at this time, although founded by the Church of England, was St James' Cemetery, behind today's Anglican Cathedral and opened in 1829. The Town Council took some of the shares for giving the abandoned ten acre quarry and donating £9000 (£0.9m today). The younger John Foster was again the architect and took full advantage of the unique location to create catacombs rising on carriageways up its eastern boundary and, as Picton tells us, "A prominent mass of rock at the entrance afforded a fine position for a Greek temple, being a sort of acropolis in miniature" (see fig.2). Picton again waxes lyrical about this cemetery but also tells us that it was a disaster financially and Hollinghurst mentions that, bizarrely, these last two cemeteries became "two of the town's main tourist attractions, particularly for those of a melancholy nature"! It is significant for future cemetery developments that neither of the above cemeteries appears to have been constructed

*Fig.2. St James Cemetery looking west, showing the 'Oratory', originally the cemetery chapel, at top right. In the centre is St Michael's Church, Upper Pitt St. Engraving by Fenner after a drawing by T. M. Baynes.*

on a minimum cost basis and that both were designed to be physically secure. Parrott says that the final burial of nearly 58,000 took place at St James in 1936.

There were several other early expansions of cemetery space in and around Liverpool at this time. In 1806, the Parish of Liverpool, its graveyards at St Nicholas's and St Peter's becoming full, opened St. Mary's on Cambridge St., close to Myrtle St., which seems to have accepted burials up to 1849. Then in 1829 the Parish opened a cemetery to the north of Liverpool, adjacent to the newly opened church of St Martin's in the Fields (as it indeed then was) on Silvester St., off Vauxhall Rd., which accepted burials up to 1861. Another early development was the opening of St. Mary's Cemetery, next to the eponymous church on Walton Rd., Kirkdale (then outside the Liverpool boundary) in 1837. Although bearing the church's name, it was a public cemetery and open to all faiths. Picton tells us that, "The entrance …consists of an arched gateway in the Gothic style, with the chapel and registrar's house on each side" and that it was "prettily laid out". By 1900, this cemetery had become a small park called Lester Gardens and nothing now remains of it except possibly the niche for a water tap just inside the entrance.

Finally, in 1837 the Old Hebrew Congregation opened a new cemetery in Deane St. (Road from 1865), off Kensington, then still outside Liverpool's boundary and, like all the new cemeteries so far mentioned, in a then sparsely populated area. This, Liverpool's third Jewish cemetery (the second had been in Oakes St., near London Rd., according to Brooke), is another secure, high walled one, which this writer remembers climbing over at the rear as a teenager! It has "a Victorian screen entrance in the Greek style. The entrance is a round arch with attached Doric columns, a frieze of triglyphs and metopes and a Hebrew inscription". (Liverpool Heritage Bureau); once again not an economy job! The last burial on a new plot here took place in 1904, bringing the total to just 1700, a surprisingly small number over nearly 70 years and perhaps explained by the ban on stacked burials in Judaism (the stacked burials at Frederick St., referred to above, were obviously an exception). This Congregation then opened a new cemetery on rural land off what became Thomas Drive in Broadgreen. Over the years the Deane Road site became extremely derelict and overgrown and it is only in

*Left: Fig.3. Refurbished entrance to Deane Road cemetery. Right: Fig.4. Rice Lane Jewish Cemetery.*

recent years, following much hard work by a group of volunteers and a £0.5m. lottery grant, that it has been resurrected as a heritage site (see fig.3).

A number of other Hebrew congregations and burial societies opened (and closed) small cemeteries locally over the years. The New Hebrew Congregation opened a now very derelict one on Green Lane, Tuebrook in 1839, moving to a site adjacent to Everton Cemetery in 1921. In that year, the Hebrew Federated Burial Society opened one next to West Derby Cemetery. The Liverpool Hebrew (Rice Lane) Burial Society Ltd., also opened one, on Hazeldale Road, in 1896, closing it in 1983 (see fig.4). Several Jewish congregations now have sections at Allerton Cemetery (see below).

By 1851, the declining capacity of the cemetery at St Martin's in the Fields, where burials ceased completely in 1861, led the Liverpool Parish to open a new cemetery in a then rural area outside the town boundary off Rice Lane in Walton. Still there, Walton Park Cemetery is probably both the least known and most unusual cemetery in Liverpool. Its grounds today are the home of a city farm and a walk around them reveals surprisingly few gravestones considering that burials were carried out there for 80 years. The reason for this is that, for most of those years, it was the final resting place of paupers, all in unmarked graves, who had died in the adjacent West Derby Poor Law Union Workhouse, which became Walton Hospital, as well as those from the Liverpool Workhouse on Brownlow Hill. The former adjacent workhouse appears to have had a private bridge access to the cemetery, across today's Merseyrail Northern railway line, and probably its own small mortuary chapel. One of the paupers, who was buried there in 1911 and whose grave is now marked, is the revered Socialist writer Robert Noonan, whose *nom de plume* was Robert Tressell, the writer of *The Ragged Trousered Philanthropists*. Its plain Gothic chapel of 1852 still survives in reasonable condition (see fig.5).

*Fig.5. Chapel at Walton Park Cemetery.*

These measures helped the situation locally for a short time but, because of the rising urban population here and elsewhere, a series of twelve Burial Acts in England from 1852 to 1885 was eventually thought to be necessary to address on a national scale the possible public health problems caused by the inadequate burial of dead bodies. Inter alia, these Acts created local Burial Boards, the then greater Liverpool area having five created in the townships of Liverpool, Toxteth Park, Everton, Kirkdale and West Derby. Not surprisingly, Picton tells us that on 1st April 1854 in Liverpool "an order in council was issued, prohibiting any further interments in the churchyards in the town". Looking at burial records, however, this order appears to have only immediately affected St Peter's, Our Lady and St Nicholas and St Paul's, others being permitted, on application, to top up family graves.

It was to be the Toxteth Park Burial Board that became the first local one to make provision under the new Acts when, in 1856, it opened a cemetery on then rural Smithdown Road (then Lane) on a thirty (subsequently forty) acre site. Writing twenty years after its opening, Picton describes it as being "pleasantly situated and laid out with taste. The chapels and entrance lodges are considerably above the average of similar structures" and then goes on to discuss the changing fashions in the design of individual graves, expressing satisfaction that the trend for iron railings had passed! The buildings are by T.D. Barry and the layout by William Gay, who exploited the natural valley through the site, using it as the main path between the entrances and elevating the two chapels on either side. This valley, interestingly, was originally the route of the now culverted watercourse, known as the Lower Brook, which partly feeds the lakes in Sefton Park, probably rising at Kensington near the Jewish cemetery, then crossing Botanic Gardens, which once had a lake, and disgorging into the Mersey at Otterspool. The subsidence damage over an arch inside nearby St. Agnes' Church, Ullet Rd., was probably caused by its being built over the course of the brook. At the cemetery, the gatehouses are still in residential use but only the Church of England chapel survives and that is too dangerous to use (see fig.6).

*Fig.6. Derelict chapel at Toxteth Cemetery, Smithdown Road.*

The next two provisions of new cemetery space near Liverpool were undertaken by the Liverpool Catholic Cemeteries Board (LCCB). The first, a rather unusual one, was in the churchyard of the then recently built St Oswald's Church, Old Swan, about 4 miles from Liverpool and in open countryside, where, one source claims, 11,000 bodies were buried in this small graveyard between 1857 and 1863. This is corroborated to some extent by Parrott, who tells us that, when a new primary school was being built on the site in the 1970s, "contractors discovered an unknown burial ground, consisting of over 3500 graves in an area only 40 yards square and in some places piled up to 16 deep beneath the ground". Local legend has it that these were plague victims from Liverpool buried a safe distance away but the idea of its being a quickfit Victorian solution to a pressing problem seems a more satisfactory answer and is reminiscent of the situation at St John's discussed above.

Father Newsham of St Anthony's Church, Scotland Road was the main mover in the LCCB's other new provision at this time, the originally 21 acre cemetery at rural Ford in Litherland, about 6 miles from Liverpool and opened in 1859. The south-west Lancashire area was a strongly Catholic one even before the Irish influx of the 19th century, with many recusants, prominent among them the Blundells of Little Crosby, who in 1611 had built a small, secret RC cemetery known as the Harkirke in their grounds. The siting of the new cemetery here, therefore, was not an unusual decision when coupled with the growing RC populations of north Liverpool and Bootle. The *Liverpool Mercury* says of what was its opening ceremony, "...the persons assembled on the ground could not number less than five thousand; and two or three hundred conveyances, including carriages, cabs, omnibuses and a large number of spring carts were stationed outside the ground". One website claims that, from 1863 to 1875, Ford had as many burials as all the other Liverpool cemeteries together and that from 1883, presumably until the opening of Yew Tree Cemetery in 1893 (see below), 80% of local Catholics were buried at Ford. Amongst the most interesting graves at Ford are the communal ones containing the remains of former sisters and inmates of the adjacent Convent of the Good Shepherd, amongst them a distant relative of the writer's wife. The convent was built a few years after the cemetery and was a home for that great Victorian cause, the fallen woman, and one of the establishments now known derogatively as a 'Magdalene laundry'. The cemetery's Chapel of the Sepulchre is long gone and no picture is readily available.

Surprisingly, in view of the supposed burial crisis, it was to be August 1856, the year Toxteth Cemetery opened, before the Liverpool Burial Board was even inaugurated. Was Liverpool, obviously the most populous and most densely populated local township, taking advantage of the provision by Toxteth and the LCCB; a subject perhaps worthy of further study? Even after its creation, the Board laboured for seven years before its *chef d'oeuvre*, Liverpool (a.k.a. Anfield) Cemetery, took its first burial. In its early days, the Board struggled to find a suitable large site. As Picton says, "The nature of the soil about Liverpool, principally rock or stiff clay, materially limited the area of selection; a light or gravelly soil, with a dry substratum, being essential". The site chosen, then in open countryside outside the then Liverpool boundary, in Walton Township, was an ample one (121 acres) with easy access from the town. Picton refers to the cemetery as "the prospective Pere la Chaise of Liverpool", an allusion to Paris's fine necropolis, and by the time he wrote this, twelve years after its opening, it must certainly have matured into a fine sight in respect of its greenery and magnificent gravestones, a true reflection of what the Liverpool Heritage Bureau calls, "the Victorian pre-occupation with death".

The landscape design competition, surprisingly not held until 1860, was won by T.D. Barry but the commission went instead to William Gay, the designer of Toxteth Cemetery. He, however, resigned after a year and Edward Kemp, soon to design the adjacent Stanley Park, took over. According to Pollard, Kemp is thought to have been responsible for a highly novel landscaping idea at the cemetery, albeit an invisible one. There was originally a large sunken area of several acres in the middle of the site and "Under the turf of this part, and the terrace to its NE, are nearly 3000 brick graves, built in order to create a platform for the chapels level with the main entrance". The competition for the buildings was won by Lucy and Littler with, according to Pollard, "amazingly ambitious Gothic designs of red sandstone, resourceful in plan and detail", including now derelict catacombs flanking the site of the now gone central Anglican chapel. The magnificent main gate on Walton Lane, complete with clock tower is well complemented by the highly novel castellated entrance under the railway line at Cherry Lane (see figs.7 and 8).

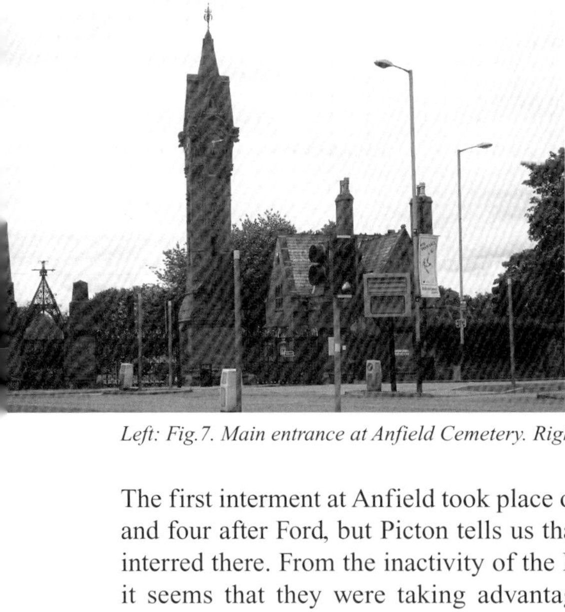

*Left: Fig.7. Main entrance at Anfield Cemetery. Right: Fig.8. Cherry Lane entrance to Anfield Cemetery.*

The first interment at Anfield took place on 5th May 1863, seven years after Toxteth and four after Ford, but Picton tells us that, by March 1870, about 30,000 had been interred there. From the inactivity of the Everton, Kirkdale and West Derby Boards, it seems that they were taking advantage of the Liverpool Board's magnificent provision and at a meeting in 1876, fearful that Anfield was "fast filling up", the Board decided that "the outgoing districts should provide burial grounds for themselves" and "face the unenviable task of incurring a large outlay of money". (All quoted in Parrott, who also tells us that, by 1888, 135,000 burials had taken place at Anfield – an average of about 5,500 a year.) The opening of Anfield had, according to Picton, cost the Liverpool Board £150,000 (about £15m. today).

The Everton Burial Board was the next to act, opening its cemetery on former farm land at Long Lane, Fazakerley, over a mile further out from the Anfield one, in July

*Left: Fig.9. Everton Cemetery's surviving chapel. Right: Fig.10. Lodges flank the entrance to Kirkdale Cemetery.*

1880, having laboured through two harsh winters. The Liverpool Heritage Bureau says of it that, "although …not as magnificent as Anfield, it does have a certain élan". The geometrical layout and buildings, all Gothic, were by Barry, his 20th cemetery commission, and financed with loans from Royal Liver and Royal Insurance (Parrott). Only the lodges at both entrances and one of the three chapels survive today, the R.C. one, but that is unsafe to use (see fig.9).

In 1881, less than a mile north of Everton Cemetery, the Kirkdale Board opened its cemetery with buildings by Duckworth and Medcalf of Liverpool and layout by William Wortley, who had been clerk of works at Anfield. The three chapels (two of which were in one building; the R.C. one being separate) are now gone but two "Tudorbethan" lodges survive on Longmoor Lane (see fig.10).

The catchment area of the West Derby Burial Board was much more extensive than the others but also then a much more rural and sparsely populated one so it is understandable that it was the last of the local boards to open a cemetery. This happened in 1884 on a site in Lower House Lane (now in Norris Green), about a mile east of Everton Cemetery and again on former farm land. The layout of its site, bigger than both Everton and Kirkdale, was again carried out by Wortley and the three chapels were by F. Bartram Payton of Bradford. Pollard tells us that, "The site is flat and the formal symmetrical plan of little interest" but that, as at Anfield, "brick graves were constructed to level the ground where it fell away in the NE corner". As elsewhere, its three Gothic chapels are long gone; indeed even a very modern 1965 replacement by City Architect Ronald Bradbury, which Pevsner described as having a "jagged roof", is no more. The cemetery's lodge, registrar's office and residence are, however, still in fine condition and it even has a clock tower (see fig.11).

*Fig.11. Entrance to West Derby Cemetery.*

An adjacent terrace of small dwellings, known as Charnock Cottages, housed cemetery workers (a school friend of the writer, whose father was a gravedigger, lived in one in the 1960s). All in all, it was a surprisingly ambitious cemetery in view of the obvious reluctance of the Board to embark upon it.

The next significant cemetery to be opened was Yew Tree, the second by the LCCB, in 1893. It is on former farm land in West Derby about six miles south of its cemetery at Ford and five miles from the city centre so would have been aimed at Catholics from a different catchment area. It is on the eastern tip of a huge tract of land purchased by that church for a number of reasons, including boys' and girls' schools, a school for blind children, a monastery and several convents. Compared to the last three cemeteries described, however, Yew Tree is a much smaller and less ambitious one with a humble Gothic chapel that is still in use. Whilst visiting there, the writer was standing next to the grave, complete with photo, of someone he had known in his youth! This cemetery's simplicity is perhaps reflected in the fact that none of the printed sources used for this article mention it.

*Fig.12. Remains of cross at Grant Gardens, formerly The Necropolis.*

The Necropolis mentioned above enjoyed 30 years of popularity and good dividends for its shareholders until it was discovered in 1857 that remains had been removed into pits to make way for new interments. This led to its forced closure to all except interments in family graves and 40 years later, in 1898, it was closed by a Liverpool Corporation Act to all interments because of its insanitary condition so close to terraced housing. By 1914, its grand entrance, rear wall and larger gravestones had been completely removed (the smaller ones being buried) and it had been converted into a public open space called Grant Gardens (much frequented by this writer as a child). It is a pity the grand entrance was removed but perhaps understandable if it was to become a welcoming place for local children! The only reminder today of its previous existence is a much vandalized, decapitated and graffitied cross (see fig.12) in a park that is now just a shabby grassed area (ironically a broken column is a funereal symbol for a young death).

Writing in 1902 about the Necropolis closure, in his update to 1900 of his father's book, J. Allanson Picton, M.P. saw its sad fate as "an illustration of the incapacity of each generation to foresee the conditions of life and death amongst even its immediate successors". Living in Conway, he was perhaps unaware that cremation, an ancient method of disposal of the dead in some parts of the world, had been modernised to take advantage of 19th century technology and had been available in Liverpool since 1896 on a site purchased from the Liverpool Burial Board adjacent to Anfield Cemetery. This was just the fourth crematorium in Britain and was run by a private company called The Liverpool Crematorium Co. Ltd., the carefully nurtured brainchild of Alfred Holt and more of a philanthropic concern than a profit making body.

The advantages of cremation are that its quick destruction of the dead body makes it much more hygienic than conventional burial and what remains can be contained in an urn so there are usually no land requirements. In its early years, however, it proved to be (if the reader will excuse the expression) a slow burner of an idea that was only taken up in the early years by Non-Conformists or those of no religious faith. The Church of England found reason until after WW1 to object on religious grounds centred on belief in the resurrection of the body after death and the R.C. Church continued objection on similar grounds until as late as 1963. In 1908, Liverpool Corporation acquired powers to run the Anfield Crematorium and, although cremation is still not a permitted practice in either Judaism or Islam, it is now much more common in Britain than burial in the ground. This writer's article about the founding and early years of the Anfield crematorium can be seen in the Liverpool History Society's 2010 Journal.

In 1906, the powers, assets and, no doubt, debts of all the township burial boards mentioned above were passed to Liverpool Corporation and it fell to the latter to provide a now much needed new cemetery for the south of the city at Allerton on a site that did not become part of Liverpool until 1913. Land was purchased from the Allerton Hall estate for £50,000 and the cemetery opened for internments in late 1909, "the red sandstone lodges, gates, superintendent's house and three chapels" being "well on their way to completion two years later" (Pollard). All the chapels are Gothic, mainly with lancets and geometrical tracery and all have steeples, the Anglican one at the head of the main drive forming the focal point (see fig.13) As Pollard says, "The extent, density and formality of the planting is in contrast to that of the Victorian cemeteries in Liverpool......It creates discrete compartments breaking down the scale of the site" with "formal planting in place of mid-C19 naturalism". The allertonoak website says of the layout that it "embodies the conclusions about good cemetery design drawn by the (Liverpool) Burials Committee during their visit to the continent in 1908" and that "It is based upon a broad central avenue, with grave spaces set back from the main walks behind planted borders to give an impression of a pleasant park". A considerable area of evergreens was also planted to retain the atmosphere during the winter. By 2003, over 74,000 burials had taken place there but today, as at most other local major cemeteries, the chapels are now all unsafe to use (services taking place at Allerton in one of the chapels at the adjacent 1975 crematorium) while all the non-ecclesiastical buildings appear to be in fine condition.

*Fig.13. Anglican Chapel at Allerton Cemetery.*

The grounds of all of Liverpool's major Victorian and Edwardian cemeteries are well-maintained today but it seems unlikely that they will ever be restored to their original splendour; indeed, it seems much more likely that some of the remaining derelict chapels and even the catacombs at Anfield will eventually be demolished for safety reasons (and many more gravestones lowered for the same reason). Subsequent urban expansion has undoubtedly taken away the original sense of remoteness and no doubt inaccessibility of many of the larger cemeteries. Although there appears in recent years to have been a renewed enthusiasm for Victorian funereal pomp and ceremony (redolent perhaps of Ogden Nash's, "It isn't the cough that carries you off; it's the coffin they carry you off in"), the final journey of most dead bodies (73% in 2008) to a cemetery in Britain today is for an hygienic cremation rather than to be interred in its grounds for an eternity. The practice of cremation has undoubtedly solved the problems of the safe and hygienic disposal of the dead in our crowded urban environment and at a very small unit cost in land terms but has it also sounded the death knell for many of the fine architectural features in our cemeteries?

***Main sources***


Brooke, Richard. *Liverpool as it was, 1775 to 1800* (1853) [2003 reprint]

Halliday, R. & Forrest, F.T. *A dead loss? The short but unusual history of The Liverpool Crematorium Company Ltd*. Liverpool History Society Journal 2010

Hollinghurst, Hugh. *John Foster and Sons, Kings of Georgian Liverpool* (2009)

Liverpool Heritage Bureau. *Buildings of Liverpool* (1978)

*Liverpool Mercury* (see text)

Marks, Saul. Talk to Liverpool History Society, December 2014

Moore, Jim. *Underground Liverpool* (1998)

O'Connor, Freddy. *Liverpool. Our city, our heritage* (1990)

Parrott, Kay. Introductions to various Old Ordnance Survey maps reprinted by The Godfrey Edition

Pevsner, Nikolaus. *South Lancashire* (1969)

Pevsner, Nikolaus & Pollard, Richard. *Lancashire: Liverpool and the South-West* (2006)

Picton, J.A. *Memorials of Liverpool*. 2 volumes (1903)

Sharples, Joseph. *Liverpool* (2004)

Stonehouse, James. *The Streets of Liverpool* (1869) [2002 reprint]

www.allertonoak.com

www.wikipedia.org


All pictures except the first two (for which I thank Ron Jones) are by the author.

# STRANGERS IN A STRANGE LAND

## *John Hussey*

*"I recognize only the Holy Pilgrimage of Science to the Land of Truths! All other pilgrimages are nothing but touristic trips!"* Mehmet Murat ildan

*John Edward Gray Hill, 1874, and Caroline Emily Gray Hill, 1873. Both portraits are by Edward Robert Hughes and are courtesy of Bruce Castle Museum, London.*

### *Laying the Foundations*

Born and educated in London, John Edward Gray Hill (1839-1914) was first articled as a solicitor in London in 1863 when he was 24 years of age. The following year he married 21-year-old Caroline Emily Hardy. Caroline's grandfather was Sir Thomas Hardy who was immortalised by Lord Nelson's final words "*Kiss me Hardy*"on the deck of HMS *Victory*.

In 1865 the young couple came to Liverpool where John had secured the post of maritime lawyer with the Duncan, Squarey and Duncan law firm. Within the space of three years the firm fell apart when the senior partner died and shortly afterwards his successor suffered a mental breakdown. The situation was a watershed in the career of the young Gray Hill who assumed the mantle of senior partner in the firm.

As the foremost maritime city in the country, Liverpool was the perfect place for a young maritime lawyer to make his mark and with the practice already having the advantage of being associated with the newly-formed Liverpool Steam Ship Owners' Association they soon represented the pioneering companies of Cunard and the Inman Steamship Company. The company thrived in their offices at Borough Buildings, 10 Water Street, which they had occupied since 1862, and it was there that Gray Hill invited John Dickinson to join him in partnership, thus forming the firm that eventually became Hill Dickinson.

*Borough Buildings (arrowed), Water Street, home of Hill Dickinson, in the era of horse-drawn trams. Other tenants included Ismay, Imrie & Co. (White Star Line) and the Liverpool Steamship Owners' Association. An article on the history of Borough Buildings appeared in the Society's 2012 Journal.*

*Hill Dickinson represented both White Star and Cunard following the sinking of the Titanic and the Lusitania respectively. (RJ).*

In the years to come, the combination of intellectual ability, expertise and sheer hard work by Gray Hill laid the foundations for Hill Dickinson which has today expanded into an international and highly respected firm of which he is acknowledged as its founder and patriarch.

As Gray Hill's prestige grew, his wealth also grew accordingly and while still living in his first home at Apsley House, Oxton, he commissioned the magnificent Mere Hall in Noctorum, Birkenhead, completed in 1880 (pictured opposite). With views of the Welsh Hills, nine acres of land and a household of seventeen domestics, coachmen and gardeners, Gray Hill proceeded to fill his home with his collection of paintings, mainly by local artists, and all manner of curios from his travels.

Although Gray Hill was a patron of local artists, favouring the landscapes of the strangely named and long-lived Liverpool artist William Joseph Julius Caesar Bond (1833-1928), his greatest patronage was reserved for his own wife, Caroline Emily Gray Hill, who was a talented painter in her own right. However, as much as he enjoyed the Fine Arts, Gray Hill's real passion was for the works of Shakespeare which he studied from childhood to old age; he had no difficulty in reciting whole plays off by heart.

Judging by his diaries, Gray Hill was a remarkably energetic and knowledgeable individual whose workload was staggering by any standards – his diary for several months in 1879 alone was a testament to his varied talents, and the people he dealt with ranged from the highest in the land to the lowliest of workmen. The diary is littered with tantalisingly abbreviated notes and the most interesting of people – "*meet Gladstone for lunch, disaster in the Zulu War, meet Prince L. Bonaparte* (who would die a few months later speared by Zulu assegais), *Lord Granville and Lowe at the British Museum, meet Disraeli and the Empress at Chislehurst* (Eugénie, whose husband Napoleon the Third had died in 1873, was in exile in England with her son, the Prince Imperial), *meet John Bright at Rochdale, journey to the Italian Lakes and Switzerland, sort out letters from Dickens, speak to Charles Darwin about investments*" and more prosaically there was "*the sale of the Leeds/ Liverpool canal, speech at Manchester, Macclesfield rents, meeting at Liverpool Art Club, cottages in Bootle,*" and so on *ad infinitum*.

*Mere Hall, Noctorum, Birkenhead.*

In between times Gray Hill communicated with Edward Burne-Jones, Matthew Arnold and William Holman Hunt – it seemed that he knew everyone and everyone knew him. Over the years Hill became Vice-President of the International Law Association, member of the International Maritime Committee, Manager and Secretary of Liverpool and London Steamship Protection Association, President of Birkenhead Liberal Unionist Association, and President of Liverpool Incorporated Law Society – how Hill managed to fit all these appointments into his daily life is a mystery only he could reveal. His special interest was as President of the Lancashire and National Sea Training Home for Poor Boys and, ably assisted by Sir Alfred Jones, owner of Elder Dempster & Co, he reciprocated by aiding Jones with his work at the School of Tropical Medicine. In 1901, Hill was elected a member of the Council of the Law Society which represented Liverpool and in 1904 his career was crowned with a knighthood bestowed by King Edward VII.

As wealthy and energetic as he undoubtedly was, Sir John's life may well have ended as a footnote in the history of Birkenhead as the founder of Hill Dickinson and the laird of Mere Hall but for his private life which was a colourful and adventurous counterpoint to his working life. For Sir John Edward Gray Hill was also a great traveller – mostly to the Holy Land and the Middle East – places which had a fascination so powerful for both Sir John and Lady Caroline that it drew them back year after year.

### *Traveller's Tales*

Only the most intrepid of travellers made their way to the Middle East in the Victorian era which made it surprising that many of them were women who took a pride in their independent spirit and travelled alone. The painter of *Fantine* which hangs in the Walker Art Gallery, Margaret Bernadine Hall, travelled to Algeria and North Africa but left few traces of her journeys. The travels of Lady Anna Brassey, who was married to the eldest son of Birkenhead's Thomas Brassey, who built many of the world's railways in the 19th century, have been well documented and Gertrude Bell's adventures with T. E. Lawrence are well known as is her soubriquet of "*The Woman Who Made Iraq*". But it was the fervent feminist and anti-vivisectionist, Frances

Power Cobbe (1822-1904), a contemporary of Sir John Gray Hill, who left the most vivid account of her travels alone throughout the Holy Land.

Apart from Egypt which was a British protectorate, the Middle Eastern countries remained a part of the declining Ottoman Empire in the Victorian era and Syria, Iraq, Libya, Jordan and the remainder of the Holy Land were daunting places, especially for a woman alone. Apart from the ever-present danger of bandits and hostile tribesmen of every denomination, the Middle East was a land of visas, firmans (local dispensations to travel), Dragomen (local guides) and, most of all, rampant bribery and corruption.

Accounts by Victorian travellers tell of arduous journeys in blistering heat across rocky crags and stony deserts and most tell of the dangers of wild tribesmen who would stop at nothing in order to steal anything they could lay their hands on. Worse still was the threat of kidnapping Westerners for ransom; Sir Arthur Conan Doyle's lesser-known novel *The Tragedy of the Korosko* written in 1898, is an enthralling tale of an eclectic group of British, French and American tourists taken hostage by a fanatical Islamic tribe of Dervish tribesmen. The clash of the two cultures as they travel through the desert could well be a template for Islamic/Christian differences but the situation is immediately recognisable in today's world when the Christian 'infidels' are finally threatened with beheading unless they convert to Islam.

### *Places No One Else Has Seen*

Although his work entailed travelling to European cities from time to time, Gray Hill was 48 years of age before he first travelled to the Middle East in 1887, accompanied by Caroline. In the opening chapter of his book *With the Bedouin*, he wrote that as he entered this new world he felt unburdened by the work he had carried out so assiduously for so many years and both he and Caroline were immediately captivated by the Holy Land. They had undoubtedly travelled firstly by steamship but once there they journeyed by horseback and mule in much the same way as Frances Cobbe had done 30 years earlier. There is reason to believe that both Sir John and Lady Caroline were both quite devout as they often quoted from the Bible and they made it their business to visit every Old Testament site that they could. Their knowledge of the ancient sites was encyclopaedic but even more impressive was their ability to associate each site with its Biblical connotations. Just a fraction of the sites that the Gray Hill's describe illustrates clearly their knowledge of those archaic places. Gray Hill curiously described Tyre in present day Lebanon, a stopping place on their biblical pilgrimage, as "*the Liverpool of the old world*."

*Landscape with Ruins and Figures c.1887-1912, by Caroline Gray Hill. Courtesy Victoria Museum & Gallery, University of Liverpool.*

Although it is true that in the larger cities of the Middle East British, American and French tourists were generally treated with respect, if not deference, every description by travellers who ventured further inland and off the beaten track tells of the danger posed by Islamic fanatics and bandits. The Hills were no exception and Gray Hill later stated in his own words "*We have had some strange adventures. We have been shot at, had bullets through our tent at night, been arrested, harassed, threatened, bullied and robbed.*" In another alarming episode the Gray Hills were held hostage by local warlord Sheik Khalil who refused to release them until he was paid the sum of 60 'Napoleon' gold coins. They had little option but to pay the ransom and travelled on, only to have the whole distressing incident repeated by another minor despot further down the road.

*Top: 'Desert Landscape with a Remote Building, Figures and Horses'; Bottom: 'Landscape with a Riverbank Town, Boats and Figures' (probably on the Nile) c. 1887–1912, both by Caroline Gray Hill. Courtesy Victoria Museum & Gallery, University of Liverpool.*

There was also the ever-present danger of illness which struck them both down at various times, not to mention snakes, but none of these things deterred the Gray Hills as they criss-crossed the land from West to East, travelling through Gaza, Jordan, Aleppo, Beyrouth (Beirut), as far north as Turkey and at one point "*...reaching to a considerable distance to the East of Haj or Mahomedan (sic) Pilgrimage Road, visiting the places no one else has seen.*"

It seemed to be common knowledge that the Gray Hill's travelled annually to the Holy Land and in 1901 before their departure they received a letter from William Holman Hunt (1827-1910) from his home in Fulham, London. The letter began, "*I imagine you must be very close upon your winter flitting to Mount Scopus...*" and expressing his regret that he could no longer travel, "*I can only envy you and Mrs Gray Hill for your sojourn there for the time for such adventures has past for me.*"

Hunt had travelled throughout the Holy Land three times in the 1850s and stayed in Jerusalem for seven years producing *The Scapegoat* (one of the Lady Lever Art Gallery's most famous pictures), *The Finding of The Saviour In The Temple* (a version can be found at Sudley House), *The Light of The World* and many landscapes of the area. Hunt then went on to mention how the railway must have brought many changes to Jerusalem and maintained that it would have been advantageous for photographers which was the real reason for his letter. He had been working from a sketch by Caroline of the heights looking down on Zuara, Fokha and Jahta and he asked the Grays to send him a photograph from an angle which included, "*...the little castle on the crag*." Whether Hunt received his picture or not is unknown.

***The Jews of Jerusalem***

In June 1912, Liverpool held a Palestine Exhibition and Sir John Gray Hill was invited to give the opening speech which said as much about Sir John as it did about Palestine itself. After briefly describing his and Lady Caroline's travels and breezily informing his audience that, "*...we eventually bought a bit of land on the Mount of Olives*" Sir John went on to describe Jerusalem; although he was not Jewish he was astute enough to realize that his mainly Jewish audience was more interested in that sacred place than anywhere else. On what he described as, "*...this dripping June of England* " Sir John transported his audience to the sunshine and sights and sounds of Jerusalem. But if they expected a rose-tinted vision of the Holy City then they were in for a disappointment and the overwhelming tone of his speech was one of bewilderment more than anything else. Sir John could never understand why the Christians, Jews and 'Mahomedans' could not get on with each other but he was particularly dismayed and mystified why the 'Mahomedans' treated the Jews with such contempt. Sir John would have known that the entrance to the Dome of the Rock had been fought over for centuries by Muslims, Christians and Jews but he still found it difficult to believe that one religion would deny access by another, "*...cruelly and unjustly the Jews are not allowed to enter that area. The Christians are allowed to enter on application to their consuls which means entrance in payment but the poor Jews are kept wailing at the bottom of the great retaining wall of that sacred enclosure. This is an injustice which I trust will someday be removed*."

*Wailing Wall, Jerusalem, by Gustav Bauernfeind (1848-1904). (WC).*

What Sir John may not have known was that for centuries the Jews were denied access to the Wailing Wall following the destruction of the Second Temple by the Romans in 70 A.D. Sometime in the Byzantine era they were allowed entry once a year on the anniversary of the razing of the Temple to the ground when they could weep against the gigantic stones of the wall which is all that remains.

Sir John was genuinely distressed at the treatment of the Jewish community in Jerusalem and he told his Jewish audience of the impoverished thousands fleeing from pogroms in Poland and Russia who were living in abject poverty in the ghettoes of the city. With more Jews arriving each day, Sir John pointed out the incongruity of Jews living in hovels next to the 'Noble Sanctuary.'

Although much of Sir John's speech initially appeared to have a wonderful naiveté completely at odds with his persona as a major player in the cut and thrust of the commercial world, it does reveal a fine humanitarian nature appalled at the sectarian violence. It is a measure of the depth of those religious differences that if Sir John returned to Jerusalem today he would find that nothing had changed.

***The House on the Hill***

The Gray Hill's "*bit of land on the Mount of Olives*" was in fact one of the finest pieces of real estate in the area, overlooking Jerusalem on one side and the Dead Sea on the other. It was renowned for its profusion of wild flowers and panoramic views and was the perfect place for Lady Caroline to have a studio for her painting. However, although all these factors were perfectly viable reasons for Sir John's choice of a place to build, he revealed the major reason in his book *With the Bedouin* when the depth of his revulsion for the religious bigotry in Jerusalem was fully expounded: "*We wanted to buy land so we would have a small place we could call our own in a land we love, a lonely quiet place that no pilgrims or tourists would visit, yet far enough from Jerusalem to be free of the religious hatred and jealousy.*"

Although the Gray Hills bought the land in 1892, five years into their lifetime love affair with the country, it was not until 1904 that they began the house-building project which would produce some surprising results. The Gray Hills would undoubtedly have been dismayed to discover that when the workmen began digging the foundations they came across a cave, but when archaeologists were called in, further excavations exposed an ossuary, or final resting place, containing bones and jewels. Slowly it became evident that the Gray Hill's proposed home stood on an important Jewish historical site and all became clear when the words "*Bones of the family of Nicanor the Alexandrian who made the gates*" were discovered above the vault; it was a story familiar to every Jewish historian.

British archaeologists in Victorian times were in the habit of removing any finds back to England no matter how incongruous they were out of their original setting, as many

*Mount of Olives c 1899. (WC)*

*Opening ceremony of the Hebrew University, Jerusalem 1925. (LOC).*

museums can testify. In that respect the burial coffins from Nicanor were reported with some bitterness by the Jews to have been transplanted to England. Despite the delay, the Gray Hill's home, which they named Ras Abou Kharoub, was built circa 1907 and became the base for their annual pilgrimage to the land they had taken to their hearts.

Sir John was only to enjoy the comforts of their home in the Holy Land for seven more years when in 1914 he was taken ill in Paris. He returned to Mere Hall where he died a few days later. Lady Caroline never returned to their home on the Mount of Olives and spent the remainder of her life at Mere Hall, later taking an active interest in the Royal Society for the Prevention of Cruelty to Animals. The house and extensive acres of land in Jerusalem were sold the same year of Sir John's death to the prospective builders of the Hebrew University. The land was totally redeveloped during construction of the University with care taken to incorporate the historic vault of Nicanor, sadly minus its ancient occupants. The University opened its doors to students in 1925 with Albert Einstein and Sigmund Freud among the founders.

***Lady Caroline Emily Gray Hill (1843-1924)***

The University and its grounds had grown to become the pride of Jerusalem. A building devoted to Jewish studies was donated by Barbara Streisand in honour of her father who was a Torah scholar. There was a synagogue and a campus surrounded by modernistic buildings and Ronald Reagan had also donated sums for the upkeep of the university; the whole conglomerate had grown into a centre of learning of national importance.

The land which Sir John Gray Hill had called the Mount of Olives was called Mount Scopus by the time the Hebrew University was surrounded by Jordanian forces during the Six Day War of 1967 and a great deal of fighting took place within the area. When the dust had settled the University area was a shambles and restoration of such an iconic site was a priority. It was at this time that another, less important, cave was discovered next to the Nicanor cave, containing the remains of Channiah Ben Yonatan the Nazir and his wife and family, interred in two sarcophagi and fourteen ossuaries.

There was another find made during this period of restoration which brought to light an aspect of the Gray Hill's occupation of the Mount which had been all but forgotten; during the restoration it was decided that the Gray Hill's original home would be torn down to make way for the new campus and it was at this time that Professor Jacob Wahrman of the Hebrew University became aware of the existence of Lady Caroline's paintings and passed the information to Irit Salmon, the curator of the Ticho House

*Left: 'Camel Rider in Mountainous Desert' (detail); Centre: 'Flowers', a break from the norm; Right: 'Resting Camels and Figures', all by Caroline Gray Hill. Courtesy Victoria Museum & Gallery, University of Liverpool.*

museum in Jerusalem who went on to trace many of the pictures. Had it not been for Professor Wahrman and Irit Salmon it is quite probable that Lady Caroline's paintings would have been lost. It was their curiosity and knowledge which quite literally brought the pictures back into the light of the Holy Land which Lady Caroline had loved so much.

Although her husband's career and life always seemed to have taken precedence over her own interests, it was apparent that Lady Caroline had left a legacy of her own and in some ways it was far more evocative of their life together, their mutual love of the Middle East and the arduous trails they had travelled together. Lady Caroline was a talented and prolific painter as much in thrall to the rugged landscapes of the Holy Land as her husband but while Sir John admired the scenery when they halted, she set up her easel and captured it all on canvas. With a few exceptions, notably the flora of Mount Scopus, most of Lady Caroline's paintings are of Bedouins, nomadic caravans and camels, set to a background of vibrant shades of golds, yellows and blues which are a feature of all her paintings, capturing the sun-baked deserts and craggy countryside in picture after picture.

***Out of the Shadows – From Obscurity to Exhibition***

Although Lady Caroline exhibited her work each year at the Walker Art Gallery's Autumn Exhibitions they were never acknowledged as of any great value and during her lifetime her paintings were little more than personal mementoes of her travels in the Middle East. It is only in latter years that they have been recognised for their aesthetic and historic value; nevertheless, the Walker has only one of her paintings, which remains in storage.

The Gray Hills were childless and following her death at Mere Hall in 1924, once again Lady Caroline's pictures were at risk with some given to relatives and others lost or sold. In a classic case of how paintings become lost, one relative came into possession of a portfolio of Lady Caroline's pictures and placed them in a Catholic monastery in London for safekeeping during World War II; the paintings still remain 'somewhere' in its safekeeping as the lady never returned for them and the name of the monastery died with her.

However, in 2002, Irit Salmon who had been instrumental in recovering the paintings in 1967, decided that Lady Caroline's paintings should be seen by a modern day Jerusalem public and over a century after she had painted them they were finally to go on exhibition. The exhibition, *The Lady and the Desert*, curated by Irit Salmon, was to be in Ticho House in the centre of Jerusalem – it could hardly have been a more fitting place.

The University of Liverpool has over one hundred of Lady Caroline's paintings in its keeping and in 2011 it held an exhibition of its own at the architectural gem of the Victoria Museum & Gallery, within the university's 'red brick' Victoria Building, designed by the Liverpool architect Alfred Waterhouse (1830–1905).

Lady Caroline is remembered in Jerusalem by a plaque on the wall of Saint George's Church. The wording is taken from John Milton's *Samson Agonistes*;

*Nothing is here for tears*
*Nothing but well and fair.*

Over a century has gone by since the Gray Hills clambered over the crags and sand dunes of the Middle East, exploring ancient sites in Libya, Iraq, Iran, Syria, Palestine, Jordan, Lebanon and as far north as Turkey. Although they may well have thought the Middle East was somewhat dangerous then, it bears no resemblance to the battleground of warring factions it has become since. The so-called Arab Spring has turned out to be no more than an illusion (that illusion resembled in some ways Sir John's romantic vision of a Utopian Palestine) and in a few short years has become a horrifying nightmare. What Sir John and Lady Caroline would have thought of their beloved oriental dreamscape in the present day can only be imagined.

### *A Grand Finale*

In keeping with Sir John Edward Gray Hill's life, his funeral was a remarkable affair and it is a measure of his deep involvement over many years in Liverpool's maritime life that so many friends and colleagues turned up to pay their respects. The funeral took place at the medieval Church of Holy Cross, Woodchurch (pictured opposite) and was attended by a seemingly endless list of the great and the good of Liverpool and the Wirral and others who had taken the trouble to travel from further afield.

The greater part of the congregation had associations with shipping and many were ship owners who are still household names, with representatives from the White Star Line, American and Dominion Line, Elder Dempster, Cunard Steamship Company, The Liverpool Steamship Owners' Association and a host of others who had been represented by Hill Dickinson over many years.

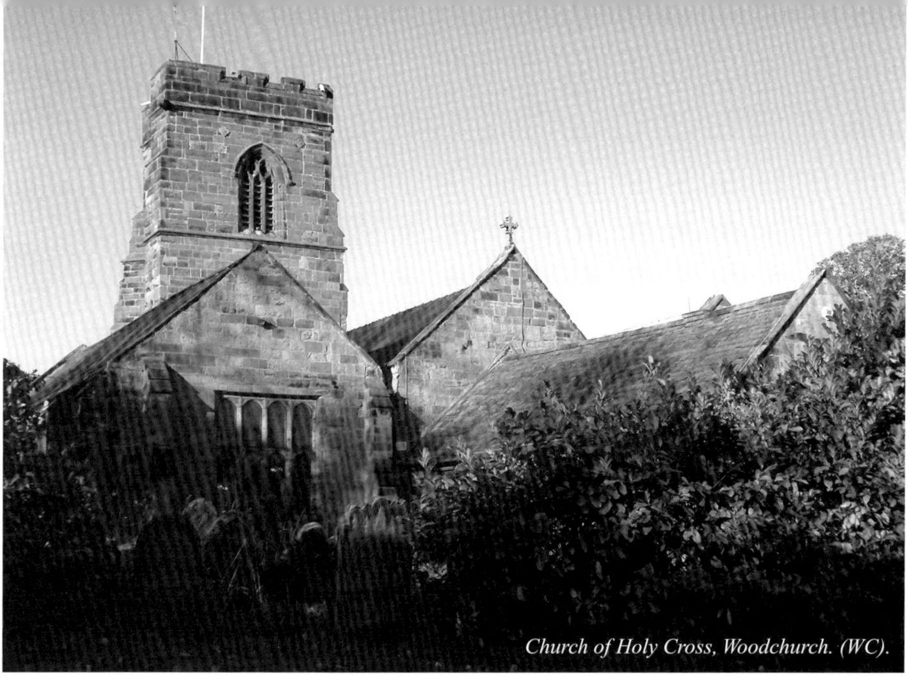


There were many other eminent men from every walk of life who filed into the tiny church in an impressive display of the circles that Sir John had moved in, representing every facet of his life: bankers, businessmen, patrons of the arts, lawyers, politicians, artists, priests and rabbis came together.

However, there were other mourners present that day who were far below the social scale of the rest; they represented a part of Sir John's life which in some ways had been far more commendable than any of his better-known achievements. They were a contingent of 200 boys from The Sea Training Homes at Liscard and another 40 boys from the training ship *Indefatigable*. They were accompanied by James Beazley, the man who had been a prime mover in the establishment of the *Indefatigable*, the *Conway* and the *Akbar* training ships which were stationed at the south end of the Birkenhead side of the Mersey.

Sir John had been closely involved with the maritime training schools and as a founder member of the Lancashire and National Sea Training Homes For Boys he travelled by horse every Sunday from Mere Hall to one of the homes in Egremont. In some ways the training ships were an adjunct to the Royal Seamen's Orphanage in Newsham Park for which Beazley could also claim to have been one of its greatest proponents. Also present at the funeral was David MacIver managing director of the Cunard Steamship Company, who had worked closely with Beazley in the founding of the Newsham Orphanage.

A decade after Sir John's death Lady Caroline followed him to the Church of Holy Cross where she was buried alongside her husband of so many years and so many adventures. Perhaps in some afterlife they are exploring the mysteries and landscapes of a different Holy Land altogether – it would be nice to think so.

# PETER ELLIS AND TWO BUILDINGS ON CATHARINE STREET

## *Graham Jones*

Recently discovered documents ('*Indentures*') at the Liverpool Record Office indicate that, in 1864-65, whilst Peter Ellis was involved in the construction of Oriel Chambers he was also the architect for two houses being built at the junction of Catharine Street and Little Saint Bride Street and which survive today.[1,2,3]

The story begins in 1835 on the east side of Catharine Street (fig. 1) which, at that stage of development, comprised no. 1 plus the terrace, nos. 3-17.

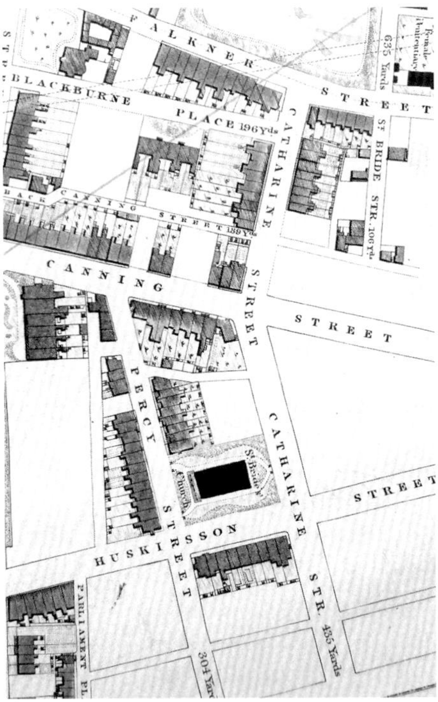


*Fig. 1. Catharine Street as surveyed in 1835 by Michael Alexander Gage. At that time it ran from Falkner Street to Upper Parliament Street (Private collection).*

*Fig. 2. The north east side of Catharine Street in 2014, left to right from Falkner Street to Little Saint Bride Street (the latter is shown in fig. 3 as a continuation of Back Canning Street). Author's image (GHJ).*

By 1847 the terrace had been completed to no. 23 (fig. 2) whilst, to the south of Canning Street, nos. 25 and 27 had arrived (to the right of the 'HE' of 'Catherine' in fig. 3) and, in between them, a church was under construction. By 1862 the remainder of the east side of Catherine Street, southwards from Canning Street to Upper Parliament Street, had appeared (fig. 4). The origin and the construction of the church – and even its name – is a story in itself. According to James Picton the building: '*was commenced in 1840, when the eastern portion was erected. It so remained incomplete for many years, when the western portion and steeple were added, on a scale much reduced from the original design*'.[4]

*Fig. 3. A portion of Catherine Street on the 1847 O.S. map. Image courtesy of the Athenaeum (ATH).*

*Fig. 4. The south east side of Catharine Street in 2014, left to right from Canning Street to Upper Parliament Street (GHJ).*

*The Builder* in 1857 indicates that the church (finally completed in that year and known subsequently as the *Catholic Apostolic Church*) had been constructed of stone from Storeton Quarry, and the account includes a view from the south-west (fig. 5).[5] It had been built for a congregation whose members were part of a religious movement which originated in England around 1831, and the English Heritage Legacy record indicates that the church was '*One of the more remarkable Non-Conformist churches of its date*'.[6]

*Fig. 5. The Catholic Apostolic Church. The building to its right is part of Napier Terrace in Canning Street; to its left is a view beyond the garden of 23 Catherine Street to the rear of properties on Saint Bride Street (see fig. 3). Image courtesy of Liverpool Central Library.*

In the church section of *Gore's Directory* this non-conformist building had an entertaining and confusing succession of names: *Catholic Church of the Holy Apostles* (from 1843), *St. Apostles' Church (Catholics)* (from 1847), *Catholic and Apostolic Church* (from 1853), and eventually – with the misleading '*and*' finally removed – *Catholic Apostolic*

*Church* (from 1881). In the directories for 1857 and 1859 its ministers were entitled Angel, Elder, Prophet, Evangelist and Pastor. In 1860 these were revised to Bishop and Priests, and from 1862 the listing was simplified to Chief Minister. And it is in that year that the name of Robert Brewster first surfaces in *Gore's Directory*, being listed as the Chief Minister at the church and as a resident of 12 Falkner Square, close to where Peter Ellis lived at no. 40.

The first of the Indentures (fig. 6) shows that on 1st August 1863 Robert Brewster obtained a lease from the Mayor, Aldermen and Burgesses for £22-2-0d (and rent of '*one pepper corn if demanded on the Feast day of Saint Michael the Archangel in every year*') for the undeveloped piece of land adjacent to the church on its northern side. By then the street that had originally been named as a continuation of Back Canning Street (fig. 3) had been renamed Little Saint Bride Street, the name that continues today.

This Indenture

*Fig. 6. The 1863 Lease to Robert Brewster (LRO, ref. 352 CLE/CON 2/28/11).*

The plan (fig. 7) shows the irregular shape of the plot that was available and upon which Robert Brewster was given the instruction to construct '*two good and substantial dwellinghouses with suitable offices thereto.*'

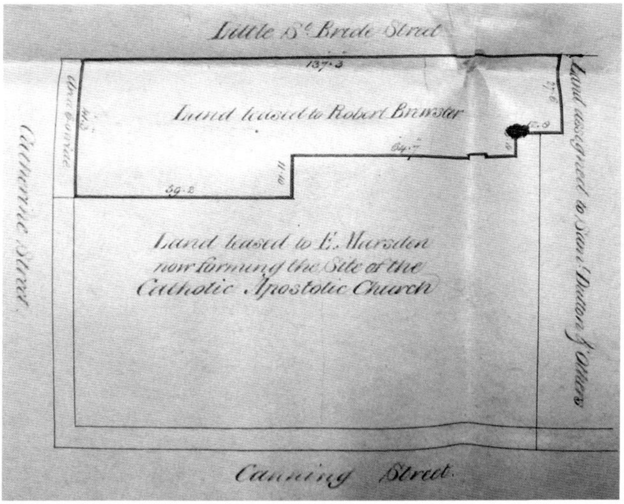


*Fig. 7. The plan on the 1863 Lease, oriented to the north (LRO).*

This was followed a year later by an '*Assignment by means of Mortgage*' (fig. 8):

*'...made the twentieth day of January one thousand eight hundred and sixty four Between Robert Brewster of Liverpool in the County of Lancaster Esquire hereinafter termed the Vendor of the first part Isaac Denton of Liverpool aforesaid Builder hereinafter termed the Purchaser of the second part and Peter Ellis of Liverpool aforesaid Architect hereinafter termed the Mortgagee of the third part...'*

*Fig. 8. The 1864 Assignment of the 1863 Lease to Peter Ellis (LRO, ref. 352 CLE/CON 2/28/13).*

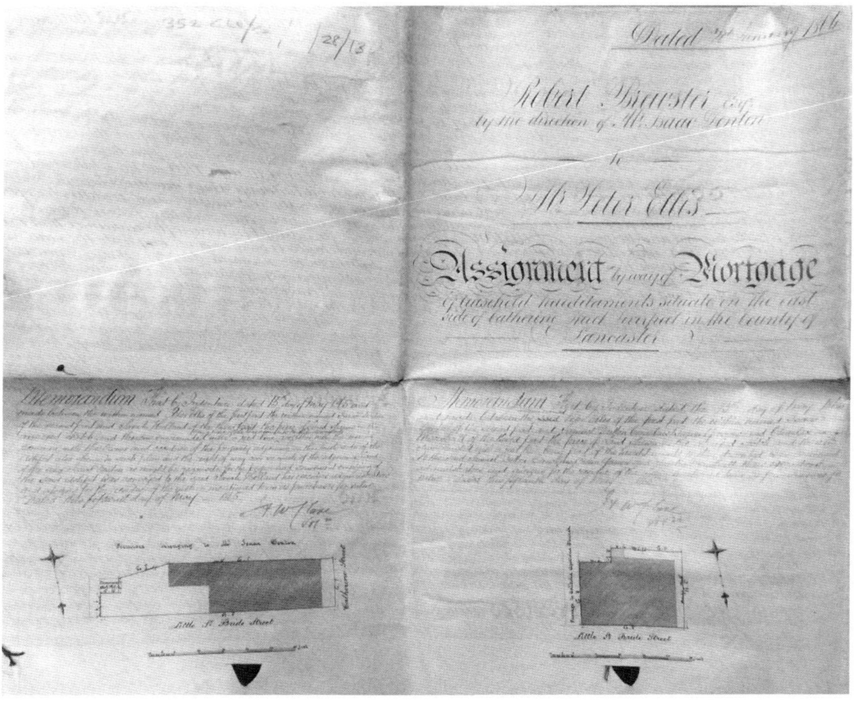

The Assignment indicates that Robert Brewster:

'*...contracted with the Purchaser for the absolute sale thereof to him at the sum of Five hundred and fourteen pounds ten shillings and the Mortgagee hath at the request of the Purchaser agreed to advance the same purchase money on having the said hereditaments assigned to him...*'

The agreement was '*subject to the proviso for redemption*', showing that if Isaac Denton repaid Peter the mortgage plus interest by 20th July 1865 (18 months later) then the land and any houses subsequently built upon it would be reassigned to Isaac.

There is no accompanying plan of the whole plot in this Assignment but the dimensions given in the text show it to be identical to that in the 1863 Indenture. However, on the cover it can be seen that there appear two Memorandums. Both are dated 15th May 1865, the first referring to the house which by that date Isaac had built adjacent to Little Saint Bride Street (bottom left in fig. 8) and the second referring to a portion of land at the eastern end of the original plot (bottom right in fig. 8 and not discussed further in this article). The first Memorandum reads:

'*That by Indenture dated 15th day of May 1865 and made between the within named Peter Ellis of the first part the within named Isaac Denton of the second part and Sarah Holland of the third part the piece of land shewn in the annexed sketch and therein surrounded with a red line being part of the hereditaments further described together with the use in common with the owner and occupier of the property adjoining on the south side of the ashpit also shewn in such plan and the right of way over so much of the adjoining land of the said Isaac Denton as might be requisite for the proper and convenient emptying of the said ashpit was conveyed to the said Sarah Holland her executors administrators and assigns for the residue of the within mentioned term as purchaser for value.*'

Sarah's purchase thus enabled Isaac to repay Peter within the redemption period. Accompanying the Memorandum is a plan of the plot and the house that had been built on it (fig. 9, oriented to the south).

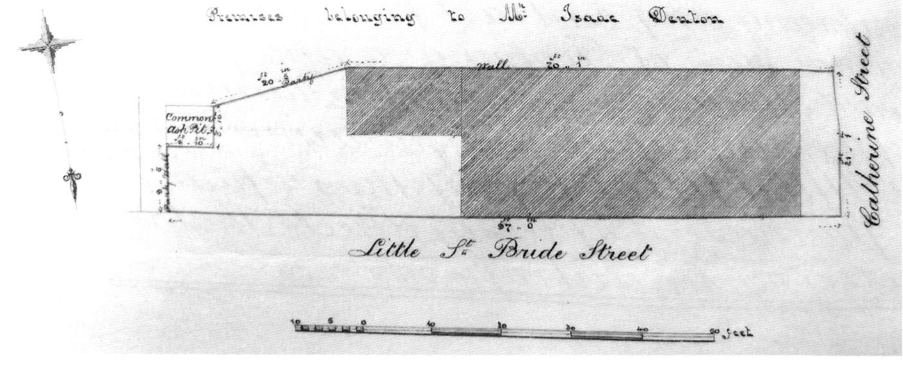


*Fig. 9. One of the 1865 Memorandum plans, oriented to the south, on the 1864 Assignment (LRO).*

Three months later, through another Indenture, Isaac sold the adjacent property to the south which he had also built. That Assignment (fig. 10) begins:

*'This Indenture made the sixteenth day of August one thousand eight hundred and sixty five Between Peter Ellis of Liverpool in the county of Lancaster Architect of the first part Isaac Denton of Liverpool aforesaid builder of the second part and Susannah Burrows of Liverpool aforesaid widow of the third part...'*

This Indenture

*Fig. 10. The 1865 Assignment to Susannah Burrows (LRO, ref. 352 CLE/CON 2/28/14).*

It goes on to indicate that Susannah purchased this dwellinghouse for £1,420. Since 25 and 27 Catharine Street had already been constructed, Susannah's house was given the number 27A. The exciting ashpit, noted in the memorandum on the 1864 Assignment, again featured prominently, and was confirmed as being held in common with Susannah's neighbour, Sarah Holland (whose house was given the number 25A).

The Assignment includes a plan of the property (fig. 11, oriented to the east), and in the bottom right hand corner Peter has written '*P Ellis, Archt &c, 9 Orange Court, Castle Street Liverpool*' (fig. 12). The signatures and seals of Peter, Isaac and Susannah appear at the foot of the document (fig. 13).

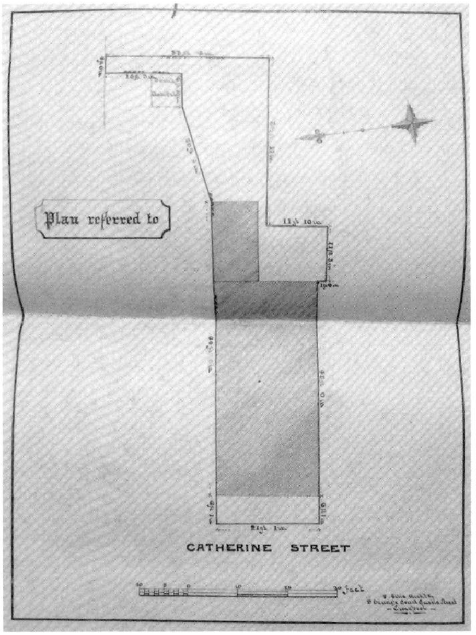


*Fig. 11. Left: The plan on the 1865 Assignment, oriented to the east (LRO).*

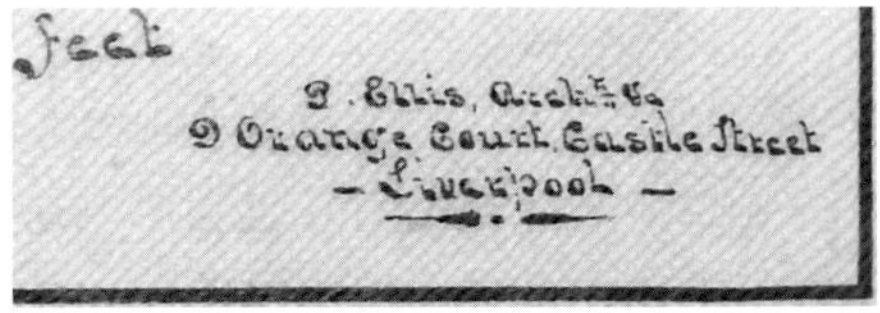


*Fig. 12. Above: Detail from the 1865 Assignment showing Peter as the architect (LRO).*

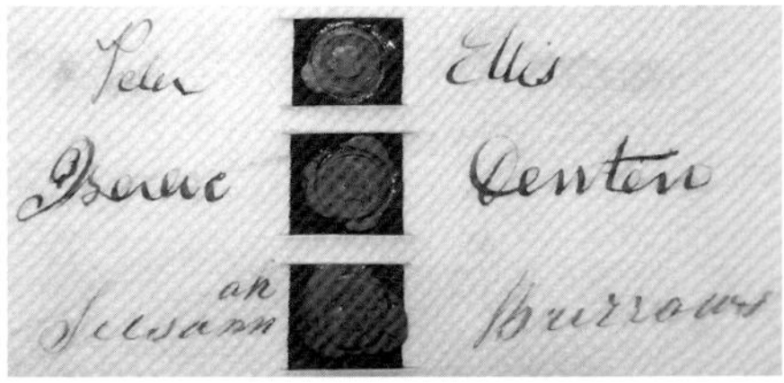

*Fig. 13. Signatures on the 1865 Assignment (LRO).*

In Robert Brewster's 1863 Lease there were quite formidable restrictions regarding what was permitted within the buildings to be erected, including the requirements that he:

'*shall not nor will at any time hereafter use or occupy cause permit or suffer any part of the said demised premises to be used occupied or appropriated for the purpose of or for carrying on any of the trades following that is to say a soap boiler tallow chandler tanner skinner currier curer of herrings or sugar boiler or for a herringhouse or slaughterhouse or as an Inn Ale house Victualling house or Beerhouse nor shall nor will cause permit or suffer any Steam Engine to be erected on the said premises...*'

Fortunately for Susannah Burrows and Sarah Holland, education was not one of the prohibited trades, for the 1867 edition of *Gore's Directory* shows that they each opened a school (fig. 14).

23 Lloyd William grocer
25A Holland Miss S. A. ladies' school
27A Burrows Mrs. Susannah boys' school
Apostolic Church
[*Canning st*
25 Maddock James gentleman
27 Hamlin George master mariner
[*Little Canning st*

*Fig. 14. From the numerical section of Gore's Directory for 1867 showing the arrival of 25A and 27A Catharine Street.*

*They were given those numbers because of the pre-existence of nos. 25 and 27. Renumbering of the street occurred in 1883 (ATH).*

Mrs Susannah Burrows is shown in the directory for 1857 as having a seminary, and in 1859 as having a boarding and day school, both in locations in Birkenhead. By 1860 she had opened a preparatory school in Canning Street and then, in the directory for 1865, she is shown as having briefly relocated to 32 Catharine Street. Although Susannah lived out the remainder of her widowhood at no. 27A, she abandoned the idea of a boys' school and later advertised her premises first as a ladies' seminary and finally as a preparatory school once more. Then, in 1873, the directory shows the Misses Emily and Annie Burrows as running the school, with Rev. George Burrows also resident there. Susannah's mortgage deed for no. 27A confirms that it was later re-granted to the Misses Burrows. In 1874, however, no. 27A is not listed and, in 1875, a tobacco merchant had arrived, and the young ladies can be seen to have relocated their preparatory school to Waterloo.[7]

Miss Sarah Holland first advertised her ladies' boarding school at Little Woolton in the Academies section of *Gore's Directory* for 1841 and stayed there until transferring to Catherine Street. She maintained her ladies' school at no. 25A until 1882 after which she disappeared from the directories, perhaps not surviving to see Catharine Street renumbered in 1883. In that year nos. 25A and 27A became nos. 25 and 27, with the remainder of the east side being renumbered from no. 29 in the sequence which remains today.

Robert Brewster remained at 12 Falkner Square until 1870 when he is shown as having moved to Prince's Park. Was it the proximity from 1862 of Robert at no. 12 and Peter at no. 40 Falkner Square that gave rise to Peter's involvement with this development on Catherine Street? Capitalising on a piece of land adjacent to a church is reminiscent of Peter's involvement a few years earlier with a similar plot next to St Philip's Church in Hardman Street.[8]

And was it Peter that chose Isaac Denton as the builder to whom to offer his mortgage? If so, with Peter's support and '*kindly advice*' (see the *Daily Post* account of Peter's funeral),[9] the work seems to have been quite a boost to Isaac's career for, in the 1865 directory and for several years afterwards, Isaac gave instructions for the list of his trades to be greatly expanded and for the entry to be placed in bold type.

Amongst the views of the Catholic Apostolic Church at the LRO there is a photograph taken towards the end of the 19th century which includes these two houses on Catharine Street (fig. 15).[10] The church became an English Heritage Grade II listed building in 1978, and the LRO folder has a photograph taken in 1982 showing it with a 'For Sale' sign. In 1986 it was burnt out, possibly as a result of arson,[11] and Freddy O'Connor photographed it in 1987 in its sad and derelict state.[12]

The site of the church is now occupied by *Mosslake*, 45A Canning Street (fig. 16), but 25 and 27 Catharine Street live on as further examples of work with which Peter Ellis was involved in his architectural career (fig. 17). Peter's choice of roof line and his decision for the houses to be built in stone (except to the rear, as commonly was the case) was clearly in order for them to blend with the church rather than with the neighbouring brick terraces. It is only as a result of the demolition of the church and its replacement with *Mosslake* that the pair now seem incongruous.

*Fig. 15. Above top: The Catholic Apostolic Church in the late 19th century, with 25 and 27 Catharine Street (as numbered post-1883) visible to its left, and the side of Napier Terrace to its right (LRO, ref. Binns Collection, vol. 30, p. 31).*

*Fig. 16. Above bottom: The equivalent view in June 2014 to that in fig. 15 (GHJ).*

*Fig.17. Above left: 25 and 27 Catharine Street in 2014 (GHJ).*

*Fig. 18. Above right: A fleur-de-lis decoration on each of the gables of 25 and 27 Catharine Street (GHJ).*

*Fig. 19. Above: A fleur-de-lis decoration on one of the window frames at Oriel Chambers. Before WWII bombing destroyed part of the Covent Garden façade there were more than 200 and, if you are keen enough to go there and count them, there are still 168 (GHJ).*

*Fig. 20. Left: A detail from the late 19th century photograph (from fig. 15) showing the original design of the bay window parapets (LRO).*

Constructed in the same years as Oriel Chambers, it is interesting to note Peter's enthusiasm for the large and oriel-style first floor windows, and his use of the fleur-de-lis emblem to decorate the gables (fig. 18).

The design was included on the gables and doorway of his St Saviour's National Schools,[13] whilst the window frames of Oriel Chambers are also adorned with rather a lot of them (fig. 19).[14]

Remembering that the Catholic Apostolic Church was constructed of stone from Storeton quarry, it would be interesting to establish whether parts of 25 and 27 Catharine Street were sourced from the same quarry.

Finally, by comparison with a detail from the late 19th century view (fig. 20), the bay window parapets (fig. 17) can be seen to have had 20th century alterations.

*Fig. 21. Left: Abney Buildings, School Lane elevation (GHJ). Fig. 22. Right: fleur-de-lis carved into the sandstone of what remains of the original 1874 building (RJ). See reference note 14 below.*


## Acknowledgements

The author wishes to thank the Athenaeum, the Liverpool Record Office and Liverpool Central Library for material reproduced from their extensive archives.


## References and notes

[1] This article is an abbreviated version of an account which appears as part of a pdf entitled *The Signatures of Peter Ellis*, published in November 2014. The pdf is a supplement to the book *In the Footsteps of Peter Ellis*, published in 2013 by the Society. *Signatures* can be downloaded from the Society's website and allows images to be viewed in colour and at a larger scale.

[2] The documents are grouped together at the Liverpool Record Office under references 352 CLE/CON 2/28/11 to 352 CLE/CON 2/28/15.

[3] In the documents and on the 1847 O.S. the spelling is 'Catherine Street'. On Gage's 1835 plan and in *Gore's Directory* it is 'Catharine Street' (as today). The two spellings are retained as they occur in the various sources.

[4] J A Picton, *Memorials of Liverpool*, G G Walmsley (Liverpool), 2nd edition, 1875, vol. II, p. 260.

[5] *The Builder*, 1857, vol. 15, p. 134. The woodcut illustration is on p. 135.

[6] English Heritage list entry no. 1356304, legacy UID 213822.

7 Further information about the Burrows family can be found in an article entitled *Emily & Annie D Burrows; Waterloo School Teachers* by Andrew Lee Hart, Journal of the Liverpool History Society, 2009, pp. 27 – 36.

[8] See *In the Footsteps of Peter Ellis*, p. 189.

[9] See *In the Footsteps of Peter Ellis*, p. 193.

[10] LRO, ref. Photographs & Small Prints: Churches: Catholic Apostolic Church. The folder also includes views of the interior.

[11] See the commentary on Colin Wilkinson's *Streets of Liverpool* website which includes an undamaged version of fig. 15 and which Colin records as being dated 1875.

[12] Freddy O'Connor, *Liverpool. It All Came Tumbling Down*, Countyvise, 2013, p. 195 (revised edition).

[13] See *In the Footsteps of Peter Ellis*, p. 112, figs. 6,11 and 6,12.

[14] Peter also employed the *fleur-de-lis* on the railings of the Catharine Street properties (a small part of which has survived) and on a building for which he was the architect in 1873 (see the *Signatures* pdf) whilst a re-examination of the School Lane building believed to have replaced Peter's 1874 warehouse (see *Footsteps* p. 181, ref. 7) suggests that at least part of the warehouse must have survived the 1883 reconstruction (figs. 21 and 22 above). Julie Robson has pointed out that *fleur-de-lis* with a Liverpudlian accent becomes *fleur d'Ellis*. Nice one Peter!

# NEW LIGHT ON CROWN STREET TERMINUS OF THE LIVERPOOL AND MANCHESTER RAILWAY


*Hugh Hollinghurst*

*Plate 8. 'Railway Office, Liverpool', from 'Coloured Views on the Liverpool and Manchester Railway' by T. T. Bury, Published by Ackermann, 1831.*

The Manchester terminus of the Liverpool and Manchester Railway survives in excellent condition but at the Liverpool end the building at Crown Street has been demolished. In spite of Bury's excellent reproductions of the most important buildings on the line, he appears not to have illustrated Liverpool's Crown Street terminus. In fact he does, but it has not universally been recognised as such because of an editorial mistake.

The construction of the line and Bury's illustrations of it must first be described. At the Liverpool end the evenly graded section of the railway finished at Edge Hill. From there the line divided into two sections worked by cable through tunnels. One went up a short distance to a passenger terminus at Crown Street, the other went down through a much longer tunnel to Wapping Dock. The expense and difficulty of constructing this indicates the overriding importance of goods traffic in the construction of the line. Later, in 1836, with the increasing importance of passenger traffic, a line was constructed at even greater expense from Edge Hill to a more central terminus at Lime Street. Thus Liverpool can claim to have the oldest continuously operated railway station in the world as recent archaeological discoveries have proved that some of the original buildings at Edge Hill are still in use.

Plate 9. *'Warehouses, etc, at the end of the tunnel towards Wapping, Liverpool', from 'Coloured Views on the Liverpool and Manchester Railway'*. Courtesy LRO.

Thomas Talbot Bury's beautiful drawings are the best record of the look of the railway at its opening. These were published by Ackermann in several editions, the best being a revision of 1831 which are the subject of this article. As an exact description of the line, they vary. Architectural details are on the whole excellent as Bury was an architect following a well-established tradition. Thus the Sankey Viaduct is shown from an angle that shows off the beautiful curves of the arches and buttresses, and the classical decoration of the pilasters and linking frieze are exactly delineated. The skew bridge at Rainhill is similarly shown from an angle that shows off its ingenious design and the pattern of brickwork on the underside of the arch.

However, his illustrations of the novel technical aspects of construction and operation have shortcomings. There was, for example, a new and remarkable method of transferring trucks from one track to another in the goods yards via revolving wooden turntables. Plates 8 and 9 demonstrate Bury's difficulties of representing the mechanism. In plate 9 the view is entitled 'Warehouses, etc. at the end of the Tunnel towards Wapping'. Because of the extreme foreshortening of the turntable, it is not immediately clear that the distance between the rails leading away from the viewer towards the tunnel must be the same as those leading from them to the side. To his credit, Bury has shown the operation in progress with the drawing of another turntable (just beyond the one in the foreground) turned through 90 degrees with two men pushing a wagon to the side, but, once again, the foreshortening makes it difficult to comprehend. The scale of the figures and track adds to the confusion as the track is more like 'broad' gauge when compared with the stature of the workmen crossing it (Stephenson's gauge is 4 feet 8½ inches and Brunel's 7 feet). However, the cable for hauling the trains up to Edge Hill is convincingly shown in the track immediately ahead as it enters the tunnel.

Plate 8 'Railway Office, Liverpool' (sic) enacts a busy, lively scene of arriving and departing passengers with more dogs than children accompanying the adults. First class carriages stand in the train shed but the lack of platforms must have caused passengers difficulties, particularly the ladies. They then board road carriages bound for town. The classical architecture of the handsome doorway and columns supporting the canopy is well depicted and the turntables are delineated. However there are no rails on them to make the operation proceed smoothly, and the cable, instead of stopping short of the turntable mechanism, cuts across it which would render cross rail movement by pedestrians extremely tricky, if not hazardous.

Unfortunately, the introduction to the 1831 version states misleadingly 'At Liverpool, the railway commences at the office, (Plate 8), *in the Company's yard at Wapping*, near the north end of the Queen's Dock by a cutting 22 feet deep and 46 wide, affording space for *four lines of rails*, between which are ranges of lofty cast-iron pillars, supporting warehouses erected over the excavation. (Plate 9).' (my italics)

However, the office cannot be 'in the company's yard at Wapping' for the following reasons.

1. Plate 8 ('Railway Office, Liverpool') shows only three lines whereas Plate 9 'Warehouses, etc. at the end of the Tunnel towards Wapping' shows four lines.

2. A map of Liverpool (courtesy of the Athenaeum) gives details of the two sites at the time (see overleaf). The detail of the Wapping area corresponds to the view depicted in Plate 9 (the dotted lines running left to right (arrowed) show the line of the Wapping tunnel) but there is no building near the tunnel that might represent the office. On the other hand, in the detail of the Crown Street site, an appropriate building is shown situated near the tunnel entrance.

3. The entrance to the tunnel at the Wapping end still exists (see photo) and corresponds both to the view of the tunnel entrance in Plate 9 and also the relationship between the tunnel and the goods yard in the map overleaf: the warehouse depicted by Bury is shown in black to the left of the area denoted as *Railway Station* and the entrance to the tunnel is to the left of that. In the map of the Crown Street area overleaf, two tunnels are shown with dotted lines coming down from the top of the map. The right hand one continues to Wapping but the left hand one emerges from under Smithdown Road to terminate in the train shed, shown in grey with the 'Railway Office' to the left of it. It will be seen that Smithdown Road crosses the railway on a slant and Bury has skilfully represented this by the diminishing lines of the entrance to the tunnel receding to the right as seen beyond the station shed in Plate 8.

*Entrance to tunnel at Wapping end. Author's photo.*

4. The 'Railway Office' as it is entitled (Plate 8) shows vibrant, high profile, passenger activity which would not have taken place in the goods traffic environment at Wapping. Admittedly, the group on the right are entering through what is labelled on the map as a coal yard and they would also be subject to the risks of being tripped up on the haulage cable. However, they are probably there for artistic reasons, balancing the travellers on the left.

5. The lines at the Wapping entrance to the tunnel (Plate 9) are curved whereas at the Crown street entrance (Plate 8) they are straight.

6. It is puzzling that in an earlier 1830 version the arch of the tunnel is shallow (like the Wapping tunnel) but in the 1831 version it has a sharper arc and is half obscured. The editor had not noticed the alteration otherwise it would have alerted him to the fact that the 'Railway Offices' were not situated at Wapping. Interestingly, there is another marked difference between the two versions. In the later one Bury has opened

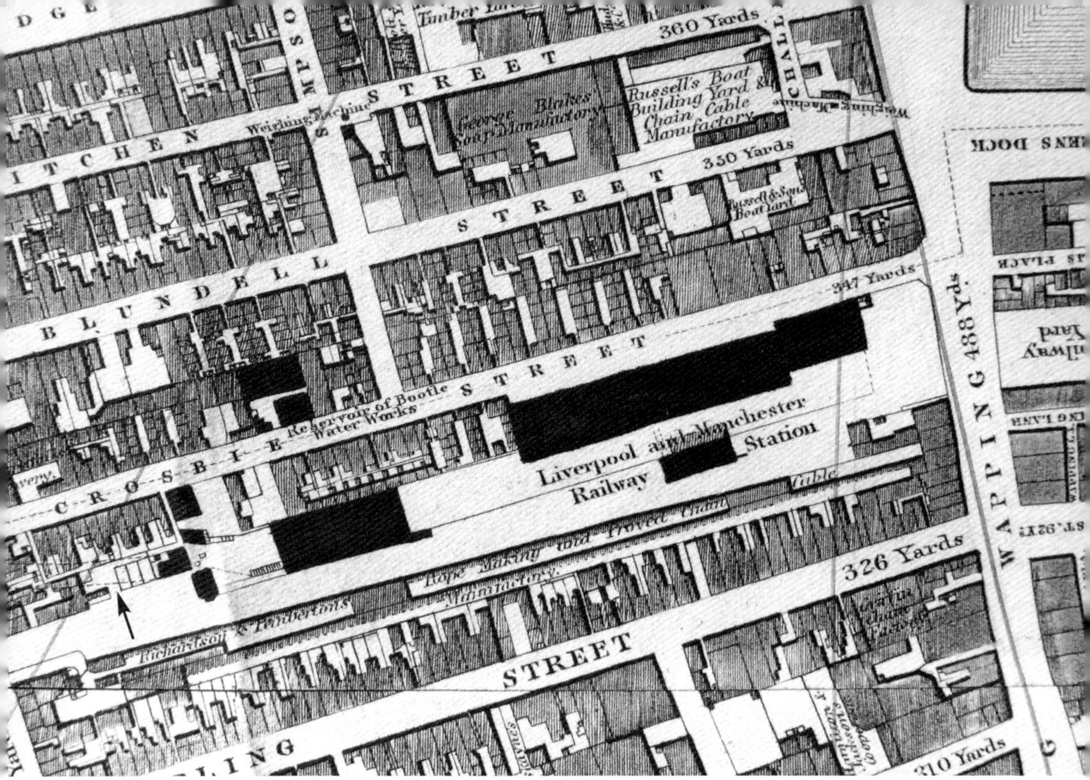
360 Yards
STREET
KITCHEN
Weighing Machine
George Blakes Soap Manufactory
Russell's Boat Building Yard & Chain Cable Manufactory
330 Yards
Russell & Sons Boat Yard
STREET
BLUNDELL
347 Yards
STREET
Reservoir of Bootle Water Works
CROSBIE
Liverpool and Manchester Railway Station
Rope Making and Proved Chain Manufactory
Cable
Richardson & Pembertons
326 Yards
STREET
WAPPING 488 Yds.
310 Yards

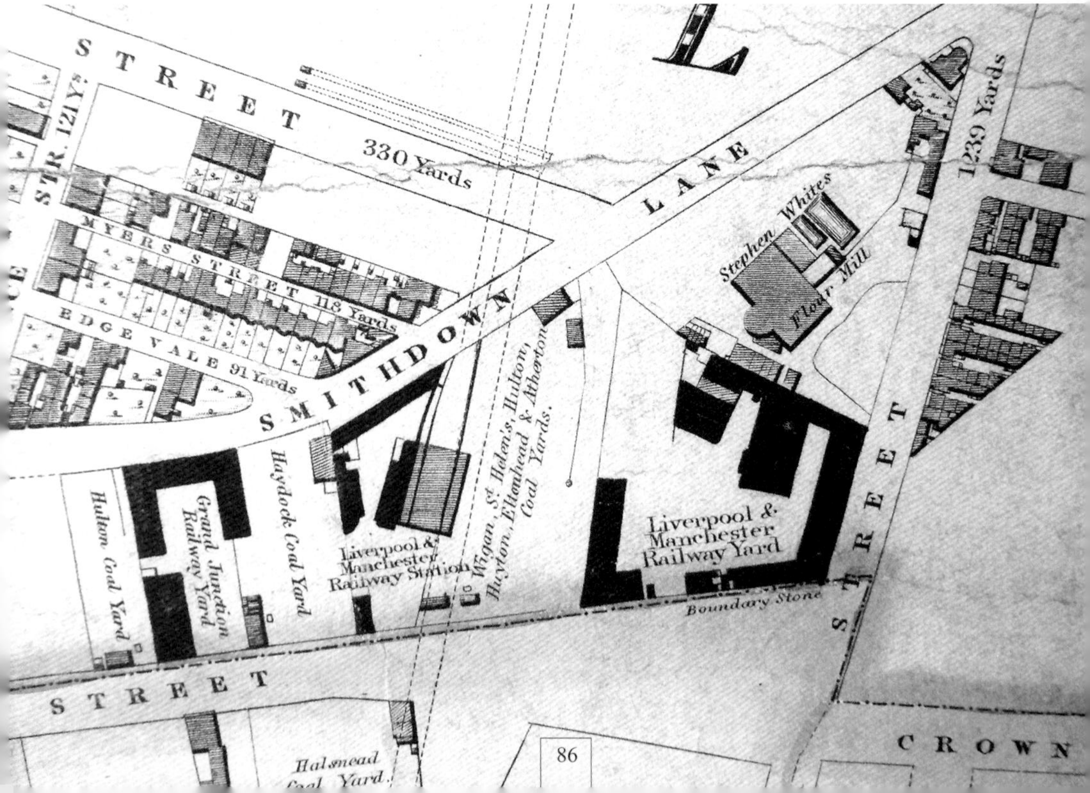
STREET
330 Yards
STR. 121 Ys
MYERS STREET 118 Yards
EDGE VALE 91 Yards
LANE
SMITHDOWN
1239 Yards
Stephen Whites Flour Mill
Haydock Coal Yard
Hulton Coal Yard
Grand Junction Railway Yard
Liverpool & Manchester Railway Station
Wigan, St. Helen's, Hulton, Huyton, Eltonhead & Atherton Coal Yards.
Liverpool & Manchester Railway Yard
Boundary Stone
STREET
STREET
CROWN
Halsnead Coal Yard.

up the shed roof to show the interior design and the method of construction but it is enclosed in the earlier version.

Frank Ferneyhough in his standard history *Liverpool & Manchester Railway 1830-1980* illustrates Plate 8 but misleadingly describes it as being at Wapping. I hope in future no one else will be puzzled or misled by the writer of the introduction to the 1831 edition of 'Coloured Views on the Liverpool and Manchester Railway'.

*Subsequent to writing this article, I have had corroboration from two other sources:*

1. Wikipedia 'Crown Street railway station'.

2. A German print in Nigel Welbourn's '*Lost Lines: Liverpool and the Mersey*' indicating the international renown of the railway.

***Bibliography*:**

*Coloured Views on the Liverpool and Manchester Railway by TT Bury: a facsimile of the original edition* published in 1831 by R Ackermann. Hugh Broadbent, Oldham 1976

*A Trigonometrical Plan of the Town and Port of Liverpool*. Michael Alexander Gage 1835 in the Athenaeum, Liverpool

*Railways began here...Stations of the Liverpool and Manchester Railway on Merseyside*. Paul Rees Edge, Hill Railway Trust 1980

*Liverpool & Manchester Railway 1830-1980*. Frank Ferneyhough, Robert Hale 1980



*Opposite, top: detail of Wapping area. Opposite, bottom: detail of Crown Street area. Both from Michael Alexander Gage's plan, surveyed in 1835 and published in 1836. Courtesy of the Athenaeum.*

# CELEBRATING THE BI-CENTENARY OF THE TOWNSHIP OF WATERLOO

***Brenda Murray***

If you wish to visit the famous Antony Gormley statues from Liverpool you will have to pass through Waterloo, a suburb six miles to its north. Before June, 1815 there was no place in Great Britain called Waterloo. The area of land between Litherland and Crosby, that was to become Waterloo, was called Crosby Seabank which was open or common land possibly having a few small cottages occupied by fishermen, of which no record survives.

Sea-bathing had become popular all over England particularly growing in fashion as King George III enjoyed it in Dorset. In 1815, to capitalise on the trend, John Kilshaw, with a company of five men, built an hotel that they called the Crosby Seabank Hotel (now the Royal Hotel) at the fine hard sands a few miles north of Liverpool. They also built six substantial cottages alongside, which are still there and in excellent condition.

*Originally called the Crosby Seabank Hotel, then the Waterloo Hotel, it finally ended up being called the Royal Hotel. This view shows the hotel and adjacent cottages in the early 1900s. (RJ).*

Originally, these were called the Marine Cottages, but shortly became known as Marine Terrace. These were the first buildings in Waterloo. Although a thatched cottage can now be seen near the junction of South Road and Mount Pleasant it is not as old as it a first appears; the earliest deeds for the house date from 1859.

Crosby Seabank Hotel began to be called the Waterloo Hotel as news of the great victory achieved by the Duke of Wellington was received everywhere with much relief as it brought to an end the 22 years of war with France that had begun in 1793. The township of Waterloo is said to have taken its name from the hotel.

More houses were built, especially in Marine Crescent in 1824, then in Adelaide Terrace in the 1830s, all along the seafront. In the 1850s, the second section of Marine Terrace, from numbers 1 to 17, was built with much bigger houses than the original six cottages. The houses at Beach Lawn were also built after 1860.

*Above: A depiction of the proposed Adelaide Terrace development from an original in Liverpool Central Library. The scheme's promoters described its prime location thus: 'The situation commands an extensive and every-varying Marine View: - a prospect of Liverpool, the River Mersey, the Cheshire Shore, the Black Rock, Fort, and Lighthouse, the West Coast, the Great and Little Ormsheads, Snowdon, and the most magnificent Mountain Scenery of the Principality of Wales.' Courtesy Liverpool Central Library. (RJ).*

The promoters of the Adelaide Terrace scheme included Charles Padley, a builder whose family were the original occupiers of nearby Picton Cottage, which was built in 1851 and is still standing. The Egyptology collection of his daughter, Anne Goodison, now on permanent display at The Atkinson, Southport, was housed in a museum room at her home on Adelaide Terrace until her death in 1906.

Streets behind the front were named after Wellington, Murat (Napoleon's brother-in-law), the Prussian General Blucher and Picton (after the British General who was shot in the head and killed at the battle).

St. John's Road (after Mont St. Jean) and Hougoumont Avenue, were both named after the places on the field of battle at Waterloo.

In effect, therefore, in Waterloo there are four terraces that stretch along its seafront and overlook the River Mersey and are listed buildings, which is unique in the country. Some of the more famous personalities associated with Waterloo made their homes in the terraces, including Thomas Ismay, owner of the ill-fated *Titanic*, who resided in 13 Beach Lawn, and its captain, Thomas Smith, who lived in 16 Marine Crescent.

*Above left: this aerial view from 1926 shows the curve of the terraces with Christ Church tower easily the tallest local landmark. The figures on the beach are flesh and blood rather than 'iron men'. Above right: Adelaide Terrace c. 1920s (RJ).*

Although many of the original frontages have been altered, the overall visual integrity of the terrace schemes has survived. One of the most interesting 'revamps' was made by Alfred Keizer a Belgian merchant specialising in decorative glass with business

*Above: Art Noveau 22 Marine Terrace.*

premises in St. Anne Street, Liverpool. He lived in Moor Lane, near Crosby Mill and in 1902 bought 22 Marine Terrace, one of the six original cottages. He enlarged it into a triple-fronted house and had it designed throughout with Charles Rennie Macintosh ideas. Below the three gables there is a long wooden balcony, pierced with the tulip design and flat top, repeated in the inside staircase. The bell-pushes and fireplace surrounds also have Art Nouveau designs.

Originally in front of each terrace were greens owned by the residents where cattle grazed (below left). The greens were gifted to the local Council by the residents to be transformed into the public gardens that are still there today. The work was financed by the Council as a work creation scheme during the Depression (below right).

The first one opened was Marine Terrace Garden in 1932. The houses and the gardens together form an outstanding local feature and are an attraction unparalleled in Lancashire. In 2009 the Friends of Waterloo Seafront Gardens was formed to safeguard the gardens, which had become sadly neglected since their heyday in the 1930s.

The whole of the seafront area was declared a conservation area in 1972. In the same year, H.R.H. Princess Anne came to open the new boating lake, constructed between the gardens and the shore, which in 2009 was further enhanced by the opening of the £10 million Crosby Lakeside Adventure Centre.

Historically, the heart of Waterloo has always been South Road which has changed enormously over its history. Seen opposite in the 1920s (with a passing ship centre stage) it was originally a mixture of residential and commercial premises but it is now entirely full of shops and restaurants. The latter serve a variety of cuisines: French, Italian, Greek, Spanish, Polish, Chinese and Indian, but above the modern shop fronts the Victorian and Edwardian red-brick façades can still be admired.

*Above left: Crosby Lakeside Adventure Centre. Above right: canopied railway station South Road c. 1907.*

A striking surviving feature of South Road is the canopy in front of the railway station. Until the opening of the railway between Southport and Waterloo in 1848 and then its extension through to Liverpool in 1850, Waterloo was very much a small, quiet residential area. In 1824 transport to Liverpool was via the Lancashire Witch Packet on the Leeds and Liverpool Canal or by coach which departed from the Waterloo Hotel at 9am daily.

However, the railways transformed Waterloo; those with the means and inclination could escape a crowded and industrial Liverpool. In particular, Waterloo extended further inland and many fine properties were built such as those in Waterloo Park.

The Liver Inn (pictured overleaf) was the only building in South Road in 1857 and it still survives today. James Dunwoody Bulloch, Confederate Agent during the American Civil War, lived in four different houses in Waterloo; he lodged at the Liver Inn for a short time and, later, when he brought his family over from the United States to join him he lived at Wellington Street and Marine Terrace.

There used to be a blacksmith's forge next to the Liver Inn and, just beyond the smithy, the Odeon (now the Plaza) Cinema was opened, and closed, just days before war broke out in 1939. The Plaza Community Cinema is the only surviving cinema in Waterloo, others such as the Winter Gardens in Church Road and the Queens Cinema in South Road having long since closed their doors.

*The Liver Inn, South Road, with blacksmith's forge on the right. (RJ).*

Waterloo boasts a number of other public houses of some antiquity; The Ship Victory Inn, of which only a small house remains, in Brunswick Terrace, and the Volunteer Canteen on East Street, which was so-called because local men gathered there to enlist during the Boer War.

As well as being the home of many well-to-do people, Waterloo was also a minor local tourist destination and many houses were rented out as holiday homes.

At one time Friedrich Engels, who did so much research for Karl Marx, stayed in 19 Bath Street for a few weeks recuperation from illness enjoying the sea air.

Between 1886 and 1898 a horse-drawn omnibus travelled along Crosby Road, Waterloo. It was later replaced by a tramcar running along a single line, from the George Hotel, Crosby to the Seaforth station of the Liverpool Overhead Railway.

A less conventional form of transport was provided by the early aviator Henry Melly. Living in Moor Lane, Crosby, beside Crosby Mill, he came down to Waterloo seashore and built two hangars for his planes at the foot of Sandheys Road, Waterloo. In 1911 he bravely made his first flight lasting twenty minutes and thereafter achieved a forty minute flight to Manchester. Subsequently, with a break during the First World War, he offered flights to the public (see below).

In 1860, a local family and their visitors produced their own pamphlets, *The Seaside Tattler or Waterloo Cracker*, for private circulation. In describing Waterloo Green, the tone of one of the contributions will be familiar to readers of the local press down the ages:

> *The grass in the summer months can hardly be said to exist, the long dresses of the ladies having completely swept it away; instead of grass the turf is covered with various odds and ends that the juvenile population have brought up from the shore, or left from their daily sports, such as tails of kites, doll's legs, arms and heads, snail shells, shells of ocean, skins of shrimps, small pebbles and unused toffee.*

Whilst the seashore is still a popular destination, particularly since the installation of Antony Gormley's *Another Place* in 2005, pictured right, there is much of architectural interest in Waterloo for the modern visitor to see and admire; some perhaps is in need of care and attention.

Probably the most interesting local building is Old Christ Church, the focus of the recently designated Christ Church Conservation Area. Designed by Paley and Austin, it dates from 1899 replacing an earlier church from the 1840s. It is described by the Council for the Care of Churches as "*a subtle blend of the Perpendicular and Arts and Crafts*".

Christ Church was declared redundant in 1982 and, in Pollard and Pevsner's view, the resulting "*absence of fittings creates a romantic, melancholy atmosphere.*" Most visitors are struck by the fabric of the church itself. Its beautiful varicolored sandstone came from Bootle Quarry, an area now covered by Derby Park, and the stained glass in the East and West windows, with its complicated tracery incorporating flowing motifs and panels, is by Shrigley and Hunt. Some 1850s glass from the original church, depicting Christ the Good Shepherd, survives in the clerestory.

The church is now listed Grade II* and is maintained by The Friends of Old Christ Church with substantial financial sponsorship from the Churches' Conservation Trust. Within the church is a fine wall-hanging created by nine lady members of the Crosby U3A which depicts nine references to Waterloo history.

*Top: one of Antony Gormley's 'Iron Men'. (RJ). Bottom: Christ Church.*

*Above left: the Town Hall. Above right: Christ Church.*

A little distance from the church, in Great George's Road, stands Christ Church School, dating from 1842 and in Waterloo Road can be found Ennis Cottages which may date from the 1830s, and was formerly the vicarage of the original Christ Church. Other notable churches are St. Mary's in Waterloo Park, St. Thomas of Canterbury in Great George's Road, St. John's in St. John's Road and St. Faith's on Crosby Road North. Other buildings of interest include the former St. John's School, now a nursery, designed by T. Mellard Reade, at the corner of Wellington Street and Oxford Road.

There is a fine Town Hall, also in Great George's Road, built in 1862. The local government of Waterloo began in 1856 with the first meeting of the Waterloo-with-Seaforth Local Board of Health (Seaforth being an adjacent township). By 1894 it was an Urban District Council until becoming part of the Municipal Borough of Crosby in 1937.

Waterloo became the name of a new parliamentary constituency in 1918, its first M.P., Albert Buckley, serving from 1918 to 1923, followed by Malcolm Bullock (1923 to 1950), until the constituency was abolished, becoming part of the Crosby parliamentary constituency. This was represented by Graham Page, followed by Shirley Williams, Malcolm Thornton, Claire Curtis-Thomas and Bill Esterson. Waterloo is currently divided between the constituencies of Bootle and Sefton Central.

In Cambridge Road can be seen the original Waterloo Grammar School for boys and girls, built in 1902 and one of the first State grammars in the country. In 1922, a separate grammar school was built for girls that became the annexe to Chesterfield High School in 1972 and was later demolished.

There are a great many other Victorian and Edwardian buildings in Waterloo that would repay inspection. In Waterloo Park, a Conservation Area since 1991, there are several handsome houses. Stone House, built in 1858, the former home of the Rollo family, of the firm of Grayson, Rollo & Clover, shipowners, was the first property in this part of Waterloo. By 1864 a residential development of large detached mansions set around an ornamental lake, which would become known as Waterloo Park, had been instigated by Seaforth merchant, Samuel Moulsdale Mellor. Stone House, like many of these properties, is currently divided into flats.

*Above left: Stone House; Above centre: Park House; Above right:Carnegie Library & Museum.*

One of the best known former private residences, Park House, stands on Crosby Road North. Run by French Augustinian nuns, during its history it has housed a school, a convalescent home, and is currently a guest house. In 1910 the Sisters established a hospital for the poor in a nearby house. Known as the Hotel Dieu of Our Lady of Hope, it was a military hospital during WWI and later became Waterloo District General Hospital.

In Church Road, adjacent to the erstwhile Police Station, are the remnants of the Waterloo Carnegie Library and Museum, built in 1908 and almost completely destroyed by an incendiary bomb in May 1941. Relatively few Waterloo buildings were lost during the Blitz but the civilian death toll still stands at 20.

Some 230 of those who perished in WWII are commemorated today on Waterloo-with-Seaforth townships' War Memorial, located at the junction of Great George's Road and Crosby Road, a site chosen in the aftermath of WWI as a central spot on the main thoroughfares through the district known to this day as the 'Five Lamps'.

The memorial was unveiled by Waterloo's first M.P., Colonel Albert Buckley, on the 29th October 1921. The design, a winged victory surmounting a sandstone pillar, is the work of Mr. F.W. Doyle Jones, R.B.S., and was exhibited at the Royal Academy in 1919. Originally it commemorated the 429 men and women from the Waterloo and Seaforth districts who died in WWI.

Unsurprisingly, the 100th Anniversary of the Battle of Waterloo was not marked in 1915 as the country was in the grip of the First World War and it was judged inappropriate to make too much of an historical Battle against the French.

*Right: war memorial at the 'Five Lamps'.*

Between 1919 and 1938 an original WWI tank stood at the entrance to Potter's Barn Park, on Waterloo's southern boundary with Seaforth. The tank was intended to permanently commemorate the achievement of the residents of Waterloo and Seaforth in raising the equivalent of £20 million for the National War Savings during the year 1918; it was sold for scrap in 1938 and the £35 raised was given to the Waterloo Branch of the British Legion.

Potters Barn, showing entrance, Seaforth

'Potter's Barn' was built by William Potter of Everton in 1841 as the entrance to a country mansion. His scheme got no further than the erection of two coachman's cottages before he became bankrupt. The buildings are now part of Potter's Barn Park and will be used as a replica for Hougoumont Farm when a Mock Battle of Waterloo takesa place in the Park in September 2015 to mark the 200th Anniversary of the original battle and the foundation of Waterloo Township.

A Waterloo Dinner will also be held at Old Christ Church to mark the occasion. The first such gathering took place at the Waterloo Hotel in 1816 to celebrate the first anniversary of the Battle. It was proposed by John Gladstone of Seaforth House that the dinner become an annual event but whether his proposal was acted upon is not known. In 1999 the 'tradition' was revived and this year's dinner will be the seventh such event in the modern era.

***Further reading and references***

Hollinghurst, Hugh. *Waterloo, Seaforth & Litherland Through Time* Amberley Publishing (2014)

Lewis, James R. *The Birth of Waterloo* Sefton Council (1973)

Pevsner, Nikolaus. The Buildings of England. *South Lancashire* Penguin (1969)

Friends of Waterloo Seafront Gardens www.fowsg.co.uk

The Friends of Old Christ Church www.oldchristchurch.moonfruit.com

Unless otherwise indicated, images used in this article are from the author's private collection or reproduced courtesy of Sefton Libraries' Information Services.

*This article is dedicated to the memory of Ian Hamilton-Fazey OBE, who sadly died last year. A retired journalist, he was a resident of Beach Lawn and was the founder and chairman of Waterloo Residents' Association that has done much to improve the area in recent years. A memorial bench will soon be installed in the public garden at Beach Lawn as a modest acknowledgment of the efforts of a man many people thought should be called 'Mr Waterloo'.*

# THE FOUNDATION OF UNIVERSITY COLLEGE, LIVERPOOL 1878 – 1882

## *Martin Strauss*

Although the foundation of a University College in Liverpool seemed to happen in a short time, between a Town Meeting in May 1878 and the official opening of the College in January 1882 at a ceremony in St George's Hall, the initiatives for a College dated from the early part of the century and involved a number of organisations and individuals who promoted education at secondary and tertiary level.

The emerging middle class were catered for by the Liverpool Royal Institution (founded by William Roscoe in 1814), Liverpool College (1840), the Royal Infirmary Medical School (1844, though this had originally been located at the Royal Institution in 1834) and the Liverpool Institute (1856). For others less fortunate, much charitable work, often facilitated by the Corporation, was done by Anglican, Catholic and Non-Conformist communities, with the work of Fr James Nugent and Canon Lester being particularly noteworthy in establishing 'Industrial' or 'Ragged' Schools. There was also educational provision at the Bluecoat School since 1708, the Welsh Charity School (1804), and the Hibernian School in Pleasant Street (1807). By the mid-century, the Mechanics Institute provided for girls at Blackburne House and boys in Mount Street. After the 1870 Education Act, the Liverpool Elementary School Board, under Christopher Bushell, set to work to provide state schools across the city (forty-two by 1902).

One important reason for the creation of civic universities and colleges (London had led the way in 1836, when University and King's Colleges combined, and Manchester followed in 1851) was the need to cater for the huge growth in industry and commerce, with a concomitant development in technology and machinery. Education was vital to service the needs of a changing and expanding Imperial nation. Alongside the growth of the iron, cotton, coal, railway and engineering industries, the professions were expanding rapidly to provide appropriate services to these industries. Bankers, lawyers, accountants, architects and surveyors were in increasing demand and these professions were providing opportunities for 'articled' students.

In 1857, Liverpool accounted for 45% of Britain's exports and 33% of her imports. Cotton, glass, chemicals, coal, salt, timber and much else passed through in huge quantities, transported by a growing number of steamship lines. It is against this background of mercantile and commercial growth in the city that the movement towards the establishment of the College gathered pace in the 1870s to meet the demands of the age.

A brief mention should be made of earlier attempts to establish a higher education institution in Liverpool by Dr James Carson in 1835-7, by Canon Abraham Hume, Vicar of All Saints, Vauxhall, in 1848 and by Richard Vaughan Yates, as part of his development of Prince's Park, in 1856. Queen's College, established in 1857, offered

*Charles Beard BA (1827-1888). Minister, Renshaw Street Chapel (1867-1888).*

a range of Arts subjects and affiliated to London University, until its demise in 1881. A School of Science was founded in 1861, with an impressive list of supporters, but it was unable to find permanent premises and closed in 1871. However, The Liverpool Ladies Educational Association of 1866 helped to further public interest in education. It was soon supported by the Association to Promote Higher Education, which held a public meeting in January 1874, addressed by William Rathbone, Emily Davies, Principal of the new Girton College in Cambridge, and James Stewart, who had started the Cambridge Extension (examination) Scheme in 1867, widely used in Liverpool in the 1870s. Thomas Waters and James Campbell-Brown of the Medical School soon joined the Committee of the Association, among whom may be noted Rathbone, Bushell, Charles Beard (Unitarian Minister at Renshaw Street Chapel), George Butler (Principal of Liverpool College and husband of Josephine), George Holt (ship-owner and merchant) and Edward Lawrence (accountant, businessman and past Lord Mayor). All these men would play a vital role in the next seven years.

All these organizations and influences came together in two significant meetings in 1877 and 1878. In November 1877 Beard presided over a conference, which resolved to form a committee to establish a 'College of Arts and Sciences'. William Rathbone then approached the Mayor, Arthur Forwood, to summon a Town Meeting to discuss the whole question of a University College. One hundred and thirty-two signatories endorsed this request and on May 11th 1878, the Daily Post announced that a meeting would be held in the Town Hall on May 24th, one of several over the next few years devoted to this matter.

The Meeting of May 1878 saw two hundred and sixty men discuss the proposal, put by Lawrence and seconded by Waters, that, "in the opinion of this meeting, it is desirable that a College be established to provide instruction in all the branches of a liberal education (to) enable residents to qualify for degrees in Arts, Sciences and other subjects...and such instruction as may be of service in professional and commercial life". A committee of sixty-five, under Forwood's chairmanship, was set up with the detailed planning undertaken by a sub-committee, chaired by Lawrence, with Beard as Vice-Chairman, Campbell-Brown and William Stewart (a barrister) as Hon. Secretaries, Robert Gladstone as Hon. Treasurer, with Sir James Picton, Waters, Butler, W.A. Jevons (a solicitor), Canon Hume, Henry Duckworth and Anthony Bower. The meeting was extensively reported in the *Liverpool Mercury* and other local papers. The Sub-Committee first met on June 3rd.

In November 1878, the Committee reported to a further Town Meeting of one hundred and forty-six men. They proposed to set up a University College with seven professorial 'chairs', in Modern Literature and History; Natural History; Classics and Ancient History; Maths and Experimental Physics; Engineering and Practical Mechanics; Chemistry; and Logic, Mental and Moral Philosophy, with lectureships, in law and physiology. No languages would be taught initially and all medical teaching would be done in the Medical School (the School wished to remain independent but to co-operate closely with the new College). Teaching costs were estimated at £3,000 per year and capital costs at £75,000. Once again this meeting was widely reported in the local press, providing much-needed publicity. Now backed by significant support, the Committee had to move fast to satisfy new requirements for the London University MB degree and to rival Owen's College in Manchester, which sought full University status.

The Committee had five tasks: to find a suitable site for the new College; to appoint an architect to modify any existing buildings or to build new premises; to raise funds for the purchase of the site, the cost of building work and to pay the salaries of the professors and other staff; to obtain a Charter of Incorporation, to establish the Governance of the new College; and to appoint a Principal, Professors and members of staff. In achieving these objectives in under four years, Thomas Kelly thinks that the most important men were Rathbone, Campbell-Brown and Beard. Yet there were many others who devoted time, energy, encouragement and much of their personal fortune to the College too. Council minutes show that a dedicated group of men were drawing up a Constitution for the new College, looking for a site and developing a campaign of fund-raising among local businessmen and industrialists for the required capital sum.

As the Committee got to work they were aided from an unexpected source, when Liverpool-born Canon Lightfoot, educated at the Royal Institution, Professor of Divinity at Cambridge and Bishop-elect of Durham, delivered a rousing speech in January 1879, when distributing prizes for the Liverpool Council of Education. He imagined a Liverpool with a University College promoted by prominent citizens; where professorial salaries were endowed by public subscription or munificent benefactors, who had given of their surplus income to educate young people in Liverpool. A pamphlet, largely written by Beard, was ready by late March, setting out the objectives of the College, listing the Chairs and costs and emphasising the proposed training of teachers and an education designed to prepare for professional examinations. The need to compete with Manchester, Leeds, Birmingham, Bristol, Nottingham, Sheffield and Newcastle was again stated strongly.

By good fortune, the Committee was able to acquire a site almost at once. After noting that possible sites in Prince's Park, Kensington Fields and St James' Mount had been rejected, the Council's Annual Report simply says: '...the College secured the buildings and four acres of land'. The story behind the acquisition is quite puzzling, involving the College Council, the City Council, the Royal Infirmary and London and

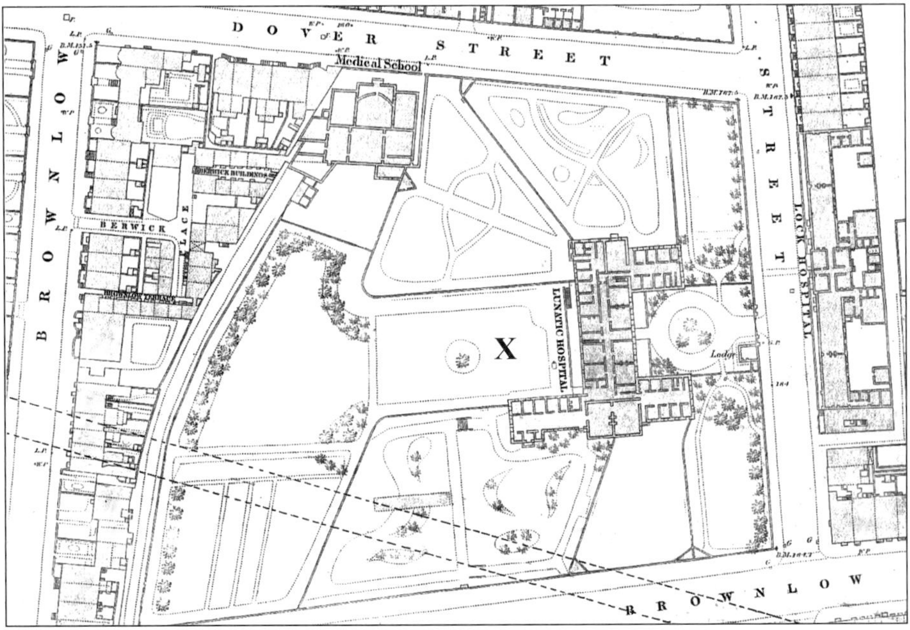

*The location chosen for the new University College, showing the 'Lunatic Hospital' (X). The site was bounded by (clockwise) Brownlow Street, Dover Street, Ashton Street and Brownlow Hill. The dotted lines show the route of the railway running into Lime Street station. From sheet 25 of the 1848 Ordnance Survey.*

North-West Railway Company in various agreements over a number of years. The Railway Company's plan was to open up the tunnel underneath the grounds of the City Lunatic Asylum. This prompted the closure of the institution which subsequently became available for the new College. The site in question still forms the hub of the University, for the College acquired the site and buildings of the Asylum on Ashton Street, adapted them for teaching and study, before opening its doors to students on 23 January 1882. To achieve this required some fast footwork by the College Council, a good deal of money and the crucial support of the City Council at a vital moment.

The College Council retained Alfred Waterhouse to adapt the Asylum buildings for the new University College. It would be the first of eight commissions. By this time, he was an architect of national standing with a reputation for providing practical buildings for his clients. In Liverpool, he had built the North-Western Hotel on Lime Street, the Seamen's Orphanage in Newsham Park and houses for several important businessmen, some of whom were involved with planning the College. The Asylum dated from 1830, and was built on two floors, with cellars. A good deal of the building was now given over to physics, with teaching rooms, offices and laboratories. In July, the Sub-Committee approved Waterhouse's alterations, costing £3,000. Detailed plans survive, dated August 18th 1881, labelled 'drawings referred to in our contract' and signed by Tomkinson and Sons, the builders. Tenders had been put out in early August and most of the building was converted and ready for use in January 1882. Oliver

Lodge, Professor of Physics, recalled that 'the Asylum did not look promising as a college, (with) makeshift laboratories in preparation', but he admitted that dedicated laboratories were rare at the time.

Meanwhile, the campaign to raise money for the new College had proceeded apace. The response from many leading citizens in the city was magnificent. Another Town Meeting in July 1880 was told that £90,000 had now been raised. A report of the meeting, chaired by the Lord Mayor, Bernard Hall, was written by E.H. Edwards of the *Liverpool Mercury*. He mentions ninety-one attendants by name. Among those present were: William, Philip and Richard Rathbone; Picton, Lawrence, Forwood, Bushell and his son, Reginald, Beard, Alexander Balfour, Samuel Smith MP, Henry Tate, Edmund Muspratt, Stephen Guion, Ralph Brocklebank, Henry Gair, James Alsop, and Butler. More industrialists and ship-owners were now supporting the College. Rathbone noted that Owen's College, Manchester, and Yorkshire College in Leeds were both developing strongly; he presented this as a challenge to Liverpool – if they can do it, so can we. His views were echoed by many. The meeting endorsed the existing plans and praised progress so far; but there was much still to be done.

Indeed there was. Some of the money had been on condition that certain targets were met. With generous supporters, they would be and by the end of 1881, seven chairs had been endowed. Kelly notes that in early 1882, £109,000 had been raised. These early benefactors set the tone for the next ten years and more. The King Alfred Chair of Modern Literature was endowed by William, Samuel and Philip Rathbone; The Derby Chair of Natural History by the Earl of Derby; The Gladstone Chair of Classics and Ancient History by Alexander Brown, William Crosfield and James Barrow; The Roger Lyon Chair of Physics by the Lyon Trust, via Edward Whitley with other trustees (and in April 1881, the Medical School Council offered to contribute too); The Grant Chair of Chemistry by Mrs F. Grant; The Roscoe Chair of Art by members of his family and the Unitarian community; the Chair of Philosophy by forty-one Scottish merchants, led by Smith and Balfour. It has been suggested that matters moved slowly until Rathbone lost his seat in Parliament in 1880 and returned to Liverpool to galvanize the 'great and good' to back the College and give generously. His own account does not dispel this version of events, but his claim is supported in the memoirs of Professor Lodge.

The General Committee changed its name to 'The Council' on April 23rd 1881 and acquired many important new members. Edmund Muspratt (chemicals), Alexander Balfour (shipping), The Rev Thom (Unitarian Minister), Thomas Cope (tobacco importer), Holbrook Gaskill (chemicals), W.R. Bateson (solicitor), Andrew Squarey (solicitor), Reginald Harrison (shipping), James Alsop (solicitor), Malcolm Guthrie (silk mercer), and David Radcliffe (industrialist). As before, the Chairman was Lawrence, the Vice-Chairman, Beard, the Honorary Treasurer, Robert Gladstone and the joint Honorary Secetaries, Campbell-Brown and Stewart. College records reflect the contribution industrialists, lawyers, merchants, ship-owners and businessmen made to establishing the College and nursing it through its formative years.

Further progress was made on June 11th 1881. A sub-committee of the Earl of Derby, Rathbone, Bushell, Lawrence and Beard chose Gerald Henry Rendall to be Principal. He was not the first choice candidate, however. The Council's preferred man was Alfred Robinson, Fellow and Bursar of New College, Oxford. Robinson declined the post in late May and Rendall accepted. Educated at Harrow, he was a Fellow, Tutor and Lecturer in Classics at Trinity College, Cambridge. It seems that James Stewart and Canon Lightfoot had strongly recommended him and presumably other opinions had been sought. Anyway the Committee clearly thought they had the right man and he would indeed prove an inspired choice during the sixteen years he served the University College. He was thirty years old and a don of five years standing, Birkbeck Lecturer in Ecclesiastical Law, with University prizes and published work to his name. A 1903 account notes: 'After anxious enquiry and fullest consideration…the post of principal was filled by (G.H. Rendall)'. Lodge writes in his memoirs: 'Rendall was appointed a fortnight before me after careful and responsible enquiry by the Council from some of the theologians involved in funding the College'. In an article of 1892, Rendall records the tremendous civic spirit and patriotic pride in Liverpool in the 1870s and 1880s, when by 1882, some £250,000 was raised by the citizens of Liverpool.

*Gerald Henry Rendall (1851–1945), MA, BD, LittD, LLD, Principal of University College, Liverpool (1881–1897). British School. Courtesy University of Liverpool.*

Once Rendall was in post, the professors could be appointed. Oliver Lodge was appointed to the Physics post in June 1881 and began teaching in the Medical School in October, with a salary of £400 p.a. plus a share of student fees. Herdman (Zoology) and Campbell-Brown (Chemistry) came in November; MacCunn (Philosophy) and Bradley (English) in December. The Registrar (Londini) was also Librarian and Lecturer in Italian and there were lecturers in French and German.

Meanwhile, another sub-committee had been working on the details of the Constitution of the new College and on July 19th the Council applied for its Charter of Incorporation, which was granted on October 18th. This established a Court of Governors, with a Council representing the Governors, in practical control of the running of the College. There was also a Senate, being the College Professors. Four members of the Medical School were to serve on the Senate – this was agreed by a joint committee of the College and Medical school in May 1881. Arrangements were put in hand to convene a meeting of the Governors on December 17th and The Earl of Derby accepted the Presidency of the College, with William Rathbone and Christopher Bushell as Vice-Presidents. (A fine statue of Bushell stands in the Victoria Building and the 'Derby Window' honours the 15th and 16th Earls.)

While all these important steps were being taken, on August 9th 1881 Edward Lawrence wrote a significant letter to the City Council, following discussions with James Picton and Arthur Forwood. Lawrence noted that the College had raised some £100,000 since May 1878, that the Charter was shortly to gain the Royal Assent and that the College had very considerable public support, with professorial chairs endorsed by prominent citizens and benefactors. Furthermore, a site had been obtained for £19,000 and Alfred Waterhouse had been retained to alter the premises. Lawrence requested that the Council purchase the land and lease it to the College for seventy-five years. This letter was reported in the *Courier* and *Post*, which endorsed the proposal. Forwood also addressed the Council on the matter, pointing out that in spite of the generosity of many, the College would not be able to erect new buildings at the present time. The City Council responded quickly and on September 7th decided to seek Parliamentary power to raise money and buy the site and other property in Brownlow and Dover streets. This power was granted by the Liverpool Improvement Act of July 1882, of which one section dealt with the University College and the land purchase.

Council Minutes for November and December 1881 show that 73 applications had been received for three of the professorships, the Royal Assent to the Charter had been granted, and a meeting of the new Governors arranged. Subject to the availability of the Earl of Derby, the new College would be officially opened on January 14th 1882, with a ceremony in St George's Hall to be planned by Lawrence, Beard, Rendall, Stewart and Harrison. Meanwhile, Picton, Rendall and others were to prepare a College Seal. The minutes for December 3rd are signed by the Earl of Derby, an indication of the close interest he was taking in the new College. During December the Ladies Educational Association had been discussing arrangements for lectures and lecturers when the new College started work. From the start, the College welcomed women students to all degree subjects, except medicine, and in 1882 eighteen of the forty-five students who enrolled were women. The College made a clear statement in the Statutes that it was non-denominational and that 'no student, professor or member of staff was to submit to any religious test'.

In the twelve months from January 1881 to January 1882, a great deal of work was undertaken by dedicated supporters of the College, on the Council and on various sub-committees. The Council met fifteen times during the year to ratify decisions and deliberate on the business being discussed in sub-committees set up tackle the details of essential work. In addition a joint Committee was formed with the Medical School, with which close relations were established. As indicated earlier, Kelly believes that Rathbone, Beard and Campbell-Brown were the key figures whereas Lodge gives pride of place to Beard, Holt and Rathbone. Between them they provided the financial stimulus, the academic focus and the philosophical energy behind the project, with which to enlist many others to the cause.

*Professor Rendall addresses the audience at the opening ceremony. From 'The Graphic' newspaper. Courtesy Liverpool Central Library.*

University College, Liverpool, was officially opened on January 14th 1882, in a ceremony in St George's Hall, with the Earl of Derby in the chair. In his Inaugural Address, Principal Rendall noted the educational provision elsewhere in Liverpool and drew very public attention to the way the College had been so well supported by its generous and numerous benefactors. The vibrant state of education in the city was proved by the new primary schools and successful secondary schools, the libraries and reading-rooms, the literary and scientific societies. He could have added that many of the men and women who had brought all these things about were probably sitting in the room as he spoke. He finished by stating that 1882 was a propitious moment to found a College in the city, to offer extensive educational opportunities and to satisfy a strong civic pride, which had been so evident for many years.

**Conclusion**

The Donor List of 1891 makes interesting reading. Those who had given in the years 1878-1882 would, in many cases, continue to do so in the years which followed. Their generosity is remarkable, given some difficult economic and trading conditions in the 1870s. The three men who would give most money to the College in the nineteenth century, George Holt, Andrew Barclay Walker and Henry Tate, scarcely appear in the years before the opening of the College, chiefly because they had committed their money elsewhere. But their generosity would dominate the next fifteen years. Membership of the College Council and the various sub-committees set up since 1878 shows that there was a fairly large group of men who gave a huge amount of time (and often money) to setting up the College. Mostly they came from the professional, industrial, merchant and commercial classes in the city, but the role of various Non-Conformist groups was important, particularly the Unitarians and Quakers. This wide-ranging support characterised the years leading to the opening of the University College in Liverpool in January 1882.

**Sources**.

I am most grateful to the staff of the University of Liverpool Special Collections Library for their help in making documents available.

*The Muniment Book* contains conveyances, indentures and documents relating to the Asylum site and other property in the area bound by Ashton Street, Brownlow Hill, Brownlow Street and Dover Street. All College/University buildings were located here until c.1910

*Minutes of the Special Committee* (later the Council) in three volumes: May 1878 – January 1881; January – December 1881; and December 1881 – 1893.

*The College Almanac* of 1902-03, which gives a history of the years 1878 - 1902.

The Council *Annual Reports*, many of which look back to the formative years after 1878.

The *List of Donors*, published in September 1891. This includes bequests from 1880.

The pamphlet written by Charles Beard, to publicise the College and its purpose.

The *College Statutes*, with a list of Governors, 1882.

*The Advancement of Learning – The University of Liverpool 1881-1981*, Thomas Kelly.

*Past Years, an autobiography*, by Oliver Lodge, Professor of Physics 1881-1900.

*Building a Better Society – Liverpool's historic institutional buildings*, Colum Giles.

Relevant issues of the *Daily Post*, *Mercury* and *Courier* relating to College matters.

# CUNARD IN WORLD WAR ONE

## David Hearn

*Located on a ground floor wall in the Merseyside Maritime Museum, this historic carved Cunard emblem is one of the first objects to be seen by visitors taking the lifts to the upper floors. (RJ)*

By 1914 the Liverpool-based Cunard Steamship Company was seventy-four years old and already a major commercial presence in Liverpool, the United States and around the world. Cunard ships carried passengers and freight principally on the lucrative trans-Atlantic routes but also from the Mediterranean and northern Europe.

The trans-Atlantic passenger and mail trade was more than just a commercial imperative; it was a matter of national pride with Britain, America and, from the beginning of the twentieth century, Germany competing to have the biggest, fastest and most luxurious ships plying between America and Europe. By 1902 Cunard had already been eclipsed by her biggest rival the White Star Line and in that year White Star had joined the International Mercantile Marine Company which was American owned and very well capitalised. A number of super liners were planned and there was a danger that an American dominated company might further damage Cunard's already secondary position. The British government intervened in an effort to re-establish Cunard's position by starting an annual subsidy of £150,000 and offering a low rate loan of £25 million to facilitate the construction of two super liners – the *Lusitania* and the *Mauritania*.

The British government subsidy and loan did not, of course, come without a price and that was an agreement, signed in 1903, under which Cunard would be obliged to hand over its fleet to government control in the event of a war. Making ships available for government use was nothing new to Cunard who only fifteen years into their business had provided eleven ships to the government during the Crimean War with ships also being requisitioned as troop transports (troopers) for the 1882 Egyptian campaign and, again, in the Boer War.

Cunard ships had, from the inception of the company, carried a Royal Navy officer in order to safeguard the mail and the 1903 agreement carried this much further in that it required all of the Cunard officers, with the exception of the engineers, and not less than half the crew to be members of the Royal Naval Reserve. This meant that the officers and majority of the crew on any Cunarder were trained to Royal Navy standards which facilitated the fleet's transfer into Royal Navy hands in the event of a war. This requirement did, however, mean that Cunarders were permitted to fly the Royal Naval Reserve flag the 'Blue Ensign' which set them apart from other British lines who flew the 'Red Ensign' of the Merchant Navy.

Immediately upon declaration of war the majority of the Cunard fleet was, in accordance with the agreement, requisitioned to be used as armed cruisers, troopers, hospital ships or prison ships. It is interesting that the Directors of Cunard decided that the ship that was, arguably, to be Cunard's most notorious casualty of the war, RMS *Lusitania*, should be retained to carry passengers, freight and mail across the Atlantic. The government not only agreed but supported the decision of the Directors because it remained important that some semblance of normality was maintained in the trans-Atlantic passenger business and that this business was seen to be in the hands of Britain and was symbolised by a large and prestigious vessel.

Cunard was not expected to simply hand over its fleet for the free use of the government. Payment was made in accordance with the 1903 agreement; these payments were known as 'subventions' and not only maintained Cunard's cash flow through the conflict but also allowed the company to grow. The Directors of Cunard had purchased shares of Thos & Jno Brocklebank in 1911 and in 1916 they bought the Commonwealth & Dominion Line, itself an amalgamation of four shipping lines that had been made in 1914. It is clear that the level of subventions was at a level beyond what Cunard needed simply to maintain its fleet despite a sharp increase in the price of coal, a general reduction in Atlantic passengers and the difficulty in finding crew.

The speed with which the Cunard fleet was prepared for war was dramatic although the more modern ships in the fleet had been built to incorporate design features that facilitated their transformation into armed cruisers. RMS *Aquitania,* pictured below at the Pier Head about to depart on her maiden voyage on 30th May 1914, had made only two further round trips before being taken over by the Admiralty. All the *Aquitania's* luxury fittings and furniture were stripped and placed in store with five thousand men filling two thousand wagon loads in only forty-eight hours. Ten 6 inch guns were

*From the Illustrated London News, 6th June 1914. (RJ)*

fitted and, in her new role as HMS *Aquitania,* she commenced patrolling the Western Approaches on 7th August 1914 – only three days after the declaration of war. However, due to her size and formidable rate of fuel consumption, the *Aquitania* was not well suited to the role of armed cruiser and later in the war was to carry out duties more fitting to her design, acting as a trooper carrying over five thousand troops at a time and, later, as a hospital ship. The *Aquitania* served throughout the first world war without mishap and went on to serve through the Second World War which it also survived undamaged.

Other Cunard ships that were converted for use in various roles include RMS *Mauretania* which became an armed cruiser for a very short time before being returned to civilian service in August 1914. Then, due to the very much reduced trans-Atlantic service, she was laid up in Liverpool for several months until she, like the *Aquitania*, became a hospital ship. The size of the *Mauritania* made her ideal as a trooper and she carried Canadian troops across the Atlantic. Following America's entry into the war the *Mauretania* again became a troop ship and carried thousands of American soldiers to Europe. After the war the *Mauretania* was also used to repatriate both American and Canadian soldiers.

RMS *Caronia* too was very quickly converted into an armed merchant cruiser and on 8th August 1914 it was on patrol on the West Indies and North American station. Initially armed with 4.7 inch guns, in May 1915 these were increased to 6 inch guns. From 1916 until the end of the war she was used as a trooper mainly between South and East Africa and India.

RMS *Laconia* was converted into an armed merchant cruiser and served out of the Simon's Town naval base in South Africa patrolling the south Atlantic and the east African coast. The ship was involved in the sinking of German light cruiser SMS

*Above: the Laconia pictured in the River Mersey. (RJ)*

*Konigsberg* in the Rufigi River in July 1915. After returning to Britain in the summer of 1916 the ship was handed back to Cunard and resumed her trans-Atlantic passenger trade in September of that year. In February 1917 *Laconia* was sunk by a German U-boat with the loss of twelve lives.

RMS *Carmania* was the sister ship of RMS *Caronia* and when they were built in 1905 they were the largest ships in the Cunard fleet. Like the *Caronia* the *Carmania* was converted into an armed merchant cruiser with eight 4.7inch guns. After conversion the ship was sent to Bermuda to patrol the West Indies. In the Battle of Trinidade off Brazil on 14th September, 1914 the *Carmania* sank the SMS *Cap Trafalgar*; ironically, the German ship had had her appearance altered so that she would resemble the *Carmania*. The *Cap Trafalgar* was manned by German Navy reservists and managed to inflict serious damage to the *Carmania* before it was hit several times below the water line and sank with the loss of 51 men. The *Carmania* lost nine crew but with many others injured and had to be helped into port by other Royal Navy ships which responded to her signals. *Carmania* was towed to Gibraltar for repair because there were no heavy ship repair facilities in the West Indies. Following repair the *Carmania* patrolled the coast of Portugal for two years before being used as a troop ship for the Gallipoli campaign. After the war the *Carmania* was used to take Canadian troops home from Europe.

RMS *Franconia* was only four years old when war was declared. *Franconia* was not requisitioned immediately but from early 1915 she served as a troop ship, a role that she continued in until she was sunk by a torpedo off Malta in October 1916. At the time of her loss she was not carrying any troops and although the majority of her crew were rescued twelve men died.

RMS *Alaunia* had undertaken her maiden voyage in December 1913 and upon outbreak of the war she became a troop ship principally carrying Canadian troops followed by service in the Gallipoli campaign and carrying troops to Bombay. In September 1916 en route between London and New York the *Alaunia* struck a mine in the English Channel and sank with the loss of two lives.

RMS *Saxonia*, which was used on the Trieste to Boston route, made one voyage as a trooper from Canada before being used to accommodate German prisoners in the Thames for a short time and again became a trooper in March 1915.

RMS *Ivernia* became a trooper as soon as war was declared and was under the command of Captain Turner who was famously the captain of the *Lusitania* when it was sunk. On New Year's Day 1917 the *Ivernia* was torpedoed off the coast of Greece and was lost at the cost of 120 men.

RMS *Carpathia*, famous as the ship that had rescued 705 survivors from the *Titanic*, became a trooper and survived until July 1918 when it was hit by three torpedoes off the coast of Ireland and sank with the loss of five crew.

1918 was a year of serious losses for Cunard with RMS *Ausonia*, RMS *Andania* and RMS *Aurania* also being sunk by German U-boats. A number of tactics were employed by Cunarders and other merchant ships against U-boat attack. Often the U-boats were first engaged by the guns that had been added to the armed merchant cruisers. U-boats had limited numbers of torpedoes and would often surface to engage a merchant ship but once on the surface the U-boat became very vulnerable to counter fire and there were many instances of U-boats being forced to break off an attack by fast and accurate gun fire. Other ships, Cunarders in particular, would simply outrun an attacker by using their superior speed. Lookouts were often doubled in number when sailing in dangerous waters and more than one Cunarder was to survive a torpedo attack when the torpedo was spotted early and speedy evasive action allowed even a large ship to avoid the attack.

*U-boat U-118, one of 329 submarines serving with the Imperial German Navy during WW1 and taking part in the first 'Battle of the Atlantic'. It was washed up on the beach at Hastings following the cessation of hostilities when its hauser broke as it was being towed to the breaker's yard during a storm.*

*Image from a contemporary stereo card.*

Probably the best known incident of the First World War which involved Cunard was the sinking of RMS *Lusitania* on 7th May 1915 by the German submarine U-20 with the loss of 1,198 passengers and crew including 128 American citizens. It was, at the time, hoped that the loss of so many Americans might have brought America into the war on the side of the Allies immediately; this, however, was not to be. The circumstances of the sinking of the *Lusitania* were controversial at the time and an examination of the facts surrounding the attack certainly reveal a more complicated story than simply a callous sinking of an unarmed passenger ship.

Although converted to an armed merchant cruiser at the outbreak of war by the installation of twelve 6 inch guns and numerous machine guns, the cost of coal to run a 31,550 ton ship was just not viable and the *Lusitania* was returned to Cunard to maintain the trans-Atlantic passenger trade even though this was very much reduced. The Germans did not need to deploy complicated intelligence techniques to plan an attack on the *Lusitania* because it sailed to a timetable that was openly published in New York. Likewise the Germans would have been well aware of who was scheduled to sail on the ship because, in common with the practice of the time, passenger lists were available for inspection by anyone.

In February 1915 the Germans declared that they were extending the sea areas that they considered to be a war zone to include the English Channel and the waters surrounding Ireland and within this area Allied merchant ships would be liable to attack and neutral ships would be stopped and searched for contraband war materiel. In order to give an idea of the size of the task taken on by the German Navy, during March 1915 five thousand ships either entered or left British ports and, of these, only twenty-one were attacked. The interception of or attacking of merchant ships at sea was governed by the 1856 Declaration of Paris as amended by the Hague Conventions of 1899 and 1907 collectively known as 'Cruiser Rules'. Under these, which were, of course, originally formulated for use by surface vessels, strict rules were put on merchant ships as well as those on warships – cruisers – intercepting them. Submarines were considered as 'cruisers' in international law and were therefore required to surface and inspect merchant ships rather than summarily sinking them.

The Germans argued that British tactics as introduced by Winston Churchill, in his capacity as First Sea Lord, made it impossible to abide by the Cruiser Rules. British ships were under instruction to attempt to ram any surfaced U-boat which made surfacing to challenge a ship an extremely dangerous manoeuvre because U-boats were very vulnerable on the surface. A further threat to U-boats was what was known as Q-ships, old merchant ships which were apparently defenceless but were crewed by Royal Navy personnel and carried concealed guns. U-boats had been tempted to surface to destroy these ships with their deck gun only to come under unexpectedly accurate fire. Although no U-boat was destroyed by a Q-ship until after the sinking of the *Lusitania*, their existence was known and U-boat skippers were naturally wary of surfacing to challenge any merchant ship. Churchill had concluded that it was inconceivable that unrestricted submarine warfare would be conducted by 'a civilised power' and yet, at the same time, his orders had made it difficult for the Germans to abide by the established maritime conventions.

RMS *Lusitania* left New York on 1st May 1915 but, prior to her departure, the German embassy in Washington had issued the following warning – 'Travellers intending to embark on the Atlantic voyage are reminded that a state of war exists between Germany and her allies and Great Britain and her allies; that, in accordance with formal notice given by the German Imperial Government, vessels flying the flag of Great Britain or any of her allies, are liable to destruction in these waters.' Neither Britain nor Cunard took this threat seriously. An attack on a specific ship was, logistically, an extremely difficult proposition and the more so when it was such a fast ship that was also taking measures to reduce attack including a doubling of lookouts and sailing on a zig zag rather than direct course.

Whilst at the time of her last voyage RMS *Lusitania* was not carrying any guns, she was carrying 4,200 cases of small arms ammunition, 1,259 cases of steel shrapnel shells, together with 3,863 boxes of cheese and 696 tubs of butter destined for the Royal Navy. It would not have been difficult for German informants to find out what was being loaded onto the ship in New York. The Germans could, subsequent to the attack, claim that the ship was carrying contraband of war in contravention of the Hague Convention which made her a legitimate target. The Germans were aware that the *Lusitania* had carried guns in the past and, in fact, the *Mauritania* had been fitted with two 4.7 inch guns even in peacetime. It is not unreasonable that the Germans might have believed that the *Lusitania* could have been carrying concealed guns.

The German U-boat which sank the *Lusitania* had already sunk three British ships on 7th May and was down to its last two torpedoes when it attacked. A single torpedo struck the *Lusitania* amidships and exploded and there was an immediate second and larger explosion slightly further forward. This second explosion was not from a torpedo and the cause of it is subject to some conjecture with coal dust in one of the bunkers or a boiler being the two most likely causes. Whatever the cause of the second explosion the ship sank very quickly and with the loss of almost twelve hundred lives.

The British were hopeful that the sinking would bring America into the war on the side of the Allies but any suggestion that the British government would 'sacrifice' such a ship to that end in some sort of trap is somewhat fanciful. In the end President Wilson was satisfied by a change in the wording of the German statement about neutral shipping. The Germans stated that: any neutral ship not carrying contraband was allowed to go to the port that it was heading to whereas a neutral ship found to be carrying contraband would be sunk but only after the passengers and crew had evacuated the vessel.

*Top: Lusitania in New York harbour. Above: Uncle Sam confronts 'Kaiser Bill' with the bodies of child victims of the Lusitania outrage, draped in the American flag. "Here lie 'the facts'" says Uncle Sam. (Both images LOC)*

The sinking of the *Lusitania* with the loss of so many crew, many of whom were from Liverpool, would have caused considerable distress in the city coming just three years after the loss of the *Titanic*. There were anti-German riots in Liverpool and other places following the sinking of the *Lusitania* and many individuals and businesses rightly or wrongly perceived to be German were attacked. The police did their best to protect possible targets but there was considerable damage and some injuries. The perpetrators who were arrested faced harsh punishment with custodial sentences being given to many. It was noted in the local press that none of those arrested in Liverpool had lost any family members in the sinking of the *Lusitania*. The stipendiary magistrate commented that a number of men brought before him were of military age and they were told that a better way of fighting the Germans was to enlist and join the army in France.

Cunard's contribution to the war effort went much further than handing over its fleet. The management and staff of Cunard had an unparalleled breadth of experience in the logistics of operating a mixed fleet of passenger and cargo vessels on various routes, a fact not lost on the Admiralty which devolved management of a considerable number of ships to Cunard. During the course of the war no fewer than one hundred and eighty ships in the North Atlantic trade were brought under Cunard management together with three hundred and fifty ships involved in the transportation of food supplies. These additional duties must have placed a huge strain on the staff of Cunard which was already stretched by employees on other war service and would have made the Cunard offices originally in Water Street and, by the end of war, in the Cunard Building, a hive of activity.

Another ship acquired by the Admiralty was RMS *Campania*, a Cunarder that had actually been sold to a ship breaking company and which in November 1914 became HMS *Campania*. In 1915 the *Campania* was fitted out as a seaplane tender and aircraft carrier. Although an older ship, launched in 1892, the *Campania* was a previous holder of the Blue Riband for the fastest crossing of the Atlantic. Cunard, in association with a number of ship builders, worked on a number of other seaplane carriers and tenders. In 1918, during high winds, *Campania* dragged her anchor, collided with another British ship and sank in the Firth of Fourth.

*RMS Campania with her distinctively tall smokestacks at the Pier Head Landing Stage. (RJ)*

*Operatives assembling shells in Cunard's shell factory at Bootle. Photo courtesy of English Heritage.*

Even something as mundane as the Cunard laundry was pressed into service. Demand by the company had lessened considerably because of the reduced trans-Atlantic passenger trade so the company undertook to deal with the laundry requirements of the various military hospitals in and around Liverpool.

Two other enterprises that were somewhat removed from Cunard's core business were undertaken during the war. The first was a shell factory in Bootle and the second an aircraft factory at Aintree. In March 1915 Cunard bought the Branch Engine Shop in Rimrose Road, Bootle and very quickly started producing shells there. By the end of the war two hundred thousand 4.5 inch shells, one hundred and seventy-five thousand 6 inch shells and thirty-four thousand 8 inch shells had been made to help satisfy the insatiable demand for ordnance. At any one time a thousand people were employed at the shell factory with by far the vast majority of them being women because, of course, so many Liverpool men were already in the forces or on work in the port.

As with the shell factory most of the staff of the aircraft factory – National Aircraft Factory No 3 – that Cunard built in Aintree in 1917/18 were also women. The first of the five hundred planned Bristol Fighter aircraft that the factory was to build was produced in June 1918 but the company quickly became frustrated with the bureaucratic requirements of the Air Board in London and they handed the factory over to the government. By the end of the war only one hundred and twenty-six aircraft out of the proposed five hundred had been built.

During World War One the contribution of the Cunard Steamship Company was huge. Cunard's own ships carried almost half a million men across the Atlantic and this figure rose to around nine hundred thousand when the total carried by ships being managed by Cunard is added. In addition to this, ten million tons of freight was also carried by Cunard or Cunard-managed ships. Cunard came out of the war in a very strong position financially and as the principal trans-Atlantic carrier of passengers. It

*Above: 1:50 scale model of the Berengaria in the Merseyside Maritime Museum. Some 900 ft long, 98 ft wide, and over 52,000 tons in weight, she was longer, wider and heavier than Titanic and, to this day, is still the biggest vessel to enter the Liverpool dock system in peacetime. (RJ)*

had, of course, been paid by the British government for all of its various activities but, as part of the German reparations, the company was handed the SS *Imperator*, the Hamburg America Line ship which was the biggest ship in the world at the time. This ship became RMS *Berengaria* and remained in service with Cunard until damaged by fire in 1938. Cunard also received the German passenger liner *Kaiserin Auguste Victoria* which it only operated for around a year before selling her on to the Canadian Pacific Steamship Company who renamed her RMS *Empress of Scotland* and operated her until 1930.

The 'gift' of these two ships was a measure of the importance placed by the British government on the contribution of a Liverpool shipping company during what was, at the time, the most desperate war that Britain had engaged in.

***Notes***

*Ship prefixes* – HMS – His/Her Majesty's Ship – a vessel of the Royal Naval; RMS – Royal Mail Ship – a ship that carries British mail items; HMTS – His/Her Majesty's Troop Ship – a ship operated by the Royal Navy specifically for trooping purposes; HMHS – His/Her Majesty's Hospital Ship – a ship operated by the Royal Navy fitted out as a hospital and casualty transport vessel.

*Further reading*

F.E. Hyde; *Cunard and the North Atlantic 1840-1973*; Macmillan Press, London, 1975.

H. Johnson; *The Cunard Story*; Whittet Books Ltd, London 1987.

*www.theshipslist.com* – the website has a very comprehensive list not only of Cunard ships but most other lines as well, including links to photographs of many ships.

# EDWIN LYON: A FORGOTTEN LIVERPOOL SCULPTOR

## *Ann Truesdale*

With wealth and a growing mercantile class came a desire to provide intellectual and aesthetic stimulation and to establish institutions in Liverpool that matched those of London. William Roscoe did much to spark a love for and interest in painting and sculpture in Liverpool and is one of the town's most remarkable citizens; much has been written about this amazingly talented man.[1] Of particular relevance here is that Roscoe took the lead in setting up a series of art societies including the Liverpool Academy of Art.[2,3,4]

It was a good time for children with artistic talent to be born and the artist of interest for this paper is the sculptor Edwin Lyon, now virtually unknown in the town of his birth.[5] He was born on 31st May 1806 into an artistic family.[6] His father George Lyon was a painter who had married Margaret Dunbill at St Mary's Church, Walton on the Hill, in 1797.[7] George and Margaret Lyon had eight children, all baptised at St Paul's Church, St Paul's Square, then a fashionable part of Liverpool, and all survived to adulthood.[8] In 1799 the family lived in Ormond Street.[9] Edwin was the fourth child, and third son of the family. By the time of Edwin's baptism the family had moved to Russell Street off Brownlow Hill.[10]

*Edwin Lyon.*

The family continued to live and work in the Brownlow Hill area for more than thirty years with both a home in Russell Place and a shop/manufactury at 62 Brownlow Hill.[11] In 1811 Edwin's father George had advertised himself as a painter. By 1824 the family were at 2 Rupert Street and the business was at 91 Brownlow Hill where George was in partnership with his second son, also George.[12] They were house, sign, and ornamental painters, glass stainers etc.[13] He would have considered himself an artist as, "*The painter might be called upon to design an ornamental ceiling, the sculptor might be engaged on hackwork of tablets, plaques or plain marble chimney pieces.*"[14]

The Lyon family would know the Brownlow Hill area very well. Of particular significance was Franceys, a firm of monumental masons. In 1811 the brothers Samuel and Thomas Franceys advertised themselves as builders and composition makers, with a marble and Italian chimney piece repository at 11 Pleasant Street and 70 Brownlow Hill.[15] Picton gives a lively reminiscence of these workshops when he describes, "*...two or three dingy shops in Brownlow Hill opposite the end of Rupert St with a labyrinth of mean sheds and workrooms behind...yet these poor feeble remains were once irradiated with the light of genius enterprise and art*".[16]

Amongst those artists was John Gibson who was to become a celebrated sculptor and Royal Academician, and whose talent had been spotted and nurtured by Roscoe. From the earliest years Edwin Lyon would have known about the Franceys family business, have walked past the workshops daily and been intrigued by the work being carried out and may even have watched Gibson at work or got to know him. He was 11 when Gibson left for Rome in 1817. Another important influence in Edwin Lyon's career was William Spence, said to have been introduced to Franceys by Gibson.[17] Spence exhibited at the 1812 exhibition of the newly-formed Liverpool Academy, promoted by Roscoe, who also commissioned a bust of himself from Spence. In 1819 Spence entered into a partnership with Franceys.[18]

Edwin Lyon may have become officially apprenticed to Spence (source not found) and was considered his pupil by the 1820s when exhibitions were once again held by the Academy.[19,20] Another important resident in the area at the same time was George Mosses, a plasterer and stucco maker. His son Alexander, 13 years senior to Edwin, became an accomplished painter and a friend, exhibiting at the Liverpool Academy as early as 1811. He lived in Brownlow Hill although by 1822 had moved to Benson Street.

Before learning to work in stone and other materials Edwin would have had some schooling. Liverpool was a rapidly growing town and George Lyon's business was probably doing well with so much building work in progress and he would have been able to afford to send his children to one of the many academies that existed in Liverpool. However, so far I have not found any evidence of where Edwin or any of his brothers and sisters were educated.

Roscoe had promoted the Liverpool Academy in 1810 as a third exhibiting art society in the town, initiated and controlled by artists and with local sculptor Bullock as its first president. The Academy held annual exhibitions between 1810-1814. Many of the paintings exhibited were from nationally renowned artists such as Constable and Turner and would have been a great visual stimulus and talking point for the gentry and artist-craftsmen of Liverpool when very few people would have had the opportunity to see original paintings or sculptures.

However, finding instruction in drawing was more difficult. There were several private drawing masters, some of whom ran drawing academies listed in 1824.[21] There was disappointment that six years following the revival of the Academy of Art in 1817 under the auspices of the Liverpool Royal Institution, a drawing school for the instruction of the youth had not been opened. Criticism from an unnamed apprentice in the *Liverpool Mercury* stung the Academy into action. It was not until 1823 that teaching began at the Academy even though the Liverpool Royal Institution had offered several rooms in its Colquitt Street premises for this purpose in 1817.

Although there had been plans to open more frequently, free tuition took place between 7-9pm on Mondays, Wednesdays and Fridays during the winter months. Pupils were taught by 'visitors' modelled on the Royal Academy scheme, much criticised by Haydon.[22] Members of the Academy who taught in rotation were unpaid and offered different perspectives on art. Initially the students drew using chalks, paint and pencil, copying from the collection of casts.

On 23rd January 1824 Edwin Lyon, then living at 70 Pleasant Street, was admitted to the drawing classes. Students drew from the collection of casts of the Elgin and the Aegina Marbles (presented by John Foster). Edwin exhibited at the Academy exhibition later that year with five items.[23] He also exhibited eleven items in 1825 giving his address as 91 Brownlow Hill.[24] In the meantime Edwin was becoming the blue-eyed boy and featured in the press on many occasions. In his address as President of the Liverpool Royal Institution in February 1827, Dr Thomas Traill reviewed the progress of the students at the drawing schools at the Academy. Edwin was considered one of the most promising pupils, such that he had been recommended for a place as a probationer at the Royal Academy School in London. Dr Traill also noted that, "*...his brother Joseph draws extremely well and both have studied human and comparative anatomy from dissection.*"[25]

Edwin must have been very excited about going to London and it is likely he travelled by the mail coach (more expensive but safer than other coaches) which left Liverpool daily and took 26 hours. He was accepted as a probationer on 23rd January 1827 and his address at registration was 35 Upper Stamford Street, Lambeth.[26] William Lawrence was the President of the Royal Academy and the Keeper was Henry Thomson who had followed Henry Fuseli. Both Keepers had exhibited at the Liverpool Academy exhibitions between 1812-14 and Fuseli and Roscoe had corresponded regularly for many years.

Students would be given access to the classical casts from the Schools and three months to produce a set of drawings from them that would then be considered by the Keeper of Schools for full enrolment. As Edwin was back in Liverpool and attending the Academy drawing classes by 2nd March he did not stay the full three months.[27] It is not known whether his drawings were considered good enough for admittance as few records were created on the life of a student in the Schools and examples of the work they produced were not collected. I can only surmise why Edwin returned to Liverpool. Maybe he expected to meet with the great artists and sculptors of the time rather than aspiring probationers and his expectations had not been met. He may have felt lonely realising that Liverpool had more to offer than London. Although tuition was free he would have had to have found living costs and would have needed to work to support himself over the six years of studentship, and it would have been several years before he could have been admitted to a life class.

Liverpool did have more to offer and 1827-30 were the years of great success for Edwin following his return. The 1827 exhibition was described in great detail by 'our correspondent' over four issues of the *Liverpool Mercury* who stated, "*...never has so fine a collection of modern art been submitted to the inhabitants of Liverpool*".

Edwin Lyon's work was highly acclaimed. Seven sculptures were exhibited which included busts of Alexander Mosses, his father George, three un-named busts, and a figure of Adonis. Alexander Mosses exhibited paintings including a portrait of George Lyon, presumably Edwin's father and not his brother; the Lyon and Mosses family were obviously good friends. At the British Institution in London in 1827, however, Lyon also exhibited a statue of Diomed going to meet the Council of the Grecians.[28]

Alexander Mosses was appointed Professor and Master of the Drawing Academy from 1828 to 1836 and would have taught Edwin who attended a number of drawing classes in 1828.[29,30] That same year Edwin's skill at drawing was recognised when he drew a series of outlines of the Aegina Marbles from casts at the Liverpool Royal Institution. These were published as an oblong folio of sixteen lithographic plates with a dedication leaf to John Foster and C.R. Cockerell who discovered the marbles in 1811 (see examples of illustrations below). The originals are in Munich Glyptothek.

Five copies of the *Outlines of the Aegina Marbles* were purchased by the Liverpool Royal Institution for distribution for the promotion of the fine arts. In January 1829 Edwin was paid £7.10s and then a further £1.[31] The publication was promoted in

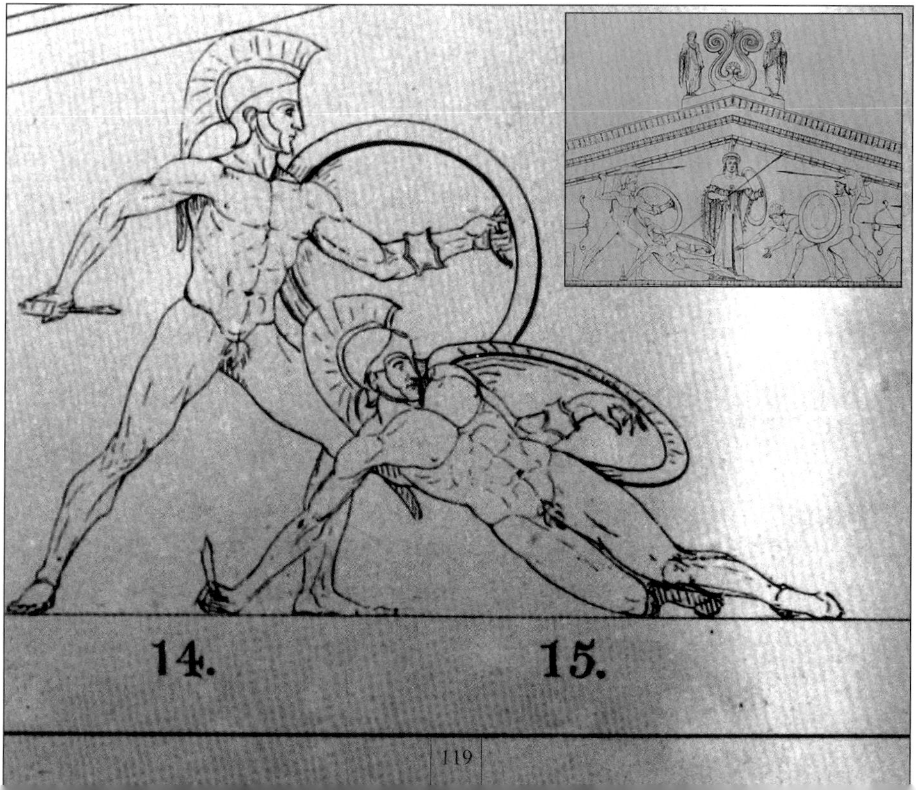

*Liverpool Mercury* editorials in 1828/9 and advertised in that newspaper frequently throughout 1829. A first edition of *Outlines* was sold at auction by Sotheby's for £5,750 in 2013 and has gone to the USA.[32] A copy of the book can be viewed digitally from the University of Heidelberg.[33]

Edwin Lyon's decision to use an outline style of drawing was probably influenced by the Liverpool cultural elite who were patrons of William Blake. Forty three subscribed to Robert Blair's book *The Grave* illustrated by Blake. Amongst these were William Roscoe and his son William, Dr Traill, John Gladstone and Samuel Franceys.[34] Blake in his turn had been influenced by Flaxman who became his lifetime friend. In his address in *Outlines* Lyon states (of himself):

> *"With a view to improvement in his profession as a Sculptor, he has long engaged in drawing from the different rare and valuable casts deposited in the Liverpool Royal Institution, before he undertook to delineate the statues of the Temple of Panhellenian Jove, from the island of Aegina. The Institution is indebted for the possession of the Casts from the Marbles of that Temple to the liberality of Mr Foster; to whom all students who have learnt to appreciate their value, will acknowledge the deepest obligation."*[35]

During the 1820s other institutions were being set up, often involving the same people who were active in the Liverpool Royal Institution such as Dr Traill. He was the first president of the Liverpool Mechanics' School of Arts established in 1825. This organisation provided evening classes, including drawing, for young working people. It was resolved in the 1828 minutes that, "*...the book of subscriptions for a bust of Dr Traill be left open in order to obtain funds to procure a Bust of Mr John Ashton Yates.*" (Director and Secretary).[36] Edwin Lyon, now highly esteemed and an Associate Member of the Academy of Art, was given the two commissions. The following year the committee meeting of 6th August 1829 with John Ashton Yates in the Chair took up Edwin Lyon's offer to superintend the Drawing Schools.

Edwin Lyon is considered to be the first fine artist to be employed teaching architectural drawing, figure drawing from casts and modelling in what was to become in the twentieth century the Liverpool College of Art.[37,38]

The 1830 half yearly report of the Mechanics' School of Arts included an item by Edwin Lyon, "*It is with feelings of great pleasure I have to state the rapid progress and increasing numbers of students in the Drawing department...The average number attending last September was about fifty but upwards of seventy or eighty are almost in constant attendance at the present time. There are ninety nine names on the list*".[39] The accounts in 1830 of the Mechanics' School of Arts show that Edwin earned a salary of £13.19s.0d in two instalments for six months' teaching.

By 1830, confident of an income, Edwin married Elizabeth Sanderson Swale (baptised in Idle, Yorkshire 24th May 1807),[40] the eldest daughter of John Henry Swale, on 21st January 1830 at St George's Church, Everton.[41] Elizabeth's father was a Professor of Mathematics and considered a distinguished Lancashire geometer by T.T. Wilkinson

*St George's, the 'Iron Church'*

who wrote an account of his life.[42] They must have felt they were on the rise as St George's was and is a lovely church commanding a wonderful position with views across the Mersey to the Welsh Hills. The newlyweds lived in Bostock Street (which used to link Scotland Road to Great Homer Street).

Edwin continued to teach at the Mechanics' School of Art and in his second report in 1830 stated:

> "*...that the pupils in the drawing class are giving very satisfactory proofs of the usefulness of this Institution the talent and ability of several would not disgrace the higher walks of art and the perseverance and good conduct of the generality of them redounds much to their credit. The attendance...not fewer than 80 or 90 being the average every night. The pupils are engaged in Architecture, Landscape, Floral, Pencil, Indian Ink and Figure Drawing...studying the Modelling of figures and ornaments.*"

Thanks are recorded in the minutes on several occasions for donations of drawings, including sketches of the Elgin Marbles, and books.[43] Edwin also felt confident enough to make requests and was given £6 to spend on books. By 1832 he was out of favour with the members of the Committee and it is recorded in the minute book, "*...that in consequence of the neglect and non attendance of Mr Lyon as well as his not answering enquiries of the Committee, the Committee consider the situation vacant.*"[44] Lyon was one of the most popular of all the teaching staff and the fees for his classes helped defray the costs of the other classes. By then it is likely that he had already left for Dublin. His last quarterly salary of £6.16s was recorded in the half yearly report following his departure. It was considered necessary to split the post and a Mr Pugh was appointed as one of two teachers to replace him at an annual salary of £30.

In 1831 a daughter, Elizabeth Sanderson, was born to Edwin and Elizabeth although it was not until 10th July 1833 that she was baptised at St Peter's Church, Liverpool, along with her brother Edwin Joseph, born probably June or July that year, and where the baptismal records describe Edwin as a sculptor living at Nelson Place, Edgehill.[45]

Edwin was back in Ireland in 1834 in what was to become a crisis year as his wife died leaving Elizabeth their daughter aged three and Edwin their son aged one. As no burial records have been found in Liverpool, it is likely that she died in Dublin. Her year of death is confirmed as 1834 in Wilkinson's paper about her father John Henry Swale who mourned the loss of his beloved daughter.[46] There is a record of Elizabeth Lyon aged 27 of 42 Anger Street buried at St Peter's Dublin on August 14 1834.[47] Following her death Edwin would have needed help with the children and it is likely that Mary, Elizabeth's sister, came to help and take the children back to Liverpool leaving Edwin in Dublin.

It could have been a lonely although productive time for Edwin. Two busts now in store in the V&A collection are of Sir William Cusack Smith 2nd Baronet (museum no. A.81:0-1965) modelled in 1834 and of Mrs. Francis Beetham (museum no. A.53-1932) in 1835 with an address of Lower Mount Street, Dublin.[48] Three other portrait busts modelled in wax had been put up for auction, that of Samuel Whit MP, Lord Massey, and Arthur H. George. Edwin Lyon is described as Irish and his address in 1834 was given as Bachelors Walk, Dublin.[49] He also produced a wax statuette of Maxwell Blacker, KC (now in the possession of Lord Dunalley at Kilboy, County Tipperary).

Tragically, in the summer of 1835 Edwin's son died at the age of two and was buried at St Paul's, Liverpool, on 10 July.[50] He may have been living at his grandfather's at Daulby Street with his sister Elizabeth, presumably looked after by their aunt Mary. Maybe Edwin was called home from Dublin in time when he heard about his son's illness. He was however in Dublin and elected an Associate of the Royal Hibernian Academy in 1836.[51] There are no known records of Edwin in Dublin after 1836.[52]

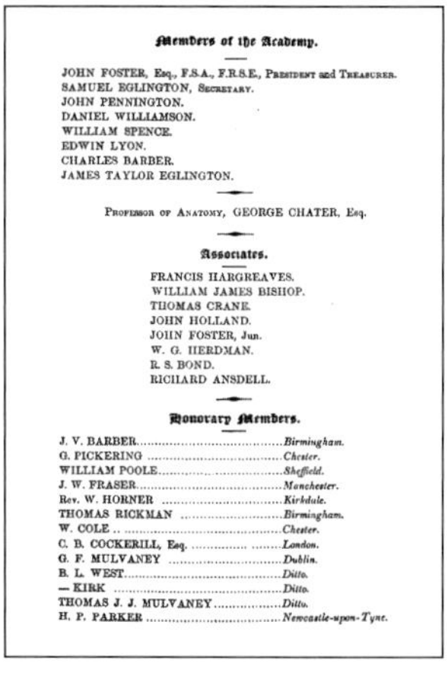

Members of the Academy.

JOHN FOSTER, Esq., F.S.A., F.R.S.E., President and Treasurer.
SAMUEL EGLINGTON, Secretary.
JOHN PENNINGTON.
DANIEL WILLIAMSON.
WILLIAM SPENCE.
EDWIN LYON.
CHARLES BARBER.
JAMES TAYLOR EGLINGTON.

Professor of Anatomy, GEORGE CHATER, Esq.

Associates.

FRANCIS HARGREAVES.
WILLIAM JAMES BISHOP.
THOMAS CRANE.
JOHN HOLLAND.
JOHN FOSTER, Jun.
W. G. HERDMAN.
R. S. BOND.
RICHARD ANSDELL.

Honorary Members.

| | |
|---|---|
| J. V. BARBER | Birmingham. |
| G. PICKERING | Chester. |
| WILLIAM POOLE | Sheffield. |
| J. W. FRASER | Manchester. |
| Rev. W. HORNER | Kirkdale. |
| THOMAS RICKMAN | Birmingham. |
| W. COLE | Chester. |
| C. B. COCKERILL, Esq. | London. |
| G. F. MULVANEY | Dublin. |
| B. L. WEST | Ditto. |
| — KIRK | Ditto. |
| THOMAS J. J. MULVANEY | Ditto. |
| H. P. PARKER | Newcastle-upon-Tyne. |

The catalogue of the Liverpool Academy exhibition which opened at the New Exhibition Rooms at Post Office Place on 11th September 1837 lists 750 entries from 269 artists together with their places of abode.[53] Edwin, a Member of the Academy, was living at 10 Pleasant Street and exhibited the following busts: Richard Butler Esq., Joseph Lyon Esq. (probably his brother), Charles Whitmore, Mrs H. Leigh, Mr John Leigh Esq., Moor Hall, Miss Eliza Leigh, Rev. H. McNeile, and busts of a friend and a gentleman. There was also one portrait of John Leigh Esq., his gamekeeper, and two famous dogs. There was one portrait by his friend Alexander Mosses who had died earlier that year.

It is not surprising that in 1838 Lyon only exhibited one sculpture at the exhibition as his daughter Elizabeth died of inflammation of the brain on 30th April aged six years eight months.[54] He registered the death from Upper Beau Street where Aunt Mary continued to live following the death of her father the previous year.[55] Edwin had now lost his only surviving child, his father-in-law and Alexander Mosses, his good friend and neighbour from Pleasant Street.

The bust he exhibited in 1838 was of Samuel Eglington Esq., a prolific Liverpool painter and a fellow member of the Academy and its secretary. Currently the location of only one English art piece is known and that is of the Rev. McNeile which is in store at the Walker Art Gallery.[56]

Top: Rev. McNeile.
Above: Zachary Taylor.

Maybe he was disheartened and even depressed as so far I have found no evidence of Edwin's activities until 1840 when the members of the Academy, "*...resolved that owing to the number of absences of Mr E. Lyon who has removed to America that he be considered no longer a member of the Academy.*"[57] Perhaps commissions had dried up and he wanted a new start after the loss of his family.

I have not yet found Edwin Lyon on any passenger lists from Liverpool but most likely he sailed to New Orleans, a popular port of call for Liverpool sailing ships at that time. By 1844 he was settled in Natchez, a town built on a bluff above the Mississippi River inhabited by rich plantation owners. He is considered an Anglo-American sculptor with his biography published by Bacot and Lambdin.[58]

On 1st November 1847 he became a naturalised citizen of the USA and married Caroline Polkinghorne Bray in Natchez in 1848. He was very successful, producing many portrait busts and eventually working in marble. His most famous work is a life size bust in marble of Zachary Taylor who became the twelfth President of the USA. This is proudly on display at Melrose Mansion in Natchez.[59] It is considered '*a most magnificent piece of art work by one of Mississippi's most renowned sculptors*'.

In 1848 he won a commission to build a monument in marble in the state capital in honour of the Mississippi Volunteers who lost their lives in the Mexican War, although, for reasons not known, the sculpture was not built. Sadly, at the height of his fame in Mississippi, Edwin Lyon died of yellow fever in 1853 at the age of 47.

He is buried in Natchez Cemetery amongst many marble funerary monuments that he had produced. See opposite for the epitaph on his grave.

For some time Edwin's widow Caroline carried on the business, known as 'The Natchez Marble Yard', possibly using skilled slaves, including one valued at $1,300 who she inherited following Edwin's death.

Edwin Lyon
A native of Liverpool
Died 29th August 1853
Aged 47 years
A death called the sculptor
Alas a chisel falls
And Lyon bids his art
And friends farewell

### *Acknowledgements*

I would like to thank the Walker Art Gallery (for inspiring me to find out more about Edwin Lyon), the Athenaeum, Liverpool John Moores University, the Liverpool Record Office and the University of Liverpool.

### *References and notes*

[1] Mayer J., Roscoe and the Influence of his writings on the Fine Arts Volume: 5 (1852-1853) *Transactions of the Historic Society of Lancashire and Cheshire* Pages: 142-155, illus.

[2] Wilson A.M., *Culture and Commerce: Liverpool's Merchant Elite c1790-1850* unpublished PhD thesis, University of Liverpool 1996

[3] Marillier H.C., *The Liverpool School of Painters* London 1904

[4] Morris E. and Roberts E., *The Liverpool Academy and Other Exhibitions of Contemporary Art in Liverpool 1774-1867* Liverpool University Press and National Museums & Galleries on Merseyside 1998

[5] Roscoe I., Hardy E., and Sullivan M.G., *A biographical Dictionary of Sculptors in Britain 1660-1851* http://217.204.55.158/henrymoore/sculptor/browserecord.php?-action=browse&-recid=1703

[6] Family Bible personal communication

[7] Family Bible

[8] Liverpool Record Office Ref No 283 PAU Ref Baptism: 29 Jun 1806 St Paul, Liverpool, Lancashire, England LDS 1656373

[9] Lancashire OnLine Parish Clerk Project City of Liverpool Baptisms St Paul 24 March 1799, Source: LDS 1656373

[10] Lancashire OnLine Parish Clerk Project City of Liverpool Baptisms St Paul 29 June 1806, Source: LDS 1656373

[11] *Gore's Directory of Liverpool 1811*

[12] *Baines' Directory of Liverpool 1824*

[13] http://www.spectrumglass.com/stained-glass/dictionary.asp. Benders produce bent glass by heating in a kiln from room temperature to a temperature high enough to cause it to soften and slump (sag) into or over a mould. The finished item takes the shape of the mould.

[14] Fawcett T., *The Rise of English Provincial Art, Artists, Patrons, and Institutions outside London 1800-1830* Clarendon Press Oxford 1974

[15] *Gore's Directory of Liverpool 1811*

[16] Picton J.A., *Memorials of Liverpool Volume II (Topographical)*. Longmans Green & Co., London, 1873.

[17] Hardy E., Roscoe I., Sullivan M.G., *Biographical Dictionary of Sculptors in Britain, 1660-1851*, Henry Moore Foundation database

[18] *Liverpool Mercury* 12 November 1819

[19] Fawcett T.

[20] Morris C., *History of Liverpool Regional College of Art 1825-1970* MPhil 1985 Liverpool John Moores University

[21] *Gore's Directory of Liverpool 1811 and 1813*

[22] http://www.liverpool-schools.co.uk

[23] Morris E. and Roberts E.

[24] Morris E. and Roberts E.

[25] Morris E. and Roberts E.

[26] *Liverpool Mercury* 23 February 1827

[27] Royal Academy Library Collections Department personal communication

[28] Walker Art Gallery Liverpool Academy of Art archives

[29] Strickland W.G. *A Dictionary of Irish Artists* 1913

[30] Morris E. and Roberts E.

[31] Walker Art Gallery Liverpool Academy of Art archives

[32] Liverpool Royal Institution Archive GB 141 LR3 Financial records Special Collection Archive University of Liverpool

[33] http://www.sothebys.com/en/auctions/ecatalogue/2011/travel-atlases-maps-natural-history/lot.109.html

[34] http://digi.ub.uni-heidelberg.de/diglit/lyon1829/0007/scroll?sid=e0bbc66bc3e72ca846fd9c5ba80b06cf

[35] Bentley G.E. *William Blake in the Desolate Market* McGill-Queen's University Press 2014

[36] http://digi.ub.uni-heidelberg.de/diglit/lyon1829/0007/scroll?sid=e0bbc66bc3e72ca846fd9c5ba80b06cf

[37] Liverpool Record Office 373 1 Minute books /1 Minutes of the Directors /1 ...June 1825 – Sep 1837

[38] Morris C.

[39] Morris C.

[40] LRO Minute Books

[41] West Yorkshire England Baptisms Marriages Burials 1806-1807

[42] Register: Marriages 1814 - 1837, Page 93, Entry 278 Source: LDS Film 2147913

[43] Wilkinson T.T. An Account of the Writings of the late J.H. Swale of Liverpool *Transactions of the Historic Society of Lancashire and Cheshire.* Volume: 7 (1854-1855) Pages: 143-64

[44] LRO Minute books

[45] LRO

[46] LDS Film 1656421

[47] Wilkinson T.T.

[48] http://churchrecords.irishgenealogy.ie/churchrecords/details/19c14c0502098

[49] http://collections.vam.ac.uk

[50] http://www.adams.ie/searchresult?keyword=Edwin%20Lyon

[51] Source: LDS Film 1656376

[52] Strickland W.G.

[53] Strickland W.G.

[54] Catalogue The Exhibition of the Liverpool Academy MDCCCXXXVII printed by Thos Kaye, Castle Street, Liverpool 1837

[55] Death Certificate DYD 776076

[56] *Liverpool Mercury* 2 February 1837

[57] Walker Art Gallery

[58] Walker Art Gallery Liverpool Academy of Art Archives

[59] Bacot H.P. and Lambdin B.B. Edwin Lyon An Anglo-American Sculptor in the Lower Mississippi River Valley in *Antiques* 111 1977 p. 554-9

[60] Bacot H.P. and Lambdin B.B.

# 'THE LIVERPOOL PHIL'
# A brief history of the Royal Liverpool Philharmonic Society
# Part 1

*Stephen A. Gent*

In 2015 the Royal Liverpool Philharmonic Society celebrates 175 years of music-making in our city. This paper seeks briefly to explore the rich history of that institution affectionately known on Merseyside – and increasingly much further afield – as the 'Liverpool Phil'.[1]

Liverpool's burgeoning middle-class society demanded genteel pursuits and entertainments which were in keeping with their social status and increasing prosperity. Consequently, a wide range of libraries, concert halls, clubs and meeting rooms was established to cater for the needs of the town's growing ranks of merchants, bankers and businessmen. There existed in Liverpool a great chasm between rich and poor, so it will come as no surprise to learn that the concert and meetings rooms were located within the town's more respectable and fashionable areas.

Towards the end of the eighteenth-century, Liverpool played host to a number of musical festivals; from 1784 these were to become triennial events.[2] A number of musical and choral societies were formed, including the Liverpool Music Society in 1820 and the Liverpool Festival Choral Society in 1836; the majority of concerts at this time were performed in churches.[3] Concerts were the domain of the wealthy and the 'well-to-do'; this point is illustrated by an article in *The Musical World* which observed that "upwards of 500 of the elite of Liverpool were present" at a concert performed in Hardman Street.[4]

Liverpool very quickly found its mark on the musical map. Three prominent nineteenth-century composers were to visit Liverpool in the period 1829-1840. In July 1829 Felix Mendelssohn visited; unfortunately he did not give a concert. Niccolo Paganini performed his third violin concert for the first time at Liverpool's Theatre Royal in 1832 and in 1834 returned to give a further two concerts at the Royal Ampitheatre. Franz Liszt, the celebrated composer-pianist, performed in Liverpool in 1840.[5]

## The Origins of the Society

Throughout the 1830s a group of 'gentlemen musical amateurs' had been meeting at St Martin's Church[6] to practice and to perform choral music. The group's numbers having increased, it was decided to formalise their gatherings and association and on 10th January 1840 the Liverpool Philharmonic Society came into being. From that point on, as Henley and McKernan observe, "Liverpool's musical life was never to look back."[7] By way of some local context the Society predates notable landmarks such as the Albert Dock (1845) and St George's Hall (1854).

The original vision and purpose of the Society was "to promote the science and practice of music", something which both the Society and its Orchestra still strive to live up to 175 years later.[8]

*Figs.1 & 2 above: interior and exterior views of the first Philharmonic Hall. Illustrated London News, 1st September 1849.*

There is some considerable debate, and inevitable consternation, as to which concert-giving organisation was established first; it all rests upon what one takes as the starting definition and is not something which will be explored here. Suffice it to say, today the (Royal) Liverpool Philharmonic Society is believed to be the oldest surviving professional symphony orchestra and the second oldest concert-giving organisation in the UK, London's Royal Philharmonic Society having been established in 1813.[9]

Following the formation of the Society, the first concert was performed on 12th March 1840 at Mr Lassell's Saloon, Great Richmond Street; the programme consisted of thirteen short orchestral and choral works, including works by Rossini, Bishop and Thomas Morley.[10] The Society was soon to outgrow the saloon and in 1843 moved its performances to the hall of the Collegiate Institute, Shaw Street.

The first symphonies to be performed in concert by the Society's orchestra were given on 23rd May 1844; they were Haydn's *Symphony No. 99 in E flat* and Beethoven's *Symphony No.1 in C major*.[11] Up until this point the Society's repertoire had, in the main, focussed upon choral works. Perhaps rather surprisingly, it seems that the early audiences were somewhat disinterested in the symphony, preferring instead the choral pieces and the much lighter glees. The lights in the hall were not dimmed during performances in order to aid the reading of programmes and the following of the score; it seems that some audience members took advantage of this and, throughout a symphony, opened up their newspapers which were "not folded again until the choir was about to give voice."[12]

Only four years after its establishment the Society had outgrown its concert venues. The committee therefore resolved to fund and build a purpose-built concert room in which to practise and perform and which to call 'home'. Arguably, a major incentive behind the decision to build its own concert venue was the sense of permanence its own premises would provide to the Society. The Society was quite literally putting itself on the musical map.

*Fig.3. Late 1800s photograph of the first Philharmonic Hall. Comparing it with the illustration on the previous page, it will be seen that the Hope Street frontage has acquired a canopy (extended to the corner of the building later) and both frontages are enclosed with iron railings and gates. On the far left a horse-drawn omnibus approaches the junction whilst to the right a hansom cab awaits a fare. Courtesy (RJ).*

## The (First) Philharmonic Hall

In 1844, the Scottish-born Liverpool-based architect John Cunningham[13] was commissioned by the Society's committee to prepare plans for a hall to be situated on Hope Street at the junction with Myrtle Street, the land being purchased from the Corporation.[14] The initial cost of purchasing the land and erecting a "Concert Room, capable of holding 1,500 persons" was estimated at £4,000 (£349,000 in 2015). The Society's committee proposed that the necessary funds be raised by issuing some 400 shares at £10 each.

The plans however swiftly changed and a second prospectus was published which proposed a Hall "intended to contain in the Audience part, two thousand one hundred persons, and on the Orchestra two hundred and fifty, and to embrace every requisite convenience in the shape of refreshment and retiring rooms."[15] The revised prospectus clearly demonstrates how forward thinking and ambitious the Society's committee was and the readiness of the membership to fund such a grand scheme. It goes without saying that as the scale of the proposed construction increased so did the cost, the eventual price tag being £30,000 (£2.72 million in 2015). *The Times* reported that whilst this was "a high figure" it "was nothing extraordinary for such a rich commercial town as Liverpool".[16]

The foundation stone of the Hall was laid in 1846, building proper commenced the following year and the Philharmonic Hall was officially opened on Monday, 27th August 1849. The programme for the opening night included performances by three of the Philharmonic's future Principal Conductors: Alfred Mellon, Julius Benedict and Charles Halle.[17] Sadly, the hall was not full on this auspicious occasion. It is believed that the audience numbers were initially impacted by rumours, which were circulating at the time of the opening, that the construction of the hall was unsafe due to the absence of centrally-supporting pillars. A correspondent from *The Times* reported upon the week-long programme concluding that the new hall was "...one of the finest and best adapted to music that I have ever entered."[18]

The Society commissioned Felix Mendelssohn to compose a cantata to be performed on the occasion of the opening of the hall, the committee prescribing that Mendelssohn use the words from Milton's *Comus*. Henley and McKernan suggest that Mendelssohn's appointment was "a sign of the Society's enormous ambition..." and "shows the determination of the committee to put Liverpool on the musical map."[19] Tragically, however, the gifted composer would die of a ruptured blood vessel before he had fulfilled the commission.

**Enforcing the 'social tone'**

Writing in *The Original Liverpool Sound: The Royal Liverpool Philharmonic Story* Henley and McKernan observed that "the Liverpool Philharmonic of the mid and late 19th century existed purely for the pleasure of the moneyed merchant class in the town, in stark contrast to the Royal Liverpool Philharmonic of today."[20] This is evident by the *Rules of the Liverpool Philharmonic Society*, a document which set out some seventeen conditions which were adopted and rigorously enforced by the Society's committee.

By and large the Society's rules served one purpose: to preserve social exclusiveness. The Society, like many other gentlemen's clubs and institutions throughout the nineteenth-century and even into the early twentieth-century, was reluctant to admit the ordinary working people into the concert hall, fearing that this would be a recipe for social disaster, because they would 'taint' the actual art of music-making and enjoyment thereof. Liverpool's bankers, merchants and factory-owners certainly did not want to 'rub shoulders' with their clerks and other underlings. The concert hall was, after all, a place to be seen, a place to mingle with one's peers; a concert provided an opportunity to demonstrate one's social standing, to display one's wealth and to establish oneself as a patron of the arts and cultural life of the town.

When the Hall opened in 1849 all sixty-five boxes and in excess of six hundred of the sixteen hundred stalls seats had been purchased in perpetuity (on condition, that is, that they continued to pay an annual subscription) by some seven hundred subscribers who would become known as 'Proprietors'. Being a 'Proprietor' of a box or a seat in the stalls, especially for those who had only relatively recently acquired their wealth as a result of the explosion of trade, commerce and industry which Liverpool witnessed in this period, brought with it social recognition that one had 'arrived'. Although Proprietors could sell their seats for a concert performance they could only do so to individuals whom the committee approved, a clear attempt at reinforcing the social tone.

On 29th August 1849, *The Times* reported that the opening night's performance was not to a full house due to "the very high price of admission – one guinea to any part of the hall not occupied by subscribers – must have kept, and will again keep, members of the general public away."[21] Two days later *The Liverpool Mercury* observed that "while possible to the general public, [access to boxes and stalls] was clearly not encouraged, and hedged in by formalities."[22]

In the early years the Society's annual programme included four 'full-dress' concerts with "metropolitan talent" and six 'non-dress' concerts "with local talent". The Rules, published in 1840, would confirm twelve concerts a year, four 'Dress' and 'eight monthly Undress Concerts'[23]. R.M. Lewis in her PhD thesis on the Society rightly noted that the "insistence upon 'dress'... was an indication of the social exclusiveness promoted by the committee."[24] Lewis, from her analysis of the Society's programmes, found that as late as 1909 there was evidence of "rigid social divisions".[25]

In fact the debate as to whether to continue to compel concert-goers to wear Evening Dress would continue on and off right up until the 1930s. In June 1932 the Society's committee, facing up to the reality of the increasingly parlous national financial situation as a consequence of the 'Depression',[26] proposed to members that it had become necessary to "make Concerts appeal to a larger public, and thereby obtain increased support". The Secretary, Mr W.J. Riley, went on to propose that Boxes and Stalls would be "more marketable if Evening Dress were optional."[27]

The proposal provoked a bitter backlash from some members and a rearguard action ensued. *The Manchester Evening News* took up the debate, interviewing one member, a Mr R.T. Golding.[28] Whilst insisting that he was not a "snob", Golding, protested that by allowing "somebody in fustian or plus-fours to sit in the stalls or boxes besides others in evening dress we are going to dissipate the atmosphere of these concerts." Golding argued that making Evening Dress optional "...would lower the dignity of the Society and its concerts". He rather pompously insisted that "evening dress does help in the appreciation of music" and that "an artist can perform better if he has before him what I can describe as a 'clean' audience."[29] To a modern reader the views of Mr Golding come across as being utterly pretentious and incongruous. A vote was conducted amongst the Society's membership, who were rather divided on the matter, which resulted in the decision to continue with the compulsory practice of wearing Evening Dress when taking seats within boxes and the stalls. It would only cease to be compulsory during the Second World War period.[31]

**Embezzlement – "fiddling at the Phil had not been confined to the ranks of the violins."**[30]

William Sudlow was a prominent early member of the Society who served as Honorary Secretary for the first fifteen years of the Society's existence. Sudlow also served as the Society's organist; he had performed at the very first concert in 1840. Additionally he was the Vocal Conductor and one of the first orchestral conductors. Suspected of having embezzled the Society's funds Sudlow submitted his letter of resignation, dated 13th January 1855.[31]

Following a thorough examination of the accounts it was discovered that Sudlow had indeed embezzled the Society's funds to the tune of £2,424 14s, roughly equivalent to £150,000 today. It would appear that Sudlow had been siphoning off funds for at least two years, a clear abuse of his trusted position. The Committee report concluded that "the examination of the accounts...has disclosed an artful and systematic course of fraud and deception..."; the Committee recorded "with deep concern their inability to discover a single extenuating fact."[32] Sudlow's resignation was accepted by the Committee, yet perhaps unsurprisingly no further action was taken against him by the Society which was probably eager to avoid the scandal of airing its affairs in public.

Ironically, out of the sixty-three applicants, a Henry Sudlow, a distant relative of William's, was appointed as his successor as Secretary, now a paid position. Henry would hold office until 1884 "without the slightest whiff of impropriety."[33]

**Philharmonic Hall: Destroyed by Fire**

Sadly the hall which had received so much critical acclaim – Sir Thomas Beecham, a Guest Conductor in the period 1913-1942, had declared the hall to be "the best in Europe"[34] – would be totally gutted by a terrible inferno on the night of 5th July 1933.

*The Manchester Guardian* on 6th July 1933 reported: "The Liverpool Philharmonic Hall, one of the finest concert halls in England, was destroyed by fire which broke out early last evening. Only the shell was left standing, and the fire is still burning at 12:30 this morning." It is perhaps worth quoting *The Manchester Guardian* at length so as to perhaps gain an understanding of the enormity of the fire which would have, at the same time, both disastrous consequences and present wonderful opportunities for the Society:

*Fig.4. Left. A large crowd fills Hardman Street to watch the fire at its peak.*

*Fig.5. Above. The aftermath.*

*Both images RLPS.*

"A workman on the roof of the new extension to the Liverpool Radium Institute, across the roadway, saw flames coming from the roof about seven o'clock. About the same time the caretaker of a neighbouring Unitarian Church noticed smoke coming up from the roof and, realising that the hall would not be heated in summer, summoned the Fire Brigade."

"Almost as soon as the brigade arrived the roof fell in. Sheets of flame were clearly visible from a great distance. Many thousands of people filled the streets, and hundreds came in from the suburbs and from Wirral to watch the fire. The heat was so intense that firemen were busy playing hoses on the lamp standards in the streets in front of the hall. Within a short time twelve engines and over a hundred firemen were on the scene. The Liverpool Salvage Corps, a private body maintained by the insurance companies to protect their interests by saving as many valuables as possible, was there almost as soon as the fire brigade."

"The Philharmonic Hall is in the middle of the hospital quarter and in one of Liverpool's two danger zones. At the city end is the School for the Blind and opposite is the Radium Institute. At one time the police thought that there was a danger to the hospitals from a threatened fall of the walls and the patients were warned and dressed so that they might be ready to leave at a moment's notice. The walls seemed to lean forward and women in the crowd shrieked in terror. Nearby a party of St. John Ambulance Brigade was drilling. They turned out with their stretchers and first-aid equipment within ten minutes of the alarm being given. When the roof collapsed several firemen and salvage men had narrow escapes from death. The only casualties were two slight cases of burning."[35]

The Philharmonic Hall was lost. Thankfully however, a number of treasures were saved by the salvage men, perhaps most notably a tablet to the memory of the musicians who lost their lives when RMS *Titanic* sank. The memorial had been erected by the Philharmonic Society from the proceeds of a special concert on 10th May 1912 for the wife and sister of viola player John Frederick Preston Clarke. Clarke had played at the Philharmonic Hall on a number of occasions although he was never in fact a member of the resident orchestra. The memorial, which is the work of J.A. Hodel and is of repousse copper, has been situated in the outer entrance foyer since 1995.[36] The greater part of the Society's extensive collection of music was also salvaged although the organ, which had only been installed some three years earlier at a cost of £2,000, was lost to the flames, as were two grand pianos.[37]

The Philharmonic Hall, as Liverpudlians know and love it today, nearly didn't get re-built at all. Firstly, there was the issue of who in fact owned the hall. As the original funds had been raised by subscription, a number of subscribers claimed partial ownership. The matter was eventually settled by the Lancashire Chancery Court in July 1934 in favour of the Society; the ruling "did not think the interest of the members in their stalls and seats was a legal interest."[38] The original aim and purpose of the Society prevailed.

The second challenge focussed on who should fund the re-building work. A fundamental difference in opinion existed between the Society and the City Council as to the function of the new building. Naturally, the Society wanted a building dedicated to the furtherance of its original aim, that is 'to promote the science and practice of music', and was prepared to surrender the lease to the Council should the Council agree to re-building the hall. The City Council meanwhile favoured a multi-purpose arts centre which would be far less exclusive than one that only promoted classical music.

A protracted and rather bitter battle between the Society and the City Council ensued.[39] Sir Henry Wood, who was one of the Philharmonic's guest conductors between 1913 and 1942, declared that "it is a crying shame to a city like Liverpool that it should turn down a proposal to provide a hall for its great Philharmonic Orchestra... The council which can do a thing like that must be composed of queer people." Sir Henry went on to argue vehemently that:

> Music should not be mixed up with anything else... In my experience serious-minded people are getting sick of the confusion of music with entertainment. Music is not entertainment. It is education in its highest sense... If the City Council members cannot realise the difference, then they are out of touch with serious minds...[40]

During the five-year period up to the opening of the new concert hall the Central Hall of the Liverpool Wesleyan Mission in Renshaw Street provided a temporary home for the Orchestra's concerts; choral concerts were held at St George's Hall.

The Society, in the end, determined to continue what it had achieved to date, proceeded alone and the insurance monies were utilised for the new building.[41]

**The New Philharmonic Hall – an architectural gem**

*Fig.6. Herbert J. Rowse. (RLPS).*

Like the proverbial phoenix a new hall rose majestically from the ashes of the old. Herbert J. Rowse (1887-1963), the exceptionally talented Liverpool-born architect, was chosen by the Society to design a new hall. There is no doubt in this author's mind that the Committee's decision to appoint Rowse was heavily influenced by the critical acclaim he had received for his earlier designs, including those for the India Buildings, Martins Bank and the ventilation tower for the Queensway Tunnel, all of which exuded the grandeur of Empire.[42]

The Transnational Architecture Group, based at the Liverpool School of Architecture, argue that Rowse "...was without doubt one of the most outstanding architects of his generation and through his work on a number of high-profile commissions he shaped the inter-war cityscape of Liverpool in a way that no other architect has done since."[43] It is therefore somewhat surprising to learn that there appears to be no book dedicated to Rowse and his contribution to Liverpool's rich architectural history. Several unpublished dissertations have however been completed by students of the City's universities.[44]

*Fig.7. A pristine Liverpool Philharmonic Hall in June 1939, the month it opened: workmen with ladders apply the finishing touches to the frontage. On the right, at the corner of Hope Street and Caledonian Street, is the Unitarian Church, completed in 1848 but since demolished. Courtesy (RJ).*

Dr Rob MacDonald of the Centre for Architecture at Liverpool John Moores University, has written that "the careful brick detailing of Rowse's Mersey Tunnel is repeated but his massing of the Hall is masterly. The interior has low relief plaster mouldings of mythical and musical images."[45]

The architectural historian Joseph Sharples suggests that the design of the new hall was influenced by the "blocky brick architecture"[46] of the Dutch Modernist architect W. M. Dudok and the speculative designs of a final year student at the School of Architecture by the name of Alwyn Edward Rice. Rowse engaged Rice to assist him with his new project. Sharples suggests that "the executed design is markedly similar to [Rice's] thesis, both in the massing of the exterior and the arrangement of the auditorium."[47] Elsewhere, Sharples notes that the hall is constructed "of brick, and starkly cubic except for two rounded stair-towers in front..."[48] The main doors and first floor windows contain etched glass by Hector Whistler and gilded relief panels by the sculptor Edmund C. Thompson are to be found on the landings and Art Deco female figures, representing the Muses are incised on the walls of the auditorium.[49]

The Liverpool-based organ builders Rushworth and Dreaper built the organ which remains in use today, making it the oldest surviving organ of its type in the world. The organ console itself is lowered below the platform where it is stored when not in use; the console has been fitted with wheels to enable the organist to face either direction. The pipes make a decorative feature to the rear of the platform and the workings, which include some 120,000 yards of insulated copper wire, 17,000 switches and contacts and 2,487 electric magnets, are hidden from view. This is a fabulous example of the care which went into designing and constructing the hall; aesthetics were certainly a number one priority.[50]

Liverpool Philharmonic Hall, which belongs to the *Streamline Moderne* school of architecture, a late type of Art Deco which emerged in the 1930s,[51] has quite rightly been recognised as an architectural treasure, the building being awarded Grade II* status in March 1981.

An extract from Hall's entry in the *National Heritage List for England* reads:

> Concert hall. 1937-9. Herbert Rowse. Fawn brick facing. Style influenced by Dutch expressionism, particularly Dudok, with engraved glass and other decoration in French taste of 1920s. Mainly of 3-storey height with receding tiers of parapets. Symmetrical front: between semi-circular stair turrets and above canopied entrance are 7 large vertical metal windows separated by piers topped by jagged abstract motifs. Interior: Auditorium walls and ceiling are moulded in curved series of undulations continuing to the back of the stage...The only decoration of the auditorium is by 3 semi-draped incised figures on each wall and geometric perforations in walls of stage... [52]

The new Philharmonic Hall opened on 19th June 1939. The total cost of the Hall amounted to £120,154. 4. 5d (£6.3 million in today's values). Rowse himself would receive payment of £6,869. The Society's Committee were very satisfied with the result recording that they had "secured a first class building at a moderate cost" [53].

Sir Thomas Beecham conducted the inaugural concert with the programme especially crafted to showcase the exemplary acoustics of the Liverpool Philharmonic Orchestra's new abode.[54] *The Guardian* newspaper wrote, "The magnificent compliment Liverpool has paid to the cause of music in England almost takes one's breath away... a hall of great size, noble proportions, and up-to-date appointments... ready to take its place among the most eminent homes of musical culture in this or any other country."[55]

Within months the continent of Europe found itself amidst the turmoil, hell and destruction of the Second World War. The Society's centenary celebrations were therefore a rather muted affair. During the 1939-40 season the orchestra gave a total of 38 performances, compared with the four concerts performed in the Society's first year.[56] The orchestra would continue to perform throughout the war; in fact the orchestra would provide hundreds of concerts at diverse locations including hospitals, camps, factories and, of course, concert halls. Many of these concerts came under the umbrella of the Council for the Encouragement of Music and the Arts, the forerunner of the Arts Council and E.N.S.A. (the Entertainment National Services Association).

A continuation of this paper, to be published in the 2016 Journal, will examine the Society's history from 1939 to the present day.[57]

*Fig.8. The interior of the new Liverpool Philharmonic Hall prior to the opening showing incomplete seating; Fig.9. Inset image shows the Proscenium in position for use; Fig.10. Right. One of Edmund C. Thompson's six Art Deco panels in the auditorium. All of the above are reproduced from the commemorative booklet for the official opening of the Hall on 19th June 1939. Courtesy (RJ).*

**Further Reading**

The author particularly recommends the following sources to those readers wanting to further explore the history of the Liverpool Phil:

Royal Liverpool Philharmonic Orchestra 'Our History' pages on the Phil's website are a useful starting point: *http://www.liverpoolphil.com/286/our-history/royal-liverpool-philharmonic-orchestra.html*

Henley, D. and McKernan, V., *The Original Liverpool Sound: The Royal Liverpool Philharmonic Story*, Liverpool University Press, Liverpool, 2009. [This is a very accessible 'coffee table book' containing rich illustrations; unfortunately the work lacks references which is rather frustrating to the historian.]

Lewis, R.M., *The Educational Functions of the Royal Liverpool Philharmonic Society 1840-1990*, unpublished PhD thesis, University of Liverpool, 1998. [Chapter 5 'a Brief Outline of the Historical Development of the Society, 1840-1990' has proved particularly useful to the author and is freely available to download via the British Library's EThOS website: *www.ethos.bl.uk* (sign-up required)]

**Author's Note**

This paper is dedicated in loving memory of two friends who were regular concert-goers at 'the Phil' – Miss Linda M. Wills and Miss Mary Cotton – both were long-standing members at the Linacre Methodist Mission (Litherland), they were called to a higher service in 2014; these ladies greatly encouraged the author to get his Philharmonic subscription series booked as a matter of priority each year.

J.S. Bach declared that "the aim and final end of all music should be none other than the glory of God and the refreshment of the soul." Amen to that.

### *Acknowledgements*

The author wishes to thank the Athenaeum, the Liverpool Record Office and Liverpool Central Library for material reproduced from their extensive archives. The author is also most grateful for the assistance provided by Jayne Garrity, Head of Communications, Royal Liverpool Philharmonic, in sourcing illustrations for this paper.


### *References and notes*

[1] Unfortunately, space does not permit a detailed examination of the contribution of the Society, its Orchestras and Choirs during the period up to 1939. The author has therefore carefully selected key events to highlight.

[2] *https://liverpool1207blog.wordpress.com/history-timelines/18th-century* – retrieved 16/01/2015.

[3] Lewis, R M, *The Educational Functions of the Royal Liverpool Philharmonic Society 1840-1990*, unpublished PhD thesis, University of Liverpool, 1998, p.107.

[4] *Ibid*., p.108.

[5] Henley, D, and McKernan, V, *The Original Liverpool Sound: The Royal Liverpool Philharmonic Story*, Liverpool University Press, Liverpool, 2009, pp.16-17.

[6] St Martin's-in-the-fields, Silvester Street.

[7] Henley, *The Original Liverpool Sound*, p.17.

[8] Copy of the original Deed of the Liverpool Philharmonic Society 1847 - Henley, *The Original Liverpool Sound*, p.27. Lewis, *The Educational Functions*, explores the educational contribution of the Society, *passim*.

[9] Henley *The Original Liverpool Sound*, p.68; Lewis, *The Educational Functions*, p.108; *http://www.liverpoolphil.com/286/our-history/royal-liverpool-philharmonic-orchestra.html* – retrieved 04/02/2015.

[10] Henley, *The Original Liverpool Sound*, pp.20-21.

[11] *Ibid*., p.25.

[12] *The Liverpolitan*, December 1934, cited Lewis, *The Educational Functions*, p.111.

[13] *http://www.scottisharchitects.org.uk/architect_full.php?id=200147* - retrieved 16/01/2015. Cunningham had designed Lime Street Station in 1836.

[14] Lewis, *The Educational Functions*, p.109.

[15] Cited Henley, *The Original Liverpool Sound*, p.25.

[16] *Ibid*., p.29.

[17] Mellon (1865-1867), Benedict (1867-1880), Halle (1883-1895).

[18] Cited Henley, *The Original Liverpool Sound*, p.30.

[19] *Ibid*., p.29.

[20] *Ibid*., p.23.

[21] Cited *Ibid*., p.32.

[22] August 31st 1849 - Cited Lewis, *The Educational Functions*, p.110.

[23] Henley, *The Original Liverpool Sound*, p.22.

[24] Lewis, *The Educational Functions*, p.108.

[25] *Ibid*., p.110 – this point was acknowledged in the 150th gala programme; Lewis makes reference to this, p.44.

[26] Henley, *The Original Liverpool Sound*, p.99, notes that 326 seats had been returned to the Society in the period 1919-1932.

[27] Cited *Ibid*., p.99.

[28] The author would like to thank F.T. Forrest for looking up R.T. Golding in the 1938 Directory, discovering that he was a chartered accountant working in Liverpool and living in Waterloo.

[29] Cited Henley, *The Original Liverpool Sound*, pp.99-100.

[30] *Ibid*., p.40.

[31] Lewis, *The Educational Functions*,p.109.

[32] Cited Henley, *The Original Liverpool Sound*, p.41.

[33] *Ibid*., p.42.

[34] *http://www.liverpoolphil.com/376/our-history/liverpool-philharmonic-hall.html* – retrieved 31/01/2015.

[35] Cited at *http://www.liverpoolpicturebook.com/2012/02/liverpool-philharmonic-hall.html* – retrieved 31/01/2015.

[36] Sharples, *Liverpool*, Yale University Press, London, 2004, p.234. For more detail on the memorial plaque see: *http://www.titanictown.plus.com/titanictown/titanic_band_memorial.htm* – retrieved 31/01/2015.

[37] Henley, *The Original Liverpool Sound*, p.101 and Lewis, *The Educational Functions*, p.118.

[38] Cited Henley, *The Original Liverpool Sound*, p.104.

[39] The Society has, at times, enjoyed very good relations with the municipal authorities, however on numerous occasions the two have been at loggerheads.

[40] Wood's comments were printed by the *Liverpool Daily Post*, cited Henley, *The Original Liverpool Sound*, p.106.

[41] The hall was insured and the insurers paid £84,000 (£5.2 million in 2015) for the hall itself, £9,503 (£589,000 in 2015) for other assets, and £6,000 (£372,000 in 2015) for the loss of two years' rental. See Henley, *The Original Liverpool Sound*, p.104 and – *http://en.wikipedia.org/wiki/Philharmonic_Hall,_Liverpool#cite_note-13* – retrieved 31/01/2015.

[42] *http://en.wikipedia.org/wiki/Herbert_James_Rowse* – retrieved 25 January 2015 and MacDonald, R, *Liverpool As Architectural Palimpsest: Rise and fall of Empire: Herbert J. Rowse* (1887-1963), *passim*.

[43] *https://transnationalarchitecturegroup.wordpress.com/tag/herbert-rowse* – retrieved 25 January 2015.

[44] See list of dissertations cited by MacDonald, *Liverpool As Architectural Palimpsest*, p.6; [A more detailed examination of Herbert Rowse's contribution to some of Liverpool most iconic buildings is demanded].

[45] MacDonald, *Liverpool As Architectural Palimpsest*, p.4.

[46] Sharples, *Liverpool*, p.31.

[47] Sharples, Joseph, ed. *Charles Reilly & the Liverpool School of Architecture 1904–1933*. Liverpool: Liverpool University Press, 1996.

[48] Sharples, *Liverpool*, p.234.

[49] *Ibid*., and *http://en.wikipedia.org/wiki/Herbert_James_Rowse* – retrieved 01/02/2015.

[50] Cited Henley, *The Original Liverpool Sound*, pp.110-113.

[51] For information on Streamline Moderne see: *http://en.wikipedia.org/wiki/Streamline_Moderne* – retrieved 31/01/2015.

[52] List Entry: 1279652 - *http://list.english-heritage.org.uk/resultsingle.aspx?uid=1279652* – retrieved 31/01/2015.

[53] Cited Henley, *The Original Liverpool Sound*, p.110.

[54] *Ibid*.

[55] *http://www.classicfm.com/artists/royal-liverpool-philharmonic-orchestra/facts-hall/opening-night* – retrieved 24/01/2015.

[56] Cited Henley, *The Original Liverpool Sound*, p.115.

[57] Lewis, *The Educational Functions*, p.123. The Arts Council is discussed in Beale, R, *The Halle*, Forsyth Brothers Ltd, Manchester, 2000, chapter 13, *passim*.

# KATE SHEPPARD: LIVERPOOL AND NEW ZEALAND

*Janet E. Hollinshead*

*Kate Sheppard. (WC)*

Most of the various denomination notes in the New Zealand currency contain portraits of men, such as the $5 where there is Sir Edmund Hillary (of Everest fame). Just two denominations carry portraits of women - the $20 note has H.M. Queen Elizabeth II, and the $10 note has Kate Sheppard. This considerable recognition is reinforced in New Zealand's capital Wellington where a street and a prestigious apartment building are named after her, and in Christchurch where her house is open to the public. Less well-known is that Kate Sheppard was born in Liverpool.

Katherine (Kate) Malcolm was born on 10 March 1847 in Liverpool. She was the second daughter of Andrew and Jemima Malcolm. According to the 1841 census both parents were in Argyleshire, Scotland. By 1851 the family was in London where Andrew Malcolm was recorded as a coal merchant. He came from Dumfries and maybe he was involved in bringing coal from south-west Scotland to London. Liverpool may have been another destination for his coal sales or a transit location en route to the capital. In any event, the Malcolm family did not re-appear in any of the Liverpool censuses.

Andrew Malcolm died in 1856 leaving a widow and five young children. Mrs Malcolm returned to Scotland and for some time the children were divided amongst relatives. Kate lived with an uncle, a minister of the Presbyterian Free Church, in Nairn. The family then re-grouped for emigration to New Zealand, possibly because Mrs Malcolm saw a new life in the southern hemisphere as providing opportunities for her two sons. In 1868 Kate found herself on board the *Matoaka* which carried many assisted passengers to Christchurch. Three years later she married Walter Sheppard, a grocer and general merchant from Christchurch.

New Zealand at this time was no easy colony to settle in. It was, and is, very far away; the journey from London or Liverpool took three months. The Maori people from Polynesia had settled the country during the thirteenth century. Some released convicts from Australia and a few free settlers from Britain were the only non-Maori residents by the 1830s. In 1840, after the Treaty of Waitangi, New Zealand began existence as a real colony, although it was not particularly attractive to new settlers. The only places to live were small coastal hamlets with very few substantial buildings. Virtually all transport was by sea around the coast of the two main islands – 1,000 miles long. This difficult environment dictated considerable isolation for individual settlements, where the economy was often at near subsistence level. Most manufactured goods had to be acquired via catalogues from Britain. It was 1915 before the population passed one million.

*A portrait of Liverpool-born Kate Sheppard graces the current New Zealand $10 dollar banknote. The $20 note carries a portrait of Queen Elizabeth II. (RJ)*

In this 'frontier' colony churches played a big part in settlers' lives as centres for social activity as well as worship. The Malcolm/Sheppard family belonged to the Trinity Congregational Church in Christchurch. Kate taught in Sunday school, organised church fund-raising activities and belonged to musical societies. Drink and the money spent on it were seen as the great evils of frontier society. From 1885 Kate became involved in the establishment of the Women's Christian Temperance Union. The WCTU evolved into a substantial organisation with local branches, then district, and then national representatives: an administration very suited to the isolated communities of New Zealand.

Kate Sheppard became a great organiser and speaker for the WCTU, at a time when it was unusual for women to speak in public. She wrote innumerable letters and a fortnightly page in the *Prohibitionist*. Another tactic was to organise petitions to be sent to local Members of Parliament, for instance against the employment of barmaids, and against the selling of alcohol to children. In 1890 in Christchurch she opened a tea and coffee shop as a base for the distribution of literature and a venue for meetings.

In order to advance its aims the WCTU became a great supporter of female suffrage. By 1887 Kate Sheppard had been appointed the National Superintendent for Franchise and Legislation. A year later she became President of the Christchurch branch of the WCTU, and her writing and advocacy of female suffrage continued apace; for instance she produced a pamphlet *Ten Reasons why the Women of New Zealand Should Vote*.

In order to counteract male opposition the WCTU wanted to petition Parliament to demonstrate the strength of support from women throughout the colony. Early in 1891 the Temperance Union got together their first petition; Kate Sheppard was a major organiser. A total of about 7,000 signatures was reached. Later a second petition was presented with 10,000 signatures, and in 1892 a third petition was collected with 20,000 signatures. In 1893 a fourth petition of 24,000 signatures was, literally, unrolled down the centre of New Zealand's Legislative Chamber; it was 270 metres long. This sustained campaign did lead to the bill that gave full voting rights to women (including Maori) in the colony. New Zealand became the first country in the world to give the vote to women.

Over the following decade Kate Sheppard continued her suffrage and reforming ambitions in both New Zealand and abroad. She became President of the National Council of Women of New Zealand and established their newspaper – *White Ribbon*. She made four trips abroad. In Britain she was puzzled as to why English women had not succeeded in getting the vote. In 1908 when in London she took part in the Grand Suffrage Procession, as well as a very large demonstration in Hyde Park. It is interesting to speculate whether Kate ever met any of the suffrage campaigners from Liverpool who were certainly in London at this time – such as Eleanor Rathbone.

From the early 1900s onwards Kate Sheppard was never in good health, although she did not die until 1934. Certainly Liverpool had little influence in Kate's life but, nonetheless, a Liverpool-born woman does feature on the New Zealand currency.

Eleanor Rathbone's achievements as Liverpool's first female Councillor (1909) and social reformer are well-known, yet a far-away colony was the first country to give all women voting rights on the same basis as men – thanks substantially to Kate Sheppard. New Zealand is so proud of the 1893 petition that it has been made available on-line with all 24,000 names.

***Sources***:


http://www.teara.govt.nz/en/biographies/2s20/sheppard-katherine-wilson

http://www.nzhistory.net.nz/media/photo/suffrage-petition-1893

http://www.nzhistory.net.nz/people/kate-sheppard

# FROM ST MARTIN'S COTTAGES TO JUVENAL DWELLINGS
## Liverpool's pioneering role in the provision of public housing
### *Bertie Dockerill*

Opened between February and April 1869, the development of the country's first purpose-built council housing for the working classes, 'St Martin's Cottages' by the Liverpool Corporation, placed the City at the vanguard of social reform within England. However, despite the laudable intentions of those who had advocated their construction, the size of the development was such that it could only ever have assisted the very smallest fraction of the town's most deprived. In focusing upon the subsequent developments at Nash Grove, this article suggests that the re-engagement of the Corporation in direct schemes to alleviate the housing conditions of the indigent is, in many ways, at least as important as the original St Martin's Cottages development. This is because their construction was accompanied by a specific policy acknowledgement by the council that it had a duty of care with regards to the housing conditions of those displaced through slum clearance programmes. This not only chimed with developments in political ideologies at a national level but would, despite the criticism contemporaneously levied against the Corporation, culminate in Liverpool leading the nation in the provision of social housing.

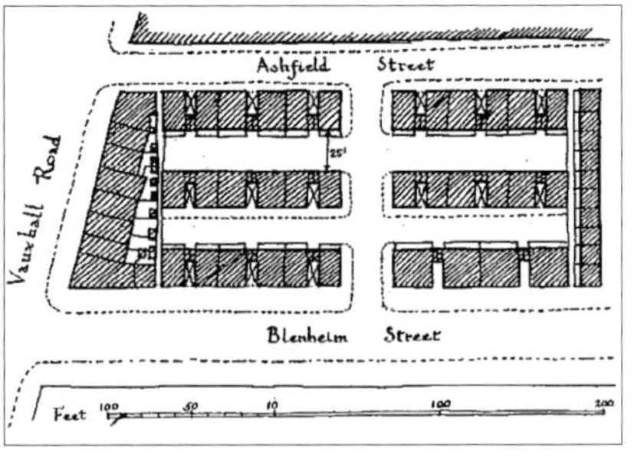


*Above left: St Martin's Cottages in 1944.*[3] *Above right: location of St Martin's Cottages.*[4]

Following an effective six-year hiatus, largely a consequence of the costs involved in the St Martin's Cottages project and the need for fiscal retrenchment by the Council, the passage of the government's 1875 Artisans' and Labourers' Dwellings Improvement Act reawakened both municipal and public opinion in Liverpool as to the urgent need to improve the living conditions of the working class. In introducing the Bill, the Home Secretary, Richard Cross, repeatedly criticised the sanitary conditions of Liverpool and their effect on mortality.[1] That Liverpool was castigated for promulgating within its environs a situation in which the working-class were,

*St Martin's Cottages facing demolition towards the end of their working life in 1968.*

"*condemned to see their children die like flies before them*",[2] was a public rebuke that stung, for within such comments was the implicit charge that the Corporation's previous endeavours had failed.

This was a humiliation for the 'second city of Empire', with Dr Playfair MP (who had previously given evidence with regard to Liverpool to the 1845 *Royal Commission on the State of Large Towns and Populous Districts*) declaring that even after 30 years of, "*much noble local effort*", Liverpool remained, "*in a terrible condition of unhealthiness*".[5] Liverpool's problems were not merely portrayed in health terms, however, for Playfair graphically illustrated that failing to resolve the underlying issue had not only cost the city £370,000 in "*preventable and wholly unnecessary sickness*", but that remedial action would safeguard the city's future prosperity through increased taxation.[6] Faced with public scrutiny and an envisaged loss of wealth, The *Liverpool Courier* harnessed local consternation, and called for the Corporation to undertake a sustained programme of civic improvement to enable, "*the ground [to be] covered with dwellings after the model of St Martin's Cottages*".[7]

In keeping with the provisions of the 1875 Act, the council concluded on the 27th October 1875 that a four-acre expanse of slums – 'The Grove' – inhabited by 1,100 people should be cleared and made available for the private sector construction of working-class dwellings.[8] Initially making representations to house some 1,700 persons, the council subsequently amended its proposals and, in August 1876, permission was granted through a Local Government Board Order, for the construction upon the site of not fewer than 1,100 working-class homes, along with a few shops.[9] By August 1878, almost three years after the council had approved the recommendations of Dr W.S. Trench, the Nash Grove site had been sufficiently cleared to enable private sector construction to commence.

Councillor A.B. Forwood, the Conservative leader of the Corporation, reported at the end of March 1879, however, that no tenders to undertake the Nash Grove tenements had been received.[10] There followed protracted discussions within council as to what to do with the site that primarily centred upon two options. The first was to leave the site barren and undeveloped until such a time as a private developer might be found to build the requisite housing. The second option, proposed by the, "*fervid Orangeman and municipal reformer*", Councillor Joseph Ball,[11] was to obtain a dispensation from the Local Government Board to sell the land, "*free from the conditions that buildings shall be erected thereon suitable for dwellings of persons of the working class*" and thereafter encourage private sector construction of replacement housing nearby.[12]

Pursuing the second course of action in May 1879, the council was unchastened both by the Local Government Board's refusal and its concurrent suggestion that, in the event of the former failing to secure private development of the land, it would be "*competent for [the council], with the consent of the Board, to erect dwellings on the site*".[13] Notwithstanding this statement, in January 1880 Liverpool sought a further relaxation of its obligations under the 1875 Act and permission was obtained at the end of May 1880. This was a consequence of the passing of the 1879 Artisans' and Labourers' Dwellings Improvement Act,[14] which permitted authorities to rehouse those displaced on alternative sites *in the vicinity of* whence they had come, and further enabled the cleared sites to be sold for commercial purposes.[15] Indeed, given the length of time that had passed since demolition, the Local Government Board further concluded that Liverpool need undertake no 'replacement' construction, for those who had been displaced had surely already moved elsewhere.[16]

Underlining individual personality dynamics within the policy-shaping process, the council would but weeks later, on the 24th June 1880, instruct the Borough Engineer Clement Dunscombe to prepare plans to facilitate the building of workmen's accommodation upon the site whilst retaining a substantial portion of the plot as open space.[17] The *Liberal Review* sought to portray this change of policy "*after five years of inglorious inactivity*" as a remarkable *volte face* inspired by Forwood's "*jealousy of Mr McDougall*" for the latter, as Chairman of the Market Committee, had sought the 'freed site' for a new wholesale fish market.[18] Forwood's actions, however, as well as the vacillation of the Health Committee, can instead be interpreted as further proof of the wider ideological battle within the Conservative Party of the time and the personal commitment of Forwood to better the living conditions of the town's most marginalised. Thus, whilst Tory traditionalists opposed to "*compulsion, centralisation, and confiscation*"[19] helped to defeat Forwood's motion by favouring the amendment brought by the Whig Councillor J.A. Picton, it was ultimately the one-nation view that triumphed with regard to the need for greater direct municipal involvement in the provision of working-class housing.

Picton's motion, supported in full council by a majority of 24-14, resulted in no further action being undertaken at Nash Grove, for the motion called for the land to be levelled and made available for general public usage.[20] Eighteen months later, the question as to the development of the Nash Grove site – in the long term – remained unanswered. Subsequent protracted discussions in both the Health and Finance Committees ensued, centring upon three propositions: to turn the land into recreation ground, which would realise no revenue; to continue to attempt to sell the land to a private developer – a course of action that might lead to its holding the plot indefinitely; or to construct artisans' dwellings itself and, through so doing, not only recoup some of the revenue hitherto expended, but also, "*get rid of a dispute on which a great deal of time ha[d] been expended to little advantage*".[21] Council decided on 7th June 1882 to build, a decision the *Liverpool Courier* declared would make the public, "*glad – if they could think that the decision arrived at... will be really carried out*". [22] With the appointment thereafter, in November 1882, of an Insanitary Property and Artisans' Dwelling Committee chaired by Forwood, progress was swift: within ten months permission was sought from the Local Government Board to construct a series of tenements. [23] Tenders duly received and contracts awarded, the dwellings at Nash Grove were finally opened on 20th October 1885 by Cross, and christened 'Victoria Square' [24] (pictured below in 1966 [25]).

Consisting of 272 tenements constructed in five, five-storey blocks, a caretaker's house and 12 ground floor shops, Victoria Square cannot, however, be evaluated as clear evidence of the success of the 1875 Act. This is because such was the lapse in time between its passage, and their opening (a little over ten years), that their construction can neither be viewed as having been a direct consequence of central government legislation, nor as having answered the rehousing needs of those originally displaced. [26] As Mr Jones, the building's superintendent, confirmed in his report to the council in March 1886, his "*careful... selection of tenants*" resulted in Victoria Square being overwhelmingly tenanted by tradesmen such as bricklayers, fitters, cabinet makers, printers, permanent labourers (by default, therefore, not dock workers), warehouse porters, retired widowers, widows with children, young childless couples, and "*good respectable people*". [27] Indeed, this process of vetting, when combined with weekly rentals of between 2s and 5s 6d, the interior design of each individual tenement, and the external finishes afforded each block, provides significant contemporaneous evidence in support of the contention that the dwellings were never truly destined for those members of the working class most in need of residential assistance. As the *Liverpool Mercury* reported, each interior benefitted from:

> *a specially-designed cooking range, with a cast-iron mantelpiece decorated with the Liverpool coat of arms, and the word 'Artisan' cast on the front... and window sills.... with ornate iron railings [upon which] tenants are expected to place pots of flowers [and] ferns with the view of cultivating a taste for horticulture for their own and the public's pleasure.*

Externally, the buildings featured:

> *handsomely decorated entrance doorway[s] of terra cotta... [and] ornate balconies [to] give quite a continental aspect to the daily life of [tenants... and] remind the imaginative visitor of the gay scenes still to be witnessed in Italian and Spanish cities during religious and other festivals.* [28]

*Above left: drawing of Victoria Square showing the quadrangle.*[29] *Above right: bird's eye view.*

Notwithstanding such 'deficiencies', Liverpool was, despite the castigation that it had received by Cross in 1875, the only provincial city in which such working-class housing was constructed. It was Liverpool's council, therefore, that had once more shown that if the working classes were to be better housed, the State was the only organ – certainly within the provinces – that could afford to do so at a price that was commensurate with that which labourers could afford to pay.

Concurrent with the commencement of the building of Victoria Square, Dr J.S. Taylor (by then the City's Medical Officer of Health) reported in November 1883 that Liverpool contained 2,684 'fever nests', 984 more than in 1875, and that whole districts were "*as plagued as the cholera-smitten cities of India*".[30] In the same month, Forwood announced to the Liverpool Diocesan Conference that the Corporation needed to replace at least 12-15,000 insanitary properties if the city was to be rid of the worst dwellings, and that if replacement houses were to be built near to places of work, they needed to be in the form of tenements for issues of geographic convenience and cost.[31] Indeed, Forwood declared that if Liverpool were to address the wider issues pertaining to the housing of the very poorest, it would need to ensure that two thirds of the accommodation replaced was at an affordable rent of one shilling per room for a three-roomed tenement for:

> *much as I deprecate over legislation or State interference with private enterprise... in the matter of sanitary houses I feel an obligation does lie upon the public authority, more particularly upon a city situated like Liverpool.*

Thus, building upon the City's primary motivating factor behind municipal slum clearance, there was now also an explicit policy acknowledgement that "*demolition and house-building had to harmonise, otherwise overcrowding was exacerbated*".[32] This was also seen in national political guidance, for the Corporation's success in obtaining a £200,000 loan from the Local Government Board in January 1884 to help fund slum demolition was contingent upon the former ensuring that there were, erected on such cleared sites "*dwellings suitable for the class of labourers who have been displaced... to be let at rentals very similar to those given for the existing dwellings viz. about one shilling per room*".[33] This was, however, a level of rent that the private sector would not tolerate, as experience at both Victoria Square and St Martin's Cottages had shown and despite the comments of both J.T. Harrison, the Local Government Board Inspector, and Forwood, regarding the preference of such building work being undertaken by private enterprise.[34]

Having, as before, failed to attain private sector interest, the Insanitary Property Committee agreed on the 13th October 1884 that if dwellings were to be built to replace those that the committee wished to demolish, the Corporation would have to build them itself.[35] Unfortunately, the Finance and Estates Committee refused, on 13th March 1885, to undertake such works. Undeterred, the Insanitary Property Committee decided to do so itself – a decision made three days thereafter, and agreed by full council on 15th April 1885.[36] The eventual result, after a further series of protracted discussions with the Local Government Board, and the allied processes of design competition, tendering, and award, was the opening three years later (in March 1888) of 50 municipal tenements called 'Juvenal Dwellings'. These were located upon part of the wider Nash Grove site that had, hitherto, remained undeveloped; a further 51 tenements followed two years later, in December 1890.

Constructed in a total of four blocks, 45 of the 101 tenements had only one room, and 53 offered two rooms. Whilst the rentals were, originally, an average of 1s 3d, this was, in percentage terms, 25 per cent higher than the level which had previously been seen as an absolute maximum for the type of tenant to which Forwood had previously alluded.[37] By 1894, rents for the one- and two-bedroomed tenements ranged from 2s and 2s 9d, to 3s 9d and 5s 3d respectively, whilst the two three-roomed tenements commanded rents of 5s 6d per week. These were rental levels that indicate that, despite the stated desire to accommodate the very poorest, this 'intent' could not be realised at a level of rent commensurate with construction costs. As richer artisans moved into tenements such as Juvenal Dwellings, the result was that any improvement felt by the indigent was only through an indirect process of 'levelling up'.

Nevertheless, in the period addressed by this article, Liverpool's reformist zeal to improve the living conditions of its most needy citizens manifested itself to a far greater extent than anywhere else in the UK. The reforms enacted should not, however, be seen as evidence of a deliberate desire to pursue a policy of municipal statism. Rather, the municipal construction of working-class dwellings in the guise of St Martin's Cottages, Victoria Square, and Juvenal Dwellings arose as a consequence of the inability of the private sector to fulfil this market niche at the price and location desired. Thus, it is clear that the Corporation intervened only when all other avenues had been exhausted. It was also, however, the case that it was increasingly apparent to those in local political control, such as Forwood, that sustained improvement to working-class living conditions could only be realised through a more coordinated approach to the process of demolition, displacement, and restoration. These were policies that could not be successfully addressed by Liverpool in isolation. Instead, they were dependent upon greater powers being bestowed by central government and a wider political recognition that state intervention to assist the poor need not, necessarily, equate to, in the words of Lord Elcho, 10th Earl of Wemyss, "*strangling the spirit of independence and the self-reliance of the people... by destroying the moral fibre of our race in the anaconda coils of state socialism*".[38] This was a realisation at a national level that would, in the early years of the twentieth century, result in the greater empowerment of authorities throughout the country to build and administer accommodation that addressed the needs of the working classes, and in which Liverpool would once more take a leading role.

*The 10th Earl of Wemyss. Vanity Fair magazine 23rd July 1870.*[39]

## ***References***


[1] Mr Richard Cross, 8th February 1875, *Hansard*, Commons, 3rd series, vol. 222, col. pp. 97-115.

[2] *Ibid.*, col. pp. 335-387.

[3] J.N. Tarn, 'Housing in Liverpool and Glasgow: The Growth of Civic Responsibility', *Town Planning Review*, 39:4 (1969), pp. 319-334, p. 329.

[4] A. Errazurez, 'Some Types of Housing in Liverpool, 1785-1890', *Town Planning Review*, 9:2 (1946), pp. 57-68, p. 65.

[5] Dr Lyon Playfair, 15th February 1875, *Hansard*, Commons, 3rd series, vol. 222, col. 382.

[6] *Ibid.*

[7] *Liverpool Courier*, 17th February 1875.

[8] Liverpool Council Proceedings, 1874-1875, p. 167.

[9] LRO 352 MIN/HEA II/1/23 Liverpool Council Health Committee, Minute Book May-October 1876, pp. 104-5, 170-174.

[10] Councillor A.B. Forwood, as cited, *Liverpool Courier*, 'Town Council: The Nash Grove Scheme', 3rd April 1879.

[11] P.J. Waller, *Democracy and Sectarianism: A Political and Social History of Liverpool 1868-1939* (Liverpool, 1981), p.113.

[12] Councillor Ball, as cited, *Liverpool Courier*, 'Town Council: The Nash-Grove Scheme', 3rd April 1879.

[13] Letter of refusal from the Local Government Board dated 18th July 1879, reproduced in full, *Liverpool Courier*, 'The Nash-Grove Scheme', 7th August 1879.

[14] Artisans' and Labourers' Dwellings Improvement Act 1879 (42 & 43 Victoria c. 63).

[15] Public Record Office, National Archives, Kew (PRO) MH 12/5991, Letter from the Local Government Board to the Liverpool Corporation, 31st May 1880.

[16] *Ibid.*

[17] *Liverpool Courier*, 'The Health Committee: The Nash Grove Site', 25th June 1880.

[18] *Liberal Review*, 'What I Thought in Council', 2nd October 1880. From 1883 onwards, the Liberal Review was known as the Liverpool Review.

[19] T.E. Kebbel, *A History of Toryism* (London, 1886), p. 405.

[20] Liverpool Council Proceedings, 1879-1880, pp. 253-254. See also *Liverpool Courier*, 'Town Council', 30th September 1880.

[21] *Liverpool Courier*, 8th June 1882.

[22] *Ibid*.

[23] PRO MH 12/5994, Letter from Liverpool Corporation Insanitary and Artisans' Property Committee to the Local Government Board, 11th May 1883.

[24] *Liverpool Daily Post*, 'Report of the Opening', 21st October 1885.

[25] Tarn, 'Housing in Liverpool', p. 330.

[26] LRO 352 MIN/INS/1/2 Minutes of the Insanitary Property and Artisans' Dwelling Committee, May 1883 - October 1885, 26th May 1884, p. 328.

[27] LRO 352 MIN/INS/1/3 Minutes of the Insanitary Property and Artisans' Dwelling Committee, November 1885 - October 1888, pp. 178-180. Superintendent's Report, 26th March 1886.

[28] *Liverpool Mercury*, 'The Nash Grove Artisans' Dwellings', 11th March 1885.

[29] Tarn, 'Housing in Liverpool', p. 330.

[30] As cited, *Liverpool Daily Post*, 5th November 1883.

[31] A.B. Forwood, *The Dwellings of the Industrial Classes in the Diocese of Liverpool and How to Improve Them* (Liverpool, 1883), pp. 19-20.

[32] Waller, *Democracy and Sectarianism*, pp. 87-88.

[33] PRO MH 12/5995 Local Government Board Inspector Harrison, Letter to the Corporation, 18th January 1884.

[34] *Liverpool Mercury*, 'Insanitary Property in Liverpool: Government Inquiry', 17th January 1884.

[35] LRO 352 MIN/INS/1/2 Minutes of the Insanitary Property and Artisans' Dwelling Committee, May 1883 - October 1885, p. 404.

[36] See respectively, LRO 352 MIN/INS/1/2 Minutes of the Insanitary Property and Artisans' Dwelling Committee, May 1883 - October 1885, p.517; Liverpool Council Proceedings, 1884-1885, pp.148-149; *Liverpool Mercury*, 'City Council', 16th April 1885.

[37] Forwood, *Dwellings of the Industrial Classes*, pp. 19-20.

[38] 10th Earl of Wemyss, 31st July 1885, *Hansard*, Lords, 3rd series, vol. 300, col. 633-650, col. 650.

[39] *Vanity Fair*, 23rd July 1870, by Carlo Pellegrini.

# THE SINKING OF THE LUSITANIA

## Merseyside 1915: The Response of Letter-Writers to the Anti-German Riots

*Lee P. Ruddin*

The sinking of RMS *Lusitania* – '"the pride of the port of Liverpool": the captain and nearly every man of the crew came from the city'[1] – by a German U-boat off the southern coast of Ireland hit Merseysiders hard. We see this most visibly in the anti-German riots which broke out on both banks of the River Mersey in the days and nights after U-20 claimed its biggest prize on 7 May 1915. But what did letter-writers think of the gutting of German premises? Did they, in short, approve of this manifestation of anti-Germanism? In a word: yes.

Questions surrounding the local – as opposed to the (inter)national – legacy of the *Lusitania* often go unanswered by authors who are too fixated on discussing life on board and loss overboard, so it is therefore timely that, as we commemorate the centenary of the ship's sinking, a discussion is provided as to why and to what extent Germanophobia manifested itself in the letter pages. Letters to the editor, it is worth reiterating, do not appear in a vacuum. As such, and in the interests of contextualisation, it is imperative that we first discuss what is commonly referred to as "invasion literature" and "atrocity reports". Such material undoubtedly contributed to an anti-German sentiment, meaning it is therefore necessary to outline the facts (not included in order to condone such sentiments, it is important to note) concerning late Victorian and Edwardian fiction as well as German atrocities which Berlin contended were purely fictitious.

The work that acted as a midwife to the birth of a new genre was George Tomkyns Chesney's *The Battle of Dorking* (1871) – pictured right. Therein, the author vividly depicts an imaginary German-speaking army successfully invading an ill-prepared Britain. The pamphlet had a 'dramatic impact',[2] selling an estimated eighty thousands copies, and kick-started an 'intense' national 'debate' about the threat posed by a unified Germany in general and about conscription in particular.[3] That readers read about the swift invasion of France by Prussian reservists only a year earlier, during the Franco-Prussian War of 1870-71, ensured this short-story had a long-term effect on the public consciousness. If Tsarist autocracy was the bogeyman of the Victorian age, Prussian militarism was to become it in the Edwardian. This was the age of "spy-fever" or '*Hysteria Germanica*'.[4]

*Book cover illustration. (WC).*

Success breeds imitation, it is said, and with *The Riddle of the Sands* (1903), Erskine Childers successfully imitates Chesney's Victorian scenario for an Edwardian audience. Fear and suspicion of Germans grew among Britons which, in turn, spawned more imitators who were even more successful: contemporary readers were part of the 'first generation [to accede] to mass literacy' thanks to the proliferation of the printed word.[5] Increase in demand was met by writers who supplied their readership with, on average, one invasion book a month between the *fin de siècle* and the outbreak of war. In an added twist, some authors elected to create a new – less overt and more covert – literary German foe: the immigrant-cum-infiltrator.

By doing this, William Le Queux, Walter Wood and E. Philips Oppenheim, authors respectively of *The Invasion of 1910* (1906), *The Enemy in Our Midst* (1906) and *The Secret* (1908), each tells 'of the threat to Britain posed by German immigrants already living in Britain's towns and cities.'[6] These individual examples of a xenophobic view of foreigners collectively contributed towards a climate of xenophobia. '[F]ear of the foreigner now lurked deep in the national psyche' and subsequently came to the surface in the form of the 1905 Aliens Act and the Official Secrets Act of 1911.[7] Ministers were fast-becoming less tolerant in their outlook; atrocity reports would ensure that Merseysiders likewise fast-became more intolerant.[8]

While it is perhaps unsafe to assume that many – if any – Merseysiders read (any of) the aforementioned works of fiction, it can be safely assumed that many – if not all – of Merseyside newspaper readers (approximately 92,000[9]) were cognisant of the facts pertaining to the use of 'asphyxiating gases on a very extensive scale' against French forces,[10] how "British prisoners [were being] abominably treated in Germany"[11] and the confirmation of alleged 'outrages [committed during the invasion of] Belgium'.[12] This was a particularly 'special time of hate in Britain' since these 'events [had] rendered Germany peculiarly repugnant'.[13] It was news of the sinking of the *Lusitania* and the loss of over 1,000 lives, though, which incited and fuelled 'a visceral hatred … towards ethnic Germans, often of long-standing acquaintance.'[14] A report in one local daily refers to this latest atrocity – too well known to be allocated space here – as 'The Pirates' Greatest Outrage'[15] while the excerpt below, taken from a second, perfectly illustrates the misery caused to those on Merseyside:

> No shipping disaster of the war affecting Liverpool has struck so wide and deep a blow as the loss of the *Lusitania*. She was the pride of the Mersey, and Liverpool loved her like a personal friend. The sense of loss will be felt by everyone, whether they had direct association with the vessel or not, because she was essentially Liverpool's own ship. For these reasons no previous disaster of the war has stirred Liverpool people so much as the loss of the great ship.[16]

A third is even more stirring in its use of language to describe the scene:

> The disaster to the *Lusitania*, in which helpless non-combatants were foully murdered, has affected Liverpool in particular. By one coward blow

> hundreds of homes in the city have been bereft. Can there be any wonder that among the less disciplined classes, who have had to freely sacrifice their menfolk on the battlefield, the feeling of bitter enmity against the Germans should be exacerbated beyond restraint?[17]

*The aftermath of rioting at the Britannia Hotel, 283 Breck Road, on the corner with Coniston Street. Courtesy Colin Wilkinson, Bluecoat Press, Liverpool.*

The ship's sinking angered many Merseysiders[18] and led directly to the 'outburst' of rioting the next day, Saturday 8 May.[19] 'If Germany had torpedoed the *Lusitania*, we certainly torpedoed everything German in our immediate vicinity – certainly all the pork butchers' shops,' recalls memoirist Pat O'Mara.[20] Now that the causes of the riots have been established, we must turn to describing their course, and for this, O'Mara's eye-witness account proves most invaluable. We pick up proceedings after he elects to bypass a dance over Paddy's Market in St. Martin's Hall, and when he notices that:

> On the corner of Scotland Road ominous gangs were gathering – men and women, very drunk and very angry. Something was afoot – we could sense that and like good slummy boys, we crowded eagerly to help in any disturbance. Suddenly something crashed up the road near Ben Johnson (sic) Street and was followed by another terrific crash of glass. We ran up the road. A pork butcher's had had its front window knocked in with a brick and a crowd of men and women were wrecking the place. A little higher up the same thing was happening – everything suggestive of Germany was being smashed to pieces.
>
> Up the road the crowd surged, some cut into Sawny (sic) Pope Street, others went into Ben Johnson (sic) Street and continued up the road. Down Scotland Road in the opposite direction, the window crashing was terrific – clear down to [Tryon] Street. Everyone had a brick or stick, or something tucked under his or her coat or apron, and there was much pilfering. The police themselves, imbued with bitterness, were the most passive guardians of law. I recall one stout little Irish sausage dealer pleading with the crowd that her husband wasn't a German; but the name was too suspicious and in the windows went and the place was wrecked.[21]

O'Mara, together with his close coterie of co-criminals, then leave the teeming thoroughfare that is Scotland Road and head towards their own neighbourhood in the South End, where:

> As soon as the tram got near Charlie Beech's pork shop, opposite St. Vincent's Church, a dense mob caused it to stop. Mr. Beech had been living in Liverpool for thirty odd years, but there was a faint suspicion that years ago, anticipating just such a riot, he had changed his name. His big shop was in a shambles when, running from the halted tramcar, we got to it; Mr. Beech and his son had made their escape.
>
> ...[W]e [then] raced on to Yaag's pork butcher's in Great George's Street. Most of us boys were at the forefront of the gang, anxious to be the first to crash the enemy's windows. Mr. Yaag, a big wholesome fellow, had allegedly been born in Germany, but I don't think he remembered much about it. Two of his nephews at the time were with my cousin Berny and the Eighth Irish over in [p.132] France. I always liked Mr. Yaag, but not quite enough, as I broke his window without fear of molestation.
>
> As we converged at the big shop, Mr. Yaag, arms akimbo and thinking some urchin was fleeing from Aeroplane Joe, came out, pipe in mouth and with his usual broad smile. This vanished instantly as someone kicked him in the belly and a volley of bricks sent in the huge windows. From the sawdust floor the astounded man had the pleasure of seeing his choice sausages kicked and thrown about and the furnishings reduced to matchwood ... We left Mr. Yaag and Yaag, Inc., in a worse mess than Charlie Beech's.
>
> Cook's pork butcher's in Mill Street came next. Mr. Cook knew as much about Germany at the time, I think, as I did. Later, investigation proved that he came from strictly Yorkshire stock and was a devoted student of Mr. Kipling – dashing off a bit of patriotic verse himself once in a while. But he had a pork butcher's shop, and as pork and Germany were identical terms, we left his shop in a shambles and himself stretched across the counter groaning.[22]

As the day began to turn into night – and with their stomachs full on all the free sausage that they had been eating – attention turned away from 'culinary stereotypes' towards private property.[23] Such scenes, alas, were not confined to one day in the South End of the city. Indeed, they started in the North End of Liverpool, where the tight-knit dockland community lived, before spreading to Bootle and Birkenhead and finished in the northern tip of the Wirral peninsula at Wallasey on Tuesday 11 May. Although separated by the Mersey, there was little to separate the treatment dished out on either side of the river to "German-looking" business- and property-owners by stick-wielding, stone-throwing vigilantes: 'Once shop premises were destroyed it ... followed that [its] living quarters ... were then attacked and looted with furniture destroyed an[d] thrown from upstairs windows to baying crowds below.'[24] Four days' (and nights') worth of rioting in Liverpool, Birkenhead and across their surrounding environs resulted in the gutting of over 200 properties and a ratepayer bill in excess of £40,000 (approximately £3 million today).

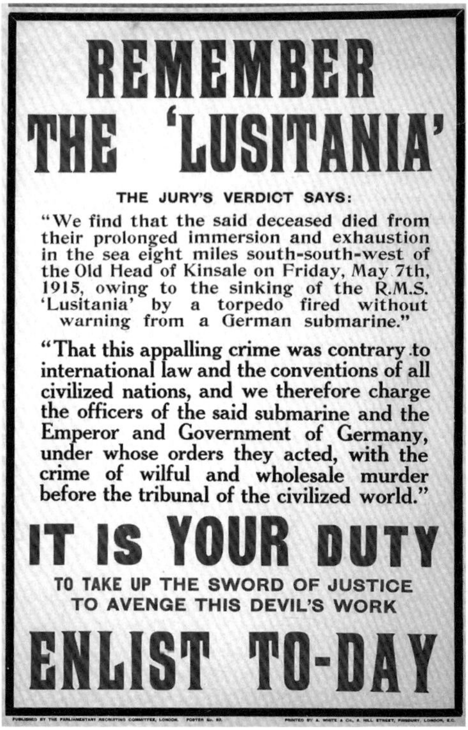


*'Remember the Lusitania' became a powerful recruiting slogan and was emblazoned on posters in Britain, Ireland and America. (LOC).*

O'Mara mockingly refers to the cost of property damage being borne by ratepayers as 'good British justice'[25] yet locals, particularly "Britisher" and "W.H.H." from Tarleton Street, consider this a bad case of injustice since they understood 'people … attacking Germans' and cannot 'find it in [their] conscience to [apportion] blame'.[26] Such opinions may well have been influenced by the Earl of Derby, the former Lord Mayor of Liverpool (1911-12), who penned an inflammatory letter in the immediate aftermath of the sinking. Therein, the Director-General of Recruitment, in an attempt to raise a "Lusitania battalion", reminds readers of the other 'diabolical', dishonourable act (the use of poisonous gas) committed by the Germans. Although Derby's efforts ultimately prove in vain, his talk of a cold-blooded Germanic 'race' is arguably on the mind of letter-writers when they discuss rates.[27] A letter by "R. Knowles" of Hamilton Square is a case in point:

> With regard to the damage already done to these aliens' property, who is to pay for it? Certainly the ratepayers of this country should not have to do so… What is my object in writing this letter[?] It is to ask my fellow country-men to say that they will not allow themselves to be taxed or rated to the extent of a single farthing to pay this accursed enemy for any damage done to their property. Damage done to British property should, of course, be paid for. Our demonical enemies must be beaten down to earth. They are lepers in the human family, and I hope, after the war is over, they will be looked upon by the nations of the world as strangers and wanderers on the face of the globe.[28]

Such a view, albeit one less pronounced, is held by "Sacrificed Enough" in Liverpool, who does not 'see why the public should be made to pay for the damage done to property occupied by Germans'.[29] With so many locals enraged with the prospect of increased rates, one letter-writer suggests – quite staggeringly – that wealthy Germans assist 'their poorer fellow-countrymen' by paying for any repairs. 'By so doing',

"CIVIS" affirms, 'they would [not only] save our ratepayers a tax which many of them at the present time can ill afford to pay[, but] would give undoubted evidence that their loyalty and gratitude go beyond mere words.'[30] The second half of this last sentence is undoubtedly in reference to the protest made only days earlier by "H.G. Gardner" of Blundellsands, a naturalised German who expresses opposition to the horrors perpetrated by the *Kaiserreich*, and who affirms his loyalty to King and Country.[31] Rather than helping social cohesion, however, such protestations hindered it, leading "An Indignant Welshwoman" to pick up her pen and pontificate about 'th[e] principle [to] never under any circumstances …trust any German.'[32]

*The 'Lusi' at the Liverpool Landing Stage. (RJ).*

Talk of Germans in "our midst", as enemy aliens not to be trusted, is widespread across the letter pages. Writing in response to "Better Late Than Never" of Liverpool, who infers that Germans 'could be possessed of a secret wireless installation,'[33] "Watchful" in Seaforth praises him 'for his warning' and wonders how 'even one German is allowed freedom amongst us.'[34] "Anti-Spy" shares such fears and likewise pleads with officials to 'hammer at internment for' all Germans.[35] Arguably most worrying is that The Church, looked upon as all that is good, provides a bad example – not unlike the venerated Lord Derby – by using anti-German language to sow disunion at a time when unity could, indeed should, have been sown. While much ink does not flow from the pen of "J. Percy Treasure" of St. Bede's Church in Toxteth Park, hatred unashamedly does: 'We didn't want these people,' the letter-writer abruptly states.[36] "Theodore A. Howard" of Dingle, goes even further by expressing his approval with the recent riots. As distasteful as the Reverend's letter indubitably is, quoting it at length will provide readers with a taste of contemporary Christian compassion:

> I witnessed yesterday the sack of two or three of the German pork shops in my own parish and district.
>
> As I notice there is a tendency to rebuke the "misguided people" who did this, will you permit me to offer a few remarks[?]
>
> First, had I possessed the power – which I had not – to have interposed in any way to prevent this form of expression of popular indignation against these Germans in our midst, brought to a head by the Lusitania crime, I would not have lifted a finger to do it. For two reasons[:] [o]ne because these people instead of being expelled or interned at the start of the war,

> have been allowed to remain petted, coddled, and protected by the police under the Home Office, and have used and abused their liberty in the most outrageous way, by insolent braggadocio … So far as these aliens or "aliens at heart" have suffered in any way, apart from personal injury, they richly deserve it.
>
> My [second] reason for satisfaction is the value this action of the "misguided people" is likely to result in … If the result of this "popular fury" is the exclusion and internment of these highly objectionable and dangerous people, it will be a blessing in disguise … If the sack of the pork shops has any part in bringing this about – and please God it shall – then it seems to me we may yet have to pass a vote of thanks to the "misguided people."[37]

As provocative as the above-referenced letter incontrovertibly was, only one reader is provoked to write to an editor in response. Yet the reply from "G.D." of Liverpool presumably proves so utterly thought-provoking that not one anti-German letter of note appears for the rest of the month.[38] It is, for this reason, worth quoting at length:

> I, like your correspondent, the Rev. Theodore A. Howard, was a witness of the disgraceful proceedings enacted in all parts of the city against the resident Germans, etc., and am ashamed at the tone of his letter[.]
>
> Permit me to point out to your correspondent that aliens in this country have not been "petted and cuddled" by the Home Office as he asserts, and further, they are entitled to police protection as citizens. True, they have established themselves in this country, but this is due to the patronage of British people, a section of which have suddenly shown their abhorrence by wrecking their premises and encumbering the ratepayers with further liability...
>
> Numbers of respectable and law-abiding citizens have to humiliate themselves in order to protect their property by explaining by poster to an ignorant, lawless mob that they are not of German nationality, with, in many cases, indifferent results.[39]

Two more voices – "Critic" and "John P. Bibby" from Bidston – rose against the popular clamour of Germanophobia in the letter pages – lamenting respectively the treatment of 'poor'[40] and 'peaceful aliens living in our midst … [by] … our own riotous element'[41] – yet these voices of tolerance are in the minority, alas, compared with the majority of those published that display intolerance. Even a letter by "H.F." of Liverpool, which at first appears tolerant, is ultimately intolerant since lambasting those behind the attacks against Jews but not Germans illuminates that letter-writers, while not generally anti-alien like the rioters, remained particularly anti-German.[42] Whether the editorial preferences of (the four) Liverpool editors contributed to this imbalance, it is impossible to know. What we do know, though, is that 'this was a time of escalating costs in the newspaper industry'[43] and 'the need to sell newspapers ensured that they printed what they believed would be popular.'[44]

Only the editor of the *Liverpool Echo* knew how many – if any – letters-writers protested against the growing calls for internment. Yet the fact his newspaper dedicates so much space to advertising a racist rant by the editor of *John Bull*, Horatio Bottomley, suggests this number was small, if a number at all.[45] Profits came before patriotism, let us not forget, so what was received (or not) permitted his paper to propagate prejudice. 'Gauging public opinion in an age when opinion polls were unheard of inevitably means turning to the press,' and, it could be added, the letter pages since this is what newspaper proprietors and policy-makers did.[46] Having sufficiently gauged the public mood, the latter introduced strict internment in 1915 and were no doubt unsurprised that it did not cause one letter-writer to dip his/her ink pen in vitriol. Merseysiders, much like those abroad, were now convinced that they were engaged in a civilisational struggle against German *Kultur*.[47] 'The pre-war stereotype of the evil and ubiquitous enemy spy had been transferred to the entire German nation' and to all Germans.[48]

There were no more anti-German riots across Merseyside in the remaining three-and-a-half years of the First World War, fortunately, but the reason for this is an unfortunate one: 'so many German shops had already been destroyed and so few enemy aliens remained free.'[49] The demise of German-owned butchers in Liverpool is a microcosm of the bigger picture: only twenty-five percent of butchers' shops were run by non-Germans on the eve of war; it was 'believed' to be one hundred percent by the time the guns had fallen silent.[50] Letter-writer "Robert Fellows" evidently got his wish that 'British butchers in Liverpool' capture 'this part of the alien enemies' trade from them'[51] – "them" being those who were largely considered as "us" before the turn of the twentieth century and prior to the sinking of the *Lusitania* fifteen years into it.

*I wish to dedicate this article to my partner's (Irish) father, Patrick Lynch, who – despite facing intolerance from many in London after arriving on these shores – is an example of tolerance to all on Merseyside and beyond.*

### *References and notes*

[1] John Belchem and Donald M. MacRaild, 'Cosmopolitan Liverpool', chapter 5, in John Belchem (ed.) *Liverpool 800: Culture, Character & History* (Liverpool: Liverpool University Press, 2006), p.366.

[2] A. Michael Matin, 'Scrutinizing *The Battle of Dorking*: The Royal United Service Institution and the Mid-Victorian Invasion Controversy', *Victorian Literature and Culture*, volume 39, issue 2 (September 2011), p.385.

[3] I.F. Clarke, 'Before and After "The Battle of Dorking"', *Science Fiction Studies*, volume 24, issue 1 (March 1997), p.42.

[4] Alfred M. Gollin, 'England Is No Longer an Island: The Phantom Airship Scare of 1909', *Albion: A Quarterly Journal Concerned with British Studies*, volume 13, number 1 (Spring 1981), p.52.

[5] Martyn Lyons, 'New Readers in the Nineteenth Century: Women, Children, Workers', chapter 12, in Guglielmo Cavallo and Roger Chartier (eds.) *A History of Reading in the West* (Cambridge, Massachusetts: University of Massachusetts Press, 1999), p.313.

[6] Panikos Panayi (ed.) *Germans as Minorities during the First World War: A Global Comparative Perspective* (Surrey: Ashgate Publishing, 2014), p.294.

[7] Gerry Docherty and Jim Macgregor, *Hidden History: The Secret Origins of the First World War* (Edinburgh: Mainstream Publishing, 2013), p.151.

[8] I say 'more' since, as John Belchem illustrates, cracks 'within Liverpool's vaunted cosmopolitanism were' beginning to appear at the end of the nineteenth century. See John Belchem, *Before the Windrush: Race Relations in 20th-Century Liverpool* (Liverpool: Liverpool University Press, 2014), pp.26-9, quote at p.26.

[9] See A.P. Wadsworth, 'Newspaper Circulations, 1800-1954', *Transactions of the Manchester Statistical Society* (1954-55), p.38.

[10] 'Deadly Suffocating Gas', *Liverpool Daily Post & Mercury*, Saturday 24 April 1915, p.5.

[11] 'German Dervishes', *Liverpool Courier*, Wednesday 28 April 1915, p.5.

[12] 'German Savages', *Evening Express*, Thursday 13 May 1915, p.5.

[13] Trevor Wilson, 'Lord Bryce's Investigation into Alleged German Atrocities in Belgium, 1914-15', *Journal of Contemporary History*, volume 14, issue 3 (July 1979), p.369.

[14] Nicoletta F. Gullace, 'Friends, Aliens, and Enemies: Fictive Communities and the Lusitania Riots of 1915', *Journal of Social History*, volume 39, issue 2 (Winter 2005), p.347.

[15] *Evening Express*, Saturday 8 May 1915, p.3.

[16] 'Liverpool Moved', *Liverpool Daily Post & Mercury*, Saturday 8 May 1915, p.5.

[17] The third newspaper being the *Liverpool Courier* (on Tuesday 11 May 1915). See Panikos Panayi, 'Anti-German Riots in Britain during the First World War', Chapter 4, in Panikos Panayi (ed.) *Racial Violence in Britain in the Nineteenth and Twentieth Centuries* (Leicester: Leicester University Press, 1996), p.70.

[18] 'Liverpool's Anger', *Liverpool Daily Post & Mercury*, Monday 10 May 1915, p.7.

[19] 'Liverpool Outburst', *Liverpool Daily Post & Mercury*, Tuesday 11 May 1915, p.3.

[20] Pat O'Mara, *The Autobiography of a Liverpool Irish Slummy* (Liverpool: The Bluecoat Press, 2007 [1934]), p.133.

[21] *Ibid.*, p.131.

[22] *Ibid.*, pp.131-2.

[23] Keir Waddington, '"We Don't Want Any German Sausages Here!" Food, Fear, and the German Nation in Victorian and Edwardian Britain', *Journal of British Studies*, volume 52, issue 4 (October 2013), p.1017.

[24] Vicki Caren, 'Anti-German Riots', Merseyside at War, 1914-1918, available at: *http://www.merseyside-at-war.org/story/anti-german-riots* (last accessed 27 March 2015).

[25] O'Mara, op. cit., p.133.

[26] 'The Liverpool Looting and Rioting', *Liverpool Echo*, Monday 17 May 1915, p.3; 'What to do with the Huns', *Liverpool Daily Post & Mercury*, Wednesday 12 May 1915, p.4.

[27] 'Cold-Blooded Murderers', *Evening Express*, Saturday 8 May 1915, p.4.

[28] 'Destroying German Shops', *Liverpool Courier*, Saturday 15 May 1915, p.7.

[29] 'Undesirable Tenants', *Evening Express*, Wednesday 12 May 1915, p.3.

[30] 'A Suggestion for Aliens', *Liverpool Daily Post & Mercury*, Saturday 15 May 1915, p.5.

[31] 'Naturalised German's Protest', *Liverpool Daily Post & Mercury*, Monday 10 May 1915, p.9.

[32] 'Protests by Naturalised Germans', *Liverpool Daily Post & Mercury*, Monday 17 May 1915, p.3.

[33] 'The Enemy Within Our Midst', *Liverpool Courier*, Thursday 13 May 1915, p.8.

[34] 'The Enemy in Our Midst', *Liverpool Courier*, Friday 14 May 1915, p.7.

[35] 'Intern All Germans', *Evening Express*, Monday 10 May 1915, p.3.

[36] 'A Nation's Anger', *Liverpool Courier*, Thursday 13 May 1915, p.8.

[37] 'Liverpool Vicar's Strong View', *Liverpool Courier*, Wednesday 12 May 1915, p.3.

[38] I say 'of note' rather than 'not at all' because, although letter-writer "A Disgusted Liverpool Terrier" expresses his shame of the 'Liverpool public' for the damage caused by rioting, he concludes by urging locals to 'leave the clearing of Liverpool of Germans to those people who get a weekly wage for doing so.' See 'Terriers Opinion of the Riots', *Liverpool Echo*, Wednesday 19 May 1915, p.4.

[39] 'Lynch Law', *Evening Express*, Tuesday 18 May 1915, p.3.

[40] 'The Looting and Riots in Liverpool', *Liverpool Echo*, Wednesday 12 May 1915, p.4.

[41] 'Anti-German Rioting', *Liverpool Daily Post & Mercury*, Friday 14 May 1915, p.9.

[42] 'Jewish Shops Attacked', *Evening Express*, Monday 17 May 1915, p.3.

[43] Panikos Panayi, 'The Lancashire Anti-German Riots of May 1915', *Manchester Region History Review*, volume 2, issue 2 (Autumn/Winter 1988/89), p.8.

[44] Waddington, *op. cit.*, p.1021.

[45] 'The Lusitania Crime … Now for the Vendetta!' *Liverpool Echo*, Wednesday 12 May 1915, p.6.

[46] Lothar Reinermann, 'Fleet Street and the Kaiser: British Public Opinion and Wilhelm II', *German History*, volume 26, issue 4 (October 2008), p.470.

[47] Tilman Dedering, '"Avenge the *Lusitania*": The Anti-German Riots in South Africa in 1915', *Immigrants & Minorities*, volume 31, issue 3 (June 2013), p.278.

[48] David French, 'Spy Fever in Britain, 1900-1915', *The Historical Journal*, volume 21, issue 2 (June 1978), p.370.

[49] Panikos Panayi, 'The Destruction of the German Communities in Britain during the First World War', chapter 7, in Panikos Panayi (ed.), *Germans in Britain since 1500* (London: The Hambledon Press, 1996), p.128.

[50] Anthony Hogan, *Merseyside at War* (Gloucestershire: Amberley Publishing, 2014), p.43.

[51] 'German Pork Butchers', *Liverpool Echo*, Monday 17 May 1915, p.3.

# About the Liverpool History Society

## Membership of the LHS

is open to anyone interested in the history of Liverpool and its environs, and is available at the following yearly rates:

**UK Ordinary £10.00 ● UK Joint £15.00 ● UK Life £100.00 (one-off payment)**

**UK Student (full–time) £5.00 ● International (ordinary) £15.00**

UK Schools, colleges, libraries, museums etc., may also become **Corporate Members** at **£25.00 per annum**.

The membership year runs from 1 April until 31 March of the following year, but for anyone joining after 1 January in any year, their first subscription covers the period until 31 March of the next year. Membership benefits include regular newsletters, one copy of *Liverpool History* and eight meetings each year.

As the LHS is a Registered Charity (No. 1093736), subscriptions may qualify as donations under the Gift Aid scheme, with the tax paid thereon being recoverable by the Society. Details are available from the Society's Treasurer: (e-mail: treasurer@liverpoolhistorysociety.org.uk)

## Applications for membership

should be sent to: membership@liverpoolhistorysociety.org.uk

## Meetings of the Society

start at 1.30 p.m. for 2.00 p.m. They are usually held on the 3rd Sunday of February to June and September to November and the 2nd Sunday of December.

Visitors are especially welcome at our meetings – admission to the first meeting is free; however, voluntary donations are gladly accepted.

Our normal venue is:
The Grace Room, 1st Floor, Cornerstone Building,
Liverpool Hope University, Shaw Street, Liverpool, L3 8QB.

For further details, including membership application form and details about paying your membership subscription by PayPal, please visit our website:

**www.liverpoolhistorysociety.org.uk**

**or e-mail: enquiries@liverpoolhistorysociety.org.uk**